IN THE AFTERMATH

IN THE AFTERMATH

Provocations and Laments

David Bentley Hart

WILLIAM B. EERDMANS PUBLISHING COMPANY

GRAND RAPIDS, MICHIGAN / CAMBRIDGE, U.K.

Published 2009 by

Wm. B. Eerdmans Publishing Co.

2140 Oak Industrial Drive NE, Grand Rapids, Michigan 49505 /

P.O. Box 163, Cambridge CB3 9PU U.K.

Printed in the United States of America

14 13 12 11 10 09   7 6 5 4 3 2 1

Library of Congress Cataloging-in-Publication Data

Hart, David Bentley

In the aftermath : provocations and laments / David Bentley Hart.

p.   cm.

Includes bibliographical references.

ISBN 978-0-8028-4573-3 (pbk. : alk. paper)

1. Theology.   I. Title.

BT80.H33   2009

230 — dc22

2008042832

www.eerdmans.com

For my father and mother,

Robert and Marianne Hart,

Gentlefolk of the Great

State of Maryland

Contents

CONTENTS

Introduction

All of the pieces assembled in this volume have been published previously, in journals or newspapers, though for the most part in slightly different forms than appear here. I have only two excuses for issuing them anew. The first is simply that a number of persons have suggested I do so. The second is that a collection of this sort allows me to restore several of these essays to something nearer the versions I originally wrote, as well as to make a few small alterations. Magazine and newspaper editors are of necessity concerned for the length of what they publish, and on more than one occasion I have had to accommodate an editor by abbreviating the text I had initially submitted. And sometimes I have succumbed to second thoughts, and moderated some of my more irresponsible rhetoric, and now in retrospect regret having done so. Editors, moreover, will insist on making small changes in what one writes, even when no particular improvement is discernible as a result. In truth, though, I have had small cause for complaint. Most of my editors have left my texts almost entirely intact, and have asked for only small revisions, if any (no doubt they know I will become unreasonable if asked to consent to anything larger). Still, to my mind the correct or definitive text is always the one stored in my hard drive, which is not necessarily the one that appeared in print; and so, in every case where there is a divergence between the two, it is the former I have included here (though with, as I have said, some slight amendments).

The articles I have published in the past several years are, broadly speaking, of two kinds: those written for publications with wide readerships, and those written for academic guild periodicals. All the pieces reproduced here belong to the former category. A collection of essays of the other sort is in the works, but that will be a very different kind of book. Here I want — at least, in part — to entertain. This is not to say that the pieces gathered here are not serious in their arguments; quite the contrary: in many ways, it is far easier to make ambitious arguments in articles for magazines, where one is at liberty to address the sort of large cultural, religious, or philosophical issues that one usually cannot in the narrower confines of academic journals. I mean only that, in these articles, I have given my natural inclinations towards satire and towards wantonly profligate turns of phrase far freer rein than academic writing permits. I hope most of my readers will not find these aspects of my "authorial voice" insufferable; I even hope they will take some pleasure in my prose (though perhaps that is most likely only if it is taken in measured doses). I have, at any rate, attempted to include only pieces that strike me as having some intrinsic interest, both in form and in content. This is true even of those written putatively as reviews of other men's books (of which there are a good number here); mere occasional reviews I would not think of including in a collection of this sort, but I have often chosen to review a book solely as a pretext for writing a small essay of my own, more in conversation with the book under examination than as a critical appraisal of that book.

One feature of my style for which I am not inclined to feel penitent, but for which reason tells me I ought to offer some apology, is an occasional want of restraint, most particularly in my expressions of distaste for an idea or for the mind that produced it. This is all attributable, I expect, to those tendencies as a writer of which I have just spoken. My only defense — apart from confessing my sense that imperturbably mild manners often make for boring copy — is that I have never intentionally used language I thought disproportionately fierce in regard to any proposition or any thinker, and that in reviewing these essays I cannot honestly find an instance of invective I particularly regret. Perhaps the most savage personal remarks I have ever committed to print are those I made regarding the bioethicist Joseph Fletcher in the article entitled "The Anti-Theology of the Body," and they astonished even me by their vehemence when I read them again in preparing this volume; I did not, however, alter them, or even soften them to the degree that the editors of *The New Atlantis* did when the article originally appeared, for the simple reason that they still do not seem unwarranted to me given the altogether loathsome nature of Fletcher's ideas, and the scandal that so many of our tenured intellectuals do not recoil from those ideas with the horror and revulsion they merit. I do not know if I believe that any quantity of abuse heaped upon persons like Fletcher is truly excessive, except in tactical terms: If one wants to convince others of the justness of one's views of anything, perhaps one ought to proceed in as moderate and cautious a manner as one can. But, then again, perhaps one occasionally should not; some ideas are simply evil, and the persons who conceive them somewhat depraved, and there may be something rather disgraceful in an unwillingness to say so.

At other times, of course, an idea or thinker is not evil or depraved, but merely silly or sanctimonious; and in these cases also a certain robustness in one's rhetoric is not necessarily a discreditable thing. The final essay in this collection is the most relentlessly satirical, I think it fair to say, and is directed at a philosopher — Daniel Dennett — who, whatever his faults, could never be indicted of the sort of moral idiocy that permeated Fletcher's work. In matters historical, religious, and even philosophical, Dennett is clearly something of an ignoramus; and he has always been a bad philosopher, however much he may be adored by journalists and book reviewers and his ideological comrades; and, since his work now belongs to that parasitic subcategory of analytic philosophy that serves simply as a sort of adjunct to the hard sciences, he no longer really writes philosophy anyway. All of that would be quite pardonable, though, were it not for the self-importance, condescension, and imperiousness of his writings on the relation between scientific reason and religious belief. Ignorance and defective logic become truly offensive only when combined with invincible and self-deluding arrogance. Moreover, whereas most of Dennett's books have something to commend them — many are quite informative on recent developments in evolutionary theory, for instance — the book I address in the article included here, *Breaking the Spell,* could scarcely be more vapid in its content or reprehensible in its tone. It is no worse, admittedly, than the books of Richard Dawkins, Sam Harris, or Christopher Hitchens (though Hitchens, even if he cannot think his way to the end of a simple syllogism, can write fairly well, as Dennett most emphatically cannot); but the arguments of a philosopher — even a bad philosopher — must be held to a higher standard. Of course, the truth is that the entire tribe of the "New Atheists" is a disappointment. A reflective and brilliant atheist is a man much to be admired, if he truly demonstrates an understanding of what it is he is rejecting; and an atheist genuinely willing to accept the full implications of his convictions (Nietzsche being a nonpareil example) should not be reviled for those convictions. But it seems obvious that among the innumerable evidences of late modern culture's lack of spiritual depths one must include its manifest impotence to produce profound atheists. Instead, the best it seems we can hope for today are dreary purveyors of historical illiteracy, theatrical indignation, subfusc moralizing, and the sort of logical confusions that Richard Dawkins has brought to a level of almost transcendent perfection.

In any event, I am allowing myself to drift beyond the proper boundaries of an introduction. I shall close simply by making a few remarks on the pieces below.

Perhaps my least favorite among them is the first, which I wrote under the title "No Other God" but which was published as "Christ and Nothing." My dissatisfaction with it follows from my never having had a chance to transform it from a public address into a magazine article; consequently it is somewhat too orotund for my taste. It is, however, the most frequently cited of the articles gathered here, and the most popular as far as I can tell, and so I have left it largely as I wrote it, though I have retained the title by which it is generally known, while relegating the original (and better) title to parentheses.

In the article "The Laughter of the Philosophers," all the translations of passages from Hamann are those of John R. Betz. To that article, moreover, I have appended an extract from my response to the letters it provoked; I have not done this out of infatuation with my own voice, but because I thought that part of my response constituted a substantial addition to my original argument.

Three of the pieces below — "Tremors of Doubt," "Tsunami and Theology," and "Where Was God?" — are related to one another, and all three are related (either before or after the fact) to my book *The Doors of the Sea*. The first was a column written just a few days after the Indian Ocean earthquake and tsunami of the second day of Christmas, 2004, and the second was a short reflection written soon after, expanding upon the earlier piece; the former was requested by Erich Eichman, the religion editor of *The Wall Street Journal*, the latter by the editors of *First Things*. These two pieces, and the response they elicited, inspired Bill Eerdmans to suggest I write a short book on the same topic. "Where Was God?" is an interview prompted by that book, conducted by Jason Byassee of *The Christian Century,* and reprinted here by the kind permission of that journal.

"Theology as Knowledge" was written in response to an article by James Stoner called "The 'Naked' University: What If Theology Is Knowledge, Not Belief?" that appeared in *Theology Today* 62 (2006); it was printed, however, as if it were in response to another piece by Stoner, written for *First Things,* which rendered a few of its arguments seemingly irrelevant.

Finally, "On the Trail of the Snark with Daniel Dennett" was written originally as the first of two public addresses that I was obliged to deliver at Providence College during my year (2006-2007) as the incumbent of that institution's Robert J. Randall Distinguished Chair in Christian Culture, which was a very happy and enlightening year for me.

The majority of the pieces reprinted here appeared originally in *First Things: A Journal of Religion, Culture, and Public Life;* these include chapters 1 (October, 2003), 2 (March, 2001), 3 (December, 2003), 4 (January, 2004), 6 (May, 2004), 7 (June/July, 2004), 9 (January, 2005), 11 (March, 2005), 13 (February, 2005), 18 (October, 2005), 20 (May, 2006), and 21 (January, 2007). Two appeared in *The New Criterion:* chapters 5 (March, 2004) and 15 (June, 2005). Two appeared in *Touchstone: A Journal of Mere Christianity:* 17 (November, 2004) and 19 (November, 2005). Two appeared in *The New Atlantis: A Journal of Technology and Society:* chapters 8 (Summer, 2004) and 16 (Summer, 2005). Two appeared in *The Wall Street Journal:* chapters 10 (December 31, 2004) and 14 (April 1, 2005). And one, as I have said, appeared in *The Christian Century:* chapter 12 (January 10, 2006). All are reprinted with permission.

In closing I shall remark that I do not necessarily still hold every view expressed here — or, at least, hold it quite as fervently as once I did — but I can nevertheless reissue all of these pieces without any great reservations. My thanks to Robert Wilken for giving me the final push to bring this volume out, and to Bill Eerdmans for taking to the idea. I hope both men are satisfied with the result.

DAVID BENTLEY HART
July, 2007

1

Christ and Nothing (No Other God)

s modern men and women — to the degree that we are modern —
we believe in nothing. This is not to say, I should add, that we do not
believe in anything; I mean, rather, that we hold an unshakable, if often
unconscious, faith in *the* nothing, or in nothingness as such. It is this in
which we place our trust, upon which we venture our souls, and onto
which we project the values by which we measure the meaningfulness of
our lives. Or, to phrase the matter more simply and starkly, our religion is
one of comfortable nihilism.

This may seem a somewhat apocalyptic note to sound, without
warning or emollient prelude, but I believe I am saying nothing not almost tediously obvious. We live in an age whose chief moral value has
been determined, by overwhelming consensus, to be the absolute liberty
of personal volition, the power of each of us to choose what he or she believes, wants, needs, or must possess; our culturally most persuasive
models of human freedom are unambiguously voluntarist and, in a
rather debased and degraded way, Promethean; the will, we believe, is
sovereign because unpremised, free because spontaneous, and this is
the highest good. And a society that believes this must, at least implicitly,
embrace and subtly advocate a very particular moral metaphysics: the
unreality of any value higher than choice, or of any transcendent Good
ordering desire towards a higher end. Desire is free to propose, seize, accept or reject, want or not want — but not to obey. Thus society must be
secured against the intrusions of the Good, or of God, so that its citizens
may determine their own lives by the choices they make from a universe

of morally indifferent but variably desirable ends unencumbered by any prior grammar of obligation or value (in America, we call this the "wall of separation"). Thus the liberties that permit one to purchase lavender bed clothes, to enjoy pornography, to become a Unitarian, to market popular celebrations of brutal violence, or to destroy one's unborn child are all equally intrinsically good because all are expressions of an inalienable freedom of choice. But, of course, if the will determines itself only in and through such choices, free from any prevenient natural order, then it too is in itself nothing. And so, at the end of modernity, each of us who is true to the times is situated thus, facing not God, or the gods, or the Good beyond beings, but an abyss, over which presides the empty, inviolable authority of the individual will, whose impulses and decisions are their own moral index, and so in a sense precede the objects in which the will manifests its mysterious powers of election and dereliction.

This is not to say that — sentimental barbarians that we are — we do not still invite moral and religious constraints on our actions; none but the most demonic, demented, or adolescent among us genuinely desires to live in a world purged of visible boundaries and hospitable shelters. Thus this man may elect not to buy a particular car because he considers himself an environmentalist; or this woman may choose not to have an abortion midway through her second trimester, because the fetus, at that point in its gestation, seems to her too fully-formed, and she — personally — would feel wrong about terminating "it." But this merely illustrates my point: we take as given the individual's right not merely to obey or to defy the moral law, but to choose which moral standards to adopt, which values to uphold, which fashion of piety to wear and with what accessories. Even our ethics are achievements of will. And the same is true of those custom-fitted spiritualities — New Age, occult, pantheist, Wiccan, or what have you — by which many of us divert ourselves from the quotidian dreariness of our lives. These gods of the boutique can come from anywhere — native North American religion, the Indian subcontinent, a Pre-Raphaelite grove shrouded in Celtic twilight, cunning purveyors of otherwise worthless quartz, pages drawn at random from Robert Graves, Aldous Huxley, Carl Jung, or that redoubtable old Aryan Joseph Campbell — but where such gods inevitably come to rest are not so much divine hierarchies as ornamental *étagères*, where their principal office is to provide symbolic representations of the dreamier sides of their votaries' personalities. The triviality of this sort of devotion, its want of dogma or discipline, its tendency to find its divinities not in glades and grottoes but in gift-shops make it obvious that this is no reversion to pre-Christian polytheism. It is a thoroughly modern religion, whose burlesque gods command neither reverence, nor dread, nor love, nor belief; they are no more than the masks worn by that same spontaneity of will that is the one unrivalled demiurge who rules this age, and alone bids its spirits come and go.

Which brings me at last to my topic. "I am the Lord thy God," says the first commandment. "Thou shalt have no other gods before me." For Israel this was first and foremost a demand of fidelity, by which God bound his people to himself, even if in later years it became also a proclamation to the nations. To Christians, however, the commandment came through — and so was indissolubly bound to — Christ. As such, it was not simply a prohibition of foreign cults, but an assault upon the antique order of the heavens — a declaration of war upon the gods. All the world was to be evangelized and baptized, all idols overturned, all worship turned towards the one God who, in these latter days, had sent his Son into the world for our salvation. It was a long and sometimes terrible conflict, occasionally exacting a fearful price in martyrs' blood, but it was, by any just estimate, a victory: the temples of Zeus and Isis alike were finally deserted, both the paean and the dithyramb ceased to be sung, altars were bereft of sacrifices, the sibyls fell silent, and ultimately all the glory, nobility, and cruelty of the ancient world lay supine under the foot of Christ the conqueror. Nor, for early Christians, was this mere metaphor. When a gentile convert stood in the baptistery on Easter's eve and, before descending naked into the waters, turned to the West to renounce the devil and devil's ministers, he was rejecting, and in fact reviling, the gods who had held him in bondage all his life; and when he turned to the East to confess Christ, he was entrusting himself to the invincible hero who had plundered hell of its captives, overthrown death, subdued the powers of the air, and been raised the Lord of history. Life, for the early Church, was spiritual warfare; and no baptized Christian could doubt how great a transformation — of the self and the world — it was to consent to serve the God revealed in Christ, and no other.

The situation of the Church has materially altered, of course, but spiritual warfare is something intrinsic to the gospel; and I suspect that, by comparison to the burden the first commandment lays upon Christians today, the defeat of the ancient pantheon, and whatever elemental

3

spirits or demons lurked behind it, will prove to have been sublimely easy. As I say, we moderns believe in nothing: the nothingness of the will miraculously giving itself form by mastering the nothingness of the world. The gods, at least, were real, if distorted, intimations of the *mysterium tremendum,* and so could inspire something like holy dread or, occasionally, holy love. They were brutes, obviously, but often also benign despots, and all of us I think, in those secret corners of our souls where all of us are monarchists, can appreciate a good despot, if he is sufficiently dashing and enigmatic, and able to strike an attractive balance between capricious wrath and serene benevolence. Certainly the Olympians had panache, as well as a rather terrible beauty whose disappearance from the world was a bereavement to devout pagans. And the divine parvenus of Egypt and Asia who had largely displaced (or absorbed) them by the time the gospel was first preached were without question excellent showmen. Moreover, in their very objectivity and elevation over their worshippers, the gods gave the Church enemies with whom it could come to grips. Perhaps they were just so many gaudy veils and ornate brocades drawn across the abyss of night, death, and nature, but they had distinct shapes and established cults, and when their mysteries were abandoned so were they. How, though, to make war on nothingness, on the abyss itself, denuded of its mythic allure? It seems to me much easier to convince a man that he is in thrall to demons and offer him manumission than to convince him that he is a slave to himself and prisoner to his own will. Surely this is a god more elusive, protean, and indomitable than either Apollo or Dionysus; and whether he manifests himself in some demonic titanism of the will, like the mass delirium of the Third Reich, or simply in the mesmerizing banality of consumer culture, his throne has been set in the very hearts of those he enslaves. And it is this god, in all likelihood, against whom the first commandment obliges modern Christians to struggle most tirelessly.

There is, however, a complication. Christians are generally quite glad to believe that the commandment to have no other god, when allied to the gospel, liberated humanity from the injustices of the divine *ancien régime;* and they are happy to believe also that this same commandment must be proclaimed again if modern persons are to be rescued from the superstitions of the modern age; but there is another, more uncomfortable truth they should also be willing to acknowledge: that humanity could not have passed from the devotions of antiquity to those of modernity but for the force of Christianity in history, and so — as a matter of historical fact — Christianity, with its cry of "no other god," had a considerable part in giving birth to the nihilism of contemporary culture. The gospel shook the ancient world to its foundations, tore down the heavens, and in just this way helped to bring about the ruin of the present moment.

THE WORD "nihilism" has a complex history in modern philosophy, but I use it in a sense largely determined by Nietzsche and Heidegger, both of whom not only diagnosed modernity as nihilism, but saw Christianity as complicit in its genesis; both, it seems to me, were penetratingly correct in some respects, if disastrously wrong in others, and both raised questions that Christians ignore at their peril. Nietzsche's case is the cruder of the two, if in some ways the more perspicacious; for him, modernity is simply the final phase of the disease called Christianity. Whereas the genius of the Greeks — so his story goes — was to gaze without illusion into the chaos and terror of the world, and respond not with fear or resignation, but with affirmation and supreme artistry, they were able to do this only on account of their nobility, which means their ruthless willingness to discriminate between the "good" — that is, the strength, exuberance, bravery, generosity, and harshness of the aristocratic spirit — and the "bad" — the weakness, debility, timorousness, and vindictive resentfulness of the slavish mind. And this same standard — "noble wisdom," for want of a better term — was the foundation and mortar of Roman civilization. Christianity, however, was a slave-revolt in morality: the cunning of the weak triumphed over the nobility of the strong, the resentment of the many converted the pride of the few into self-torturing guilt, the higher man's distinction between the good and the bad was replaced by the lesser man's spiteful distinction between good and "evil," and the tragic wisdom of the Greeks sank beneath the flood of Christianity's pity and pusillanimity. This revolt then, joined to an ascetic and sterile devotion to positive fact, would ultimately slay even God. And, as a result, we have now entered the age of the Last Men, whom Nietzsche depicts in terms too close for comfort to the banality, conformity, and self-indulgence of modern mass culture. Heidegger's tale is not as catastrophist, and so emphasizes less Christianity's novelty than its continuity with a nihilism implicit in all Western thought, from at least the time of Plato (something that Nietzsche, in his way, also acknowledged).

Nihilism, says Heidegger, is born in a forgetfulness of the mystery of being, and in the attempt to capture and master being in artifacts of reason (the chief example — and indeed the prototype of every subsequent apostasy from true "ontology" — being Plato's ideas). Scandalously to oversimplify his argument, it is, says Heidegger, the history of this nihilistic impulse to reduce being to an object of the intellect, subject to the will, that has brought us at last to the age of technology, for which reality is just so many quanta of power, the world a representation of consciousness, and the earth a mere reserve awaiting exploitation; technological mastery has become our highest ideal, and our only real model of truth. Christianity, for its part, is not so much a new thing as a prolonged episode within the greater history of nihilism, notable chiefly for having brought part of this history's logic to its consummation by having invented the metaphysical God, the form of all forms, who grounds all of being in himself as absolute efficient cause, and who personifies that cause as total power and will. From this God, in the fullness of time, would be born the modern subject who has usurped God's place.

I hope I will be excused both for so cursory a *précis* and for the mild perversity that causes me to see some merit in both of these stories. Heidegger seems to me obviously correct in regarding modernity's nihilism as the fruition of seeds sown in pagan soil; and Nietzsche correct to call attention to Christianity's shocking — and, for the antique order of noble values, irreparably catastrophic — novelty; but neither grasped why he was correct. For indeed Christianity was complicit in the death of antiquity, and in the birth of modernity, not because it was an accomplice of the latter, but because it, alone in the history of the West, constituted a rejection of and alternative to nihilism's despair, violence, and idolatry of power; as such, Christianity shattered the imposing and enchanting façade behind which nihilism once hid, and thereby, inadvertently, called it forth into the open.

I am speaking (impressionistically, I grant) of something pervasive in the ethos of European antiquity, which I would call a kind of glorious sadness. The great Indo-European mythos, from which Western culture sprang, was chiefly one of sacrifice: it understood the cosmos as a closed system, a finite totality, within which gods and mortals alike occupied places determined by fate; and this totality was, of necessity, an economy, a cycle of creation and destruction, oscillating between order and chaos, form and indeterminacy: a great circle of feeding, preserving life through a system of transactions with death. This is the myth of "cosmos" — of the universe as a precarious equilibrium of contrary forces — which undergirded a sacral practice whose aim was to contain nature's promiscuous violence within religion's orderly violence. The terrible dynamism of nature had to be both resisted and controlled, by rites at once apotropaic — appeasing chaos and rationalizing it within the stability of cult — and economic — recuperating its sacrificial expenditures in the form of divine favor, a numinous power reinforcing the regime sacrifice served. And this regime was, naturally, a fixed hierarchy of social power, atop which stood the gods, a little lower kings and nobles, and at the bottom slaves; the order of society — which was continuous with the natural and divine order of reality — was a fixed and yet somehow fragile "hierarchy within totality" that had to be preserved against the forces that surrounded it, while yet drawing on those forces for its spiritual sustenance. Gods and mortals were bound together by necessity; we fed the gods, who required our sacrifices, and they preserved us from the forces they personified and granted us some measure of their power. There was, surely, an ineradicable nihilism in such an economy: a tragic resignation before fate, followed by a prudential act of cultic salvage, for the sake of social and cosmic stability.

The word "tragic," incidentally, is especially apt here. A sacrificial mythos need not always express itself in slaughter, after all. Attic tragedy, for instance, began as a kind of sacrificial rite. It was performed during the festival of Dionysus, which was a fertility festival, of course, but only because it was also an apotropaic celebration of delirium and death: the *Dionysia* was a sacred negotiation with the wild, antinomian cruelty of the god whose violent orgiastic cult had once, so it was believed, gravely imperiled the city; and the hope that prompted the feast was that, if this devastating force could be contained within bright Apollonian forms and propitiated through a ritual carnival of controlled disorder, the polis could survive for another year, its precarious peace intact. The religious vision from which Attic tragedy emerged was one of the human community as a kind of besieged citadel preserving itself through the tribute it paid to the powers that both threatened and enlivened it. There is no better epitome of this vision of things than *Antigone,* in which the tragic crisis is the result of an insoluble moral conflict between familial piety (a sacred obligation) and the civil duties of kingship (a holy office): Antigone, as a woman, is bound to the chthonian gods (gods of the dead, so of family and household), and Creon, as king, is bound to Apollo (god of the city), and so both are adhering to sacred obligations. The conflict between them, then, far from involving a tension between the profane and the holy, is a conflict within the divine itself, whose only possible resolution is the death — the sacrifice — of the protagonist. Necessity's cruel intransigence rules the gods no less than us. In general, Attic tragedy's great power is that of reconciling us to this truth, to what must be, and to the violences of the city that keep at bay the greater violence of cosmic or social disorder.

Nor does one require extraordinarily penetrating insight to see how the shadow of this mythos falls across the philosophical schools of antiquity. To risk a generalization even more reckless than those I have already ventured: from the time of the pre-Socratics, all the great speculative and moral systems of the pagan world were, in varying degrees, confined to this totality, to either its innermost mechanisms or outermost boundaries; rarely did any of them catch even a glimpse of what might lie beyond such a world; and none could conceive of reality except as a kind of strife between order and disorder, within which a sacrificial economy held all forces in tension. This is true even of original Platonism, at least in its more dualistic moments, with its dialectic of change and the changeless (or of limit and the infinite) and its equation of truth with eidetic abstraction; the world, for all its beauty, is the realm of fallen vision, separated by a great *chorismos* from the realm of immutable reality. It is true of Aristotle too: the dialectic of act and potency that, for sublunary beings, is inseparable from decay and death, or the scale of essences by which all things — especially various classes of persons — are assigned their places in the natural and social order. Stoicism offers an obvious example: a vision of the universe as a fated, eternally repeated divine and cosmic history, a world in which finite forms must constantly perish simply in order to make room for others, and which in its entirety is always consumed in a final *ecpyrosis* (which makes a sacrificial pyre, so to speak, of the whole universe). And Neoplatonism furnishes the most poignant example, inasmuch as its monism merely inverts earlier Platonism's dualism, and only magnifies the melancholy: the mutable world is separated from its divine principle — the One — by intervals of emanation that descend in ever greater alienation from their source, and so — inasmuch as the highest truth is a secret identity between the human mind and the One — the labor of philosophy is one of escape: all multiplicity, change, particularity, every feature of the living world, is not only accidental to this formless identity, but a kind of falsehood, and to recover the truth that dwells within, one must detach oneself from what lies without, including the sundry incidentals of one's individual existence; truth is oblivion of the flesh, a pure nothingness, to attain which one must sacrifice the world.

IN ANY EVENT, the purpose behind these indefensibly broad pronouncements — however elliptically pursued — is to aid in recalling how shatteringly subversive Christianity was of so many of the certitudes of the world it entered, and how profoundly its exclusive fidelity to the God of Christ transformed that world. This is, of course, entirely in keeping with the New Testament's Paschal triumphalism: "Now is the judgment of this world, now will the prince of this world be cast out" (John 12:31); "I have overcome the world" (John 16:33); he is "far above all principality, and power, and might, and dominion" and all things are put "under his feet" (Eph. 1:21-22); "having spoiled principalities and powers, he made a show of them openly, triumphing over them in it" (Col. 2:15); "he led captivity captive" (Eph. 4:8); and so on. Still we can largely absorb scripture's talk of the defeat of the devil, the angels of the nations, and the powers of the air, and yet fail to recognize how radically the Gospels reinterpreted (or, as Nietzsche would say, "transvalued") everything in the light of Easter.

Read in the context of its time, for example, what could be more seditious than the account John's Gospel gives of the dialogue between Christ and Pilate (John 18:28-19:12)? Nietzsche, the quixotic champion of the old standards, thought jesting Pilate's "What is truth?" to be the only moment of actual nobility in the New Testament, the wry taunt of an acerbic ironist rightly repelled by the pathetic fantasies of a deranged peasant. But one need not share Nietzsche's sympathies to take his point; one can certainly see what is at stake when Christ, scourged and mocked, is brought before Pilate a second time. The latter's "Whence art thou?" has about it something of a demand for a pedigree, which might at least lend some credibility to the claims Christ makes for himself; for want of which, Pilate can do little other than pronounce his truth: "I have power to crucify thee" (which would under most circumstances, to be fair, be an incontrovertible argument). It is worth asking ourselves what this *tableau*, viewed from the vantage of pagan antiquity, would have meant? A man of noble birth, representing the power of Rome, endowed

9

with authority over life and death, confronted by a barbarous colonial, of no name or estate, a slave of the empire, beaten, robed in purple, crowned with thorns, insanely invoking an otherworldly kingdom, and some esoteric truth, unaware of either his absurdity or his judge's eminence. Who could have doubted where, between these two, the truth of things was to be found? But the Gospel is written in the light of the resurrection, which reverses the meaning of this scene entirely. If God's truth is in fact to be found where Christ stands, the mockery visited on him redounds instead upon the emperor, all of whose regal finery, when set beside the majesty of the servile shape in which God reveals himself, shows itself to be just so many rags and briars. This slave is the Father's eternal Word, whom God has vindicated with victory, and so ten thousand immemorial certainties are unveiled as lies: the first become last, the mighty are put down from their seats and the lowly exalted, the hungry are filled with good things while the rich are sent empty away. Nietzsche was quite right to be appalled. Almost as striking, for me, is the tale of Peter, at the cock's crow, going apart to weep. Nowhere in the literature of pagan antiquity, I assure you, had the tears of a rustic been regarded as worthy of anything but ridicule; to treat them with reverence, as meaningful expressions of real human sorrow, would have seemed grotesque from the perspective of all the classical canons of good taste. Those wretchedly subversive tears, and the dangerous philistinism of a narrator so incorrigibly vulgar as to treat them with anything but contempt, were most definitely signs of a slave-revolt in morality, if not quite the one against which Nietzsche inveighed — a revolt moreover that all the ancient powers proved impotent to resist.

In a narrow sense, then, one might say that the chief offense of the Gospels is their defiance of the insights of tragedy — and not only because Christ does not fit the model of the well-born tragic hero. More important is the incontestable truth that, in the Gospels, the destruction of the protagonist emphatically does not restore or affirm the order of city or cosmos. Were the Gospels to end with Christ's sepulture, in good tragic style, it would exculpate all parties, including Pilate and the Sanhedrin, whose judgments would be shown to have been fated by the exigencies of the crisis and the burdens of their offices; the story would then reconcile us to the tragic necessity of all such judgments. But instead comes Easter, which rudely interrupts all the minatory and sententious moralisms of the tragic chorus, just as they are about to be uttered to full effect, and which moreover cavalierly violates the central tenet of sound economics: rather than trading the sacrificial victim for some supernatural benefit, and so the particular for the universal, Easter restores the slain hero in his particularity again, as the only truth the Gospels have to offer. This is more than a dramatic peripety. The empty tomb overturns all the "responsible" and "necessary" verdicts of Christ's judges, and so grants them neither legitimacy nor pardon.

In a larger sense, then, the entire sacrificial logic of a culture was subverted in the Gospels. I cannot attempt here a treatment of the biblical language of sacrifice, but I think I can safely assert that Christ's death does not, in the logic of the New Testament sources, fit the pattern of sacrifice I have just described. The word "sacrifice" is almost inexhaustible in its polysemy, particularly in the Old Testament, but the only sacrificial model explicitly invoked in the New Testament is that of the Atonement offering of Israel, which certainly belongs to no cosmic cycle of prudent expenditure and indemnity. It is, rather, a *qurban,* literally a "drawing nigh" into the life-giving presence of God's glory. Israel's God requires nothing, he creates, elects, and sanctifies without need; and so the Atonement offering can in no way contribute to any sort of economy; it is instead a penitent approach to a God who gives life freely, and who not only does not profit from the holocaust of the particular, but who in fact fulfills the "sacrifice" simply by giving his gift again. This giving again is itself, in fact, a kind of "sacrificial" motif in Hebrew scripture, achieving its most powerful early expression in the story of Isaac's *aqedah,* and arriving at its consummation, perhaps, in Ezekiel's vision in the valley of dry bones. After all, a people overly burdened by the dolorous superstitions of tragic wisdom could never have come to embrace the doctrine of resurrection. I am tempted to say, then, that the cross of Christ is not simply *a* sacrifice, but the place where two opposed understandings of sacrifice clashed. Christ's whole life was a reconciling *qurban:* an approach to the Father, and a real indwelling of God's glory in the temple of Christ's body, and an atonement made for a people enslaved to death; in pouring himself out in the form of a servant, and in living his humanity as an offering up of everything to God in love, the shape of the eternal Son's life was already sacrificial in this special sense; and it was this absolute giving, as God and man, that was made complete on Golgotha. While, from a pagan perspective (on the other hand), the crucifixion itself could be viewed as a sacrifice in the most proper sense — destruction of the agent of social instability for the sake of peace, which is always a profitable exchange — Christ's life of charity, service, forgiveness, and righteous judgment could not; indeed, it would have to be seen as the very opposite of sacrifice, an aneconomic and indiscriminate inversion of rank and order. Yet, at Easter, it is the latter God accepts and the former he rejects; what then of all the hard-won tragic wisdom of the ages?

Naturally, also, with the death of the old mythos, metaphysics too was transformed. For one thing, while every antique system of philosophy had to presume an economy of necessity binding the world of becoming to its inmost or highest principles, Christian theology taught from the first that the world was God's creature in the most radically ontological sense: that it is called from nothingness, not out of any need on God's part, but by grace. The world adds nothing to the being of God, and so nothing need be sacrificed for his glory or sustenance. In a sense, God and world alike were liberated from the fetters of necessity; God could be accorded his true transcendence and the world its true character as divine gift. The full implications of this probably became visible to Christian philosophers only with the resolution of the fourth-century Trinitarian controversies, when the subordinationist schemes of Alexandrian Trinitarianism were abandoned, and with them the last residue within theology of the late antique metaphysical vision of a descending scale of divinity mediating between God and world — the both of them comprised in a single totality. That is a technical and disputable point, though; one more general, and uncontroversial, is that theology rejected nothing good in the metaphysics, ethics, or method of antique philosophy, but — with a kind of omnivorous glee — assimilated such elements as served its ends, and always improved them in the process. Stoic morality, Plato's language of the Good, Aristotle's metaphysics of act and potency — all became richer and more coherent when emancipated from the morbid myths of sacrificial economy and tragic necessity. In truth, Christian theology nowhere more wantonly celebrated its triumph over the old gods than in the use it made of the so-called *spolia Aegyptorum;* and, by despoiling pagan philosophy of its most splendid achievements, and integrating them into a vision of reality more complete than philosophy could attain on its own, theology took to itself irrevocably all the intellectual glories of antiquity. The temples were stripped of their gold and precious ornaments, the sacred vessels were carried away into the precincts of the Church and turned to better uses, and nothing was left behind but a few grim, gaunt ruins to lure back the occasional disenchanted convert and to shelter a few atavistic ghosts.

THIS LAST OBSERVATION returns me at last to my earlier contention: that Christianity assisted in bringing the nihilism of modernity to pass. The command to have no other god but the God of Christ was never for Christians simply an invitation to forsake an old cult for a new, but was an announcement that the shape of the world had changed, from the depths of hell to the heaven of heavens, and all nations were called to submit to Jesus as Lord. In the great "transvaluation" that followed, there was no sphere of social, religious, or intellectual life that the Church did not claim for itself; much was abolished, and much of the grandeur and beauty of antiquity was preserved in a radically altered form, and Christian civilization — with its new synthesis and new creativity — was born. But what is the consequence, then, when Christianity, as a living historical force, recedes? We have no need to speculate, as it happens; modernity speaks for itself: with the withdrawal of Christian culture, all the glories of the ancient world that it baptized and redeemed have perished with it in the general cataclysm. Christianity is the midwife of nihilism, not because it is itself nihilistic, but because it is too powerful in its embrace of the world and all of the world's mystery and beauty; and so to reject Christianity now is, of necessity, to reject everything except the barren anonymity of spontaneous subjectivity. As Ivan Karamazov's Grand Inquisitor tells Christ, the freedom that the gospel brings is too terrible to be borne indefinitely. Sin makes us feeble and craven, and we long to flee from the liberty of the sons of God; but where now can we go? Everything is Christ's.

It is tempting to take the history of modern philosophy — at least in its continental (and, so to speak, proper) form — as a particularly vivid illustration of this point. There is something of a theological fashion at present of attempting precise genealogies of modernity, which would be a task far too ambitious for this essay; but it does seem clear to me that the special preoccupations and perversities of modern philosophy were incubated in the age of late scholasticism, with the rise of nominalism and voluntarism: whereas earlier theology spoke of God as Goodness as such, whose every act (by virtue of divine simplicity) expresses his nature, the specter that haunts much of late scholastic thought is a God

13

whose will precedes his nature, and whose acts then are feats of pure spontaneity. It is a logically incoherent way of conceiving of God, as it happens, but it is a powerful idea, elevating as it does will over all else and redefining freedom — for God and, by extension, for us — not as the unhindered realization of a nature (the liberty to "become what you are"), but as the absolute liberty of the will in determining even what its nature is. Thus when modern philosophy established itself anew as a discipline autonomous from theology, it did so naturally by falling back upon an ever more abyssal subjectivity. Real autonomy could not be gained by turning back to the wonder of being or to the transcendental perfections of the world, for to do so would be to slip again into a sphere long colonized by theology; and so the new point of departure for reason had to be the perceiving subject rather than the world perceived. Descartes, for instance, explicitly forbade himself any recourse to the world's testimony of itself; in his third Meditation, he seals all his senses against nature, so that he can undertake his rational reconstruction of reality from a position pure of any certitude save that of the ego's own existence. The world is recovered thereafter only insofar as it is posited, as an act of will. And while God appears in that reconstruction, he does so only as a logical postulate following from the idea of the infinite. From there, it is a short step to Kant's transcendental ego, for whom the world is the representation of its own irreducible "I think," and which (inasmuch as it is its own infinity) requires God as a postulate only in the realm of ethics, and merely as a regulative idea in the realm of epistemology. And the passage from transcendental idealism to absolute idealism, however much it involved an attempt to escape egoistic subjectivity, had no world to which to return; even Hegel's system, for all that it sought to have done with petty subjectivism, could do so only by way of a massive metaphysical myth of the self-positing of the Concept, and of a more terrible economy of necessity than any pagan antiquity had imagined. This project was, in every sense, incredible, and its collapse inevitably brought philosophy, by way of Nietzsche and Heidegger, to its "postmodern condition" — a "heap of broken images." If Heidegger was right — and he was — in saying that there was always a nihilistic core to the Western philosophical tradition, the withdrawal of Christianity leaves nothing but that core behind, for the gospel long ago stripped away both the deceits and the glories that had concealed it; and so philosophy becomes, almost by force of habit, explicit nihilism.

Modern philosophy, however, merely reflects the state of modern culture and modern cult. And here, I should admit, I feel a certain sympathy for Nietzsche's melancholy plaint, "Nearly two-thousand years and no new god"; and for Heidegger's mournful, twilight oracle: "Only a god can save us." No new gods, of course, will come. The Christian God has taken up everything into himself; all the treasures of ancient wisdom, all the splendor of creation, every good thing has been assumed into the story of the incarnate God, and every stirring towards transcendence is soon recognized by the modern mind — weary of God — as leading back towards faith. Antique pieties cannot be restored, for we moderns know that the hungers they excite can be sated only by the gospel of Christ crucified. To be a Stoic today, for instance, is simply to be a soul *in via* to the Church; a Platonist, most of us understand, is only a Christian *manqué;* and a polytheist is merely a truant from the one God he hates and loves. The only cult that can truly thrive in the aftermath of Christianity is a narrow service of the self, of the impulses of the will, of the nothingness that is all that the withdrawal of Christianity leaves behind. The only futures open to post-Christian culture are conscious nihilism, with its inevitable devotion to death, or the narcotic banality of the Last Men, which is a kind of death in life. Surveying the desert of modernity, it would be a kind of moral dereliction for Christians to fail to acknowledge that Nietzsche was right in holding Christianity responsible (even if he misunderstood why) for the catastrophe around us. Christians should be willing to confess that the failure of Christian culture to live up to its victory over the old gods has allowed the dark power that once hid behind them to step forward *in propria persona.* And everyone with some consciousness of cultural history should certainly dread whatever rough beast it is that is being bred in our ever coarser, crueler, more inarticulate, more vacuous popular culture; because, cloaked in its anodyne insipience, lies a world increasingly devoid of merit, wit, kindness, imagination, or charity.

These are, I admit, extreme formulations; but I do not intend them simply as provocations. When recently I made these very remarks from a speaker's podium, two theologians (neither of whom I would consider a champion of modernity) raised objections to them. From one quarter, I was chided for forgetting the selflessness of which modern persons are capable; on 11 September 2001, I was reminded, we had seen plenteous demonstrations of that selflessness; and those of us who teach undergraduates must be aware that, for all the cultural privations they suffer, they are often decent and admirable. From the other quarter I was cautioned that too starkly stated an alternative of "Christianity or nihilism" amounted to a denial of the goodness of natural wisdom and virtue, and seemed to suggest that *gratia non perficit, sed destruit naturam*. As fair, however, as such remarks may seem, they are not apposite to the argument I mean to advance.

To the former objection, I would wish to reply by making clear that I do not intend to suggest that, because modernity has lost the organic integrity of Christianity's moral grammar, every person living in modern society must therefore become heartless, violent, or unprincipled. My observations are directed at the dominant language and ethos of a culture, not at the souls of individuals. Many among us retain some loyalty to ancient principles, most of us are in some degree pre-modern, and there are always and everywhere to be found examples of natural virtue, innate nobility, congenital charity, and so on; if Christian teaching is correct, the light of God is ubiquitous and the image of God is impressed upon our nature. The issue for me is whether, within the moral grammar of modernity, any of these good souls could give an account of his or her virtue. I wish, that is, to make a point not conspicuously different from Alasdair MacIntyre's in the first chapter of his *After Virtue:* that is, what an odd *bricolage* ethics has become in the wake of a morality of the Good. As far as I can tell, *homo nihilisticus* may often be in several notable respects a far more amiable rogue than *homo religiosus,* exhibiting a far smaller propensity for breaking the crockery, destroying sacred statuary, or slaying the nearest available infidel. But, love, let us be true to one another: even when all of this is granted, it would be a willful and culpable blindness for us to refuse to recognize how culturally arid and spiritually impoverished our society has become — which any unprejudiced survey of the artifacts of popular culture will effortlessly confirm. How, after all, should Christians regard the present age when, in America alone, more than 40 million babies have been killed in the womb since the Supreme Court invented the right to abortion, and when there are many who see these deaths not just as tragic necessities, but as blameless consequences of a moral social triumph? When the Carthaginians were prevailed upon to cease sacrificing their babies, at least the place vacated by Baal reminded them that they should seek the divine above themselves; but our culture offers up its babies to "my" freedom of choice, to "me." Surely a Christian must doubt that any other society's moral vision has ever shown itself to be more degenerate.

To the latter objection, I would make three responses. First, my remarks here do not concern the entirety of human experience, nature, or culture; they concern one particular location in time and space: late Western modernity. Nor have I anything to say about cultures or peoples who have not suffered the history of faith and disenchantment we have, or who do not share our particular relation to European antiquity or the heritage of ancient Christendom. "Nihilism" is simply a name for post-Christian sensibility and conviction (and not even an especially opprobrious one). Second, the alternative between Christianity and nihilism is never, in actual practice, a kind of Kierkegaardian either/or posed between two absolute antinomies, incapable of alloy or medium; it is an antagonism that occurs along a continuum, whose extremes are rarely perfectly expressed in any single life (else the world were all saints and satanists). Third, and most important, my observations do not concern nature at all, which is inextinguishable and which, at some level, always longs for God; they concern culture, which has the power to purge itself of the natural in some considerable degree. Indeed, much of the discourse of late modernity — speculative, critical, moral, and political — consists precisely in an attempt to deny the authority, or even the reality, of any general order of nature or natures. Nature is good, I readily affirm, and is itself the first gift of grace. But that is rather the point at issue: modernity is profoundly unnatural.

Which is why I repeat that our age is not one in danger of reverting to paganism (would that we were so fortunate). If we turn from Christ today, we turn only towards the god of absolute will, and embrace him under either his most monstrous or his most vapid aspect. A somewhat more ennobling retreat to the old gods is not possible for us; we can find no shelter there, nor can we sink away gently into those old illusions and tragic consolations that Christ has exposed as falsehoods. To love or be nourished by the gods, we would have to fear them; but the ruin of their glory is so complete that they have been reduced — like everything else — to commodities. Nor will the ululations and lugubrious platitudes and pious fatalism of the tragic chorus ever again have the power to recall us to sobriety. The gospel of a God found in broken flesh, humility, and measureless charity has defeated the old lies, rendered the ancient order visibly insufficient and even slightly absurd, and instilled in us a longing for transcendent love so deep that — if once yielded to — it will never grant us rest anywhere but in Christ. And there is a real sadness in this, because the consequences of so great a joy rejected are a sorrow, bewilderment, and anxiety for which there is no precedent. If the nonsensical religious fascinations of today are not, in any classical or Christian sense, genuine pieties, they are nevertheless genuine — if deluded — expressions of grief, encomia for a forsaken and half-forgotten home, the prisoner's lament over a lost freedom. For Christians, then, to recover and understand the meaning of the command to have "no other god," it is necessary first to recognize that the victory of the Church in history was not only incomplete, but indeed set free a force that the old sacral order had at least been able to contain; and it is against this more formless and invincible enemy that this commandment urges Christians today.

This commandment has always been a hard discipline: it destroys, it breaks in order to bind; like a cautery, it wounds in order to heal. In practical terms, I suspect that this means that Christians must make an ever more concerted effort to recall and recover the wisdom and centrality of the ascetic tradition. It takes formidable faith and devotion to resist the evils of one's age, and it is to the history of Christian asceticism — especially, perhaps, the apothegms of the Desert Fathers — that all Christians, whether married or not, should turn for guidance. To have no god but the God of Christ, after all, means today that we must endure the Lenten privations of what is most certainly a dark age, and strive to resist the bland solace, inane charms, brute viciousness, and dazed passivity of post-Christian culture — all of which are so tempting precisely because they enjoin us to believe in and adore ourselves. It means also to remain aloof from many of the moral languages of our time, which are — even at their most sentimental, tender, and tolerant — usually as decadent and egoistic as the currently most fashionable vices. It means, in short, self-abnegation, contrarianism, a willingness not only to welcome but to condemn, and a refusal of secularization as resolute as the refusal of the ancient Christians to burn incense to the genius of the emperor. This is not an especially grim prescription, I should add: Christian asceticism is not, after all, a cruel disfigurement of the will, contaminated by world-weariness or malice towards creation; it is a different kind of detachment, the cultivation of the pure heart and pure eye, which allows one to receive the world, and rejoice in it, not as a possession of the will or an occasion for the exercise of power, but as the good gift of God. It is, so to speak, a kind of Marian waiting upon the Word of God and its fruitfulness. Paradoxical as it may seem to modern temperaments, Christian asceticism is the practice of love, what Maximus the Confessor calls learning to see the logos of each thing within the Logos of God, and it leads most properly to the grateful reverence of a Bonaventure or the lyrical ecstasy of a Thomas Traherne.

Still, it is a discipline for all that; and for modern Christians it must involve the painful acknowledgement that neither they nor their distant progeny will live to see a new Christian culture rise in the Western world, and to accept this with both charity and faith. After all, in the mystery of God's providence, all of this has followed from the work of the Holy Spirit in time. Modern persons will never find rest for their restless hearts without Christ, for modern culture is nothing but the wasteland from which the gods have departed, and so this restlessness has become its own deity; and, deprived of the shelter of the sacred and the consoling myths of sacrifice, the modern person must wander or drift, vainly attempting one or another accommodation with death, never escaping anxiety or *ennui,* and driven as a result to a ceaseless labor of distraction, or acquisition, or willful idiocy. And, where it works its sublimest magic, our culture of empty spectacle can so stupefy the intellect as to blind it to its own disquiet, and induce a spiritual torpor more deplorable than mere despair. But perhaps Christians — while not ignoring how appalling such a condition may be — should actually rejoice that modernity offers no religious comforts to those who seek them. If this is a time of waiting, marked most deeply by the absence of faith in Christ, it is perhaps good that the modern soul should lack repose, piety, peace, or nobility, and should often find the world outside the Church barren of spiritual rapture or mystery, and should go about vainly looking for beautiful or terrible or merciful gods to adore. With Christ came judgment into the world, a light of discrimination from which there is neither retreat nor sanctuary. And this means that, as a quite concrete historical condition, the only choice that remains for the children of post-Christian culture is not whom to serve, but whether to serve the God Christ has revealed or to serve nothing — *the* nothing. No third way lies open now, because — as all of us now know, whether we acknowledge it consciously or not — all things have been made subject to him, all the thrones and dominions of the high places have been put beneath his feet, until the very end of the world, and — simply said — there *is* no other god.

2

Notes on John Paul II's Pontificate, 2001

As John Paul II's extraordinary pontificate enters its twilight (one hopes a long and golden one), it is well to reflect upon his enormous achievements and celebrate them with the grateful admiration they merit. But it is also well to recall the sobering truth that the one aim that, by his own avowal, has always lain closest to his heart — reconciliation between the Eastern and Roman Churches — has proved to be the source of his gravest disappointment, and probably the only manifest failure that can be placed in the balance over against his innumerable successes. As an Orthodox Christian in the ecumenical "left wing" of my Church, I cannot speak for all my coreligionists; but I can record my own perplexity regarding the failure of most Orthodox hierarchs at least to recognize the remarkable gesture made by John Paul II in *Ut Unum Sint,* in openly soliciting advice on how to understand his office (even indeed the limits of its jurisdiction), or to respond with anything like comparable generosity of spirit. However, the pope has perhaps always been somewhat quixotic in his reckoning of the severity of the differences between the communions, and so of the effort required to effect any real reciprocal understanding between them (let alone *rapprochement*).

Anyone familiar with the Eastern Christian world knows that the Orthodox view of the Catholic Church is often a curious *mélange* of fact, fantasy, cultural prejudice, sublime theological misunderstanding, resentment, reasonable disagreement, and unreasonable dread: a misty phantasmagoria of crusades, predestination, "modalism," a God of wrath, flagellants, Grand Inquisitors, and those *blasted* Borgias. But, still, and from my own perspective *ab oriente,* I must remark that the greater miscalculation of what divides us is almost inevitably found on the Catholic side, not always entirely free of a certain unreflective condescension. Often Western theologians, justifiably offended by the hostility with which their advances are met by certain Orthodox, assume that the greatest obstacle to reunion is Eastern immaturity and divisiveness. The problem is dismissed as one of "psychology," and the only counsel offered one of "patience." Fair enough: decades of communist tyranny set atop centuries of other, far more invincible tyrannies have effectively shattered the Orthodox world into a contentious confederacy of national churches struggling to preserve their own regional identities against every alien influence, and under such conditions only the most obdurate stock survives. But psychology is the least of our problems.

In truth, so vehement is this pope's love of Eastern Christianity that it has often blinded him to the most inexorable barriers between the churches. As an error of judgment, this is an endearing one, but also one possible only from the Western vantage; for there is an obvious and even necessary asymmetry in the way the Christian East and the Christian West regard one another. *Of course* a Catholic who looks eastward finds nothing to which he objects, because what he sees is the Church of the Seven Ecumenical Councils (but — here's the rub — for him, this means the *first* seven of twenty-one). When an Orthodox turns his eyes westward he sees what appears to him a Church distorted by innovation and error: the *filioque* clause, the pope's absolute primatial authority, Purgatory, indulgences, priestly celibacy. . . . Our deepest divisions concern theology and doctrine, and this problem admits of no immediately obvious remedy, because both Churches are so fearfully burdened by infallibility. Of course, *theological* disagreements can be mitigated: Western theologians now freely grant that the Eastern view of original sin is more biblical than certain Latin treatments of the matter, and openly lean towards the Eastern view of grace; only the most obtusely truculent Orthodox still believe that the huge differences in Trinitarian theology that a previous generation found everywhere in Latin tradition indeed actually exist; etc. But *doctrine* is more intractable. The Catholic Church might plausibly contemplate the suppression of the *filioque,* but could it repudiate the claim that the papacy ever possessed the authority to allow such an addition? The Eastern Church believes in sanctification after death, and perhaps the doctrine of Purgatory really asserts nothing more; but can Rome ever say that in speaking of it as "temporal punishment," which the pope may in whole or part remit, it was in error? And so on.

Even if we retreat to the issue of psychology again, here too Catholic ecumenists often misconstrue the nature of the Orthodox distrust of their good will. It is not simply the case that the Orthodox are so fissiparous and jealous of their autonomy that the Petrine office appears to them a dangerous principle of homogeneity, a *regula oboedientiae* to which their fractious Eastern wills cannot submit. Jurisdictional squabbling aside, the Orthodox world enjoys so profound a unity — of faith, worship, spirituality, and ecclesiology — that the papacy cannot but appear to it as a dangerous principle of plurality. After all, under the capacious canopy of the papal office, so many disparate things find common shelter. Eastern rites huddle alongside liturgical practices (hardly a peripheral issue in the East) disfigured by rebarbative banality, by hymnody both insipid and heterodox, and by a style of worship that looks flippant if not blasphemous. Academic theologians explicitly reject principles of Catholic orthodoxy, but suffer no adverse consequences for their acts. At least three men are called Patriarch of Antioch in the Roman communion — there would be four, but the Latin Patriarchate has been suppressed — which suggests that the very title of patriarch, even as regards an apostolic see, is merely an honorific bauble, attached to the metropolitan bishop of a particular liturgical rite, because the only unique patriarchal office is the pope's. As unfair as it may seem to some Catholic observers, to Orthodox Christians it often appears as if, from the Catholic side, so long as the pope's supremacy is acknowledged, all else is irrelevant ornament. Which yields the sad irony that the more the Catholic Church strives to accommodate Orthodox concerns, the more disposed many Orthodox are to see in this merely the advance embassy of an omnivorous ecclesial empire.

All of which sounds rather grim. But I say it so that — proper qualifications made — I can praise John Paul II for all he has done for the unity of the apostolic Churches. He is, one likes to think, a visionary on this matter. True, human beings cannot overcome the obstacles dividing East from West; but the unity of the Church is never — even when it is only two or three gathered in Christ's name — a human work. Each Church is grievously wounded by its separation from the other, and only those who have allowed pride and infantile anger to displace love in their hearts are blind to this.

Moreover, our need for one another grows greater with the years. It is occasionally asserted that the future of society in the West — and perhaps of the world — is open to three "options": Christianity, Islam, and a consumerism so devoid of transcendent values as to be, inevitably, nothing but a pervasive and pitiless nihilism. The last of these has the singular power of absorbing some of the energies of almost any cultural reality without at first obviously draining it of its essence; the second enjoys a dogmatic warrant for militancy and a cultural cohesiveness born both of the clarity of its creed and the refining adversities of political and economic misfortune; but the only tools at Christianity's disposal will be evangelism and unity. The confrontation between the Church and modern consumerism will continue to expand principally from the West, where a fresh infusion of Orthodoxy's otherworldliness may prove a useful inoculant; but the encounter or confrontation with Islam, though it is global, will continue to move outward from the East. It is impossible to say what peace will be wrought there or what calamity, but it may well be that the papal office, with its special capacity for "strengthening the brethren" and speaking the truth to the world, will prove indispensable. The present pope has long been the great, indefatigable voice of Christian conviction in a faithless age. If future popes follow his lead, and speak out forcibly on behalf of the Christians — in Egypt, Syria, Turkey, and elsewhere — who will most acutely suffer the pressure of this difficult future, love will ever more drive out suspicion, and the vision of unity that inspires John Paul II *will* bear fruit. *Sic*, at any rate, *oremus*.

3

A Most Partial Historian:
On Maurice Cowling's Religion and Public
Doctrine in Modern England

Volume III: *Accommodations* (Cambridge University Press, 2001);
Volume II: *Assaults* (Cambridge University Press, 1985); Volume I
(Cambridge University Press, 1980)

Maurice Cowling (b. 1926) has never gained wide celebrity in Britain, and is all but unknown beyond its shores, even though he is
arguably among the most accomplished historians of the twentieth century. In part, this is a neglect attributable to something indefinably elliptical in his work — his concern for topics that often excite only other
scholars, perhaps, or the simultaneous subtlety and diamantine hardness of his prose — but in far greater part, I suspect, it is attributable to
the unfashionable cast of his ideas. His intellectual convictions are conservative and "Christian," if idiosyncratically so in both respects, and neither quality endears him to those many British academics and assorted
savants to whom this can mean only that he is a dangerous reactionary;
and, even among the Christian intelligentsia of those isles, his importance may occasionally be acknowledged, but often with more than a little suspicion, or even hostility.

I, for one, can attest to the latter reality. I was a postgraduate at Cambridge in the middle '80s, at some remove from Cowling's haunts but still
within range of many of the ripples that spread from him, and while
there I learned how pronounced was the distaste the earnest English
Christians in the Divinity School — students and faculty alike — were ca-

pable of feeling towards whatever it was they imagined Cowling represented. Occasionally the rhetoric he inspired was positively hysterical, if not slightly lunatic. No one denied his reputation for erudition, clarity of mind, and impatience with vagary — as well as for the profound influence he had on those who chose to expose themselves to his thought — but somehow this reputation was taken as something sinister. In the minds of certain of my colleagues, he seemed a kind of Klingsor in his castle, weaving unwholesome spells with which to ensnare innocent souls (an impression given added strength by the fact of his being a fellow of Peterhouse, of all the colleges the most cordially loathed, regarded by all right-thinking persons as an impregnable citadel of criminal nostalgias).

Not that any of my acquaintances had been Cowling's student or, as far as I could tell, knew him personally. The real scandal of Cowling for those of my fellow theologians who had any sense of him was not simply that he was in some undefined sense a man of the right, or even that he was by all accounts a rather severe personality, but that — in addition — he presumed to present himself as a Christian thinker. Devout and studious British Christians, after all, are as a rule creatures of the left, and it can often seem as if there is no form of social meliorism that the clergy and theologians of England are not eager to embrace, whether or not it has any of the actual effects they desire from it; but Cowling has the temerity to demur from the cozy consensus, to cast a cold eye upon the facile equation of Christian morality with sentimentality, sincerity, or "activism," and to do so with a power of argument that is disturbingly difficult to resist. And this is one reason, I imagine, for the relative obscurity in which his work languishes — which is a pity, most especially for Christian thinkers, who could profit much from an unprejudiced encounter with his work. Were they to grant him more of a hearing than they generally have to this point, they might find him to be a thinker intelligently and skeptically absorbed in vital questions, and an interpreter of Christian culture who, whatever one makes of his politics, deserves the attention of anyone concerned to understand the fate of faith in the modern age.

WHICH BRINGS ME to the present; for, if the time for a proper critical appreciation of Cowling's importance is ever to come, it may as well be now. With the publication in 2001 of the third and final volume of his immense *magnum opus, Religion and Public Doctrine in Modern England,*

Cowling has completed a work of history not only in many ways *sui generis,* but truly magisterial. Its focus is quite rigorously limited, un-questionably, but its scope is vast: it is an attempt to gain an encompass-ing perspective on the transition of England's cultural consensus, over a little more than a century and a half, from that of a Christian country to that of one decidedly post-Christian, and to do so entirely by way of the literary remains of the intellectual classes.

Indeed, this last aspect of the trilogy is in a sense its governing logic and its most significant challenge to historiographical conventions. From the first, Cowling eschews all social or material history, sequesters his study from political, economic, or class theory, refuses every invita-tion to subordinate ideas to events, and fixes his gaze with almost as-cetic intensity on the published beliefs, speculations, fantasies, convic-tions, and modest proposals of the caste of literati who mold the opinions and prejudices of their times. His interest is, as his title an-nounces, "public doctrine," by which he means the entire spectrum of or-thodoxies and heterodoxies propounded by the literature of popular, lit-erary, and scholarly discourse in the public forum; today, as Cowling remarks, "reading, viewing and reflecting are more central than prayer or worship," and so it is exclusively of texts and their authors that he chooses to write.

What this method produces, one must immediately say, is in no sense a work of impartial history; indeed, Cowling regards such impar-tiality as a pretense, and views the opinionated historian as the more honest and probative practitioner of the craft. In the trilogy's first vol-ume — which is something of an intellectual autobiography — he speaks of his desire to "describe the contours of a narrow mind"; and in the final volume confesses to being "a cynical Conservative who has never had the slightest enthusiasm for the rhetoric of progress, virtue and improve-ment." Not that he needs to inform his readers of these things: his treat-ment of writers is frequently, as he freely concedes, venomous, and he is not the sort to suffer from any excessive anxiety over the prominence of his own personality within his commentary. While the range of his inves-tigations is huge — making no distinctions among philosophers, psy-chologists, historians, novelists, or any other tradesmen of the written word — the range of his sympathies most emphatically is not. He is a Christian by intellectual conviction (though not necessarily, he ruefully acknowledges, by virtue of devout observance), and a conservative by philosophy and temperament, and it is only where these two currents fruitfully intersect that he is obviously at peace with his subjects.

That said, no one should mistake Cowling for a rigid dogmatist, much less for an apostle of reaction. There is not even any sense in which he could be said to cling to any particular conservative "theory"; he is a pure exemplar of H. Stuart Hughes's maxim that conservatism is "the negation of ideology." Not the sort who vests his confidence in any general political or economic principle equally applicable to — and equally abstracted from — all societies, he represents a conservatism of the concrete, historically and socially specific. One is tempted to characterize it simply as an attachment to certain traditions, memories, customs, habits of usage and association, cultural forms, and even perhaps particular landscapes; or as a belief in the organic integrity of civilization, and of the adherences upon which civilization depends, and a stern distaste for the damage done when the coherence of culture is carelessly or callously assailed. He is a royalist, naturally, a believer in the established church, a defender of worthy institutions and traditions, and is unimpressed by those who think in terms of grand designs for refashioning the social order from the top down or bottom up; but it would be imprudent to assay an account of his political "philosophy."

Most importantly, though, Cowling's conservatism is (at least, institutionally) Christian — a sober fidelity to English Christian culture. He sees that the decline of Christian belief and disintegration of the social authority of the state-church accommodation have been ruinous to "the historic English personality," and have "flooded the providential causeway which divides dignity and cosmic confidence from hopelessness, boredom and despair." And, since this is the moral concern with which his history is engaged, his intellectual alliances and enmities are not necessarily at the beck of his personal loyalties and aversions. When, at the end of his history, he lists the figures he has discussed for whom "the reader will detect anything resembling sympathy," he does not simply name fellow conservatives. He mentions, for instance, the resolutely socialist theologian John Milbank because Milbank is so blithely uncompromising an enemy of modernity, as unwilling as Cowling to grant secularity any of the intellectual, moral, or historical claims it makes for itself. At the same time Roger Scruton, whom an inattentive reader might expect to appear in the same company, is excluded from it, and is treated earlier in the text as, in some sense, an accomplice of that "post-

Christian consensus" upon which Cowling's trilogy pronounces so damning a verdict.

That verdict, incidentally, is one not so much of apostasy as of heresy. It may be the case, Cowling believes, that the Christian epoch has descended deep into its twilight and that when the sun rises again it will be — at least, in England — upon a world evacuated of transcendence, but he refuses to concede that this is a result of natural necessity, advances in cultural rationality, social progress, or (certainly) "enlightenment." In fact, Cowling treats belief in progress as itself little more than a sordid superstition, and he excels at exposing the secret little fideisms (many of them parasitic on religious habits of speech and thought) that inform the minds of "advanced" thinkers and the rhetoric of triumphalist secularism. Religion cannot be escaped, he argues, even if Christianity is now in retreat, and "whatever post-Christian and anti-Christian thinkers may have thought they were doing, they were in fact contributing to a transformation within religion."

THE STRUCTURE of *Religion and Public Doctrine* is elegantly simple, for all the vastness of its exposition; the longueurs are surprisingly few, the narrative rarely flags, and the work as a whole succeeds at being exhaustive without being tedious (though, admittedly, opinions on this last point are likely to vary).

The first volume, as I have said, is in a sense autobiographical, though it records few details of Cowling's life; rather, it situates his project within the field of intellectual forces that exerted an influence — for good or ill — over the evolution of his opinions. Hence it is governed by no chronology except that of Cowling's own formation: the first two major treatments in the volume are of Alfred North Whitehead and Arnold Toynbee, but the last drifts well back into the nineteenth century, to Lord Robert Cecil (Salisbury). And, by any standard other than the author's own peculiar intellectual history, the assortment of subjects is an eccentric one: in addition to the figures just named, the "three Anglican reactionaries" Kenneth Pickthorn, Edward Welbourne, and Charles Smyth, as well as T. S. Eliot, David Knowles (whose works this book, one hopes, will revive), R. G. Collingwood, Herbert Butterfield, Michael Oakeshott, Winston Churchill, Elie Kedourie, and Evelyn Waugh; and, *inter alia,* Hugh Trevor-Roper, Christopher Hill, Lord Acton, Norman Sykes, Owen Chadwick, Enoch Powell, and so on.

Though it introduces most of the themes that will recur throughout the trilogy, the chief pleasure this volume affords — being more diffusive than its successors — lies in the judgments it renders upon individual authors. Here, as elsewhere, Cowling's willful defiance of the dull, dry, judicious manner of the modern historian is absolute — as is, in consequence, his critical candor. It would be difficult to find a more pitiless dissection of Whitehead's "organism," or of the emptily idealistic optimism that allowed it to float with such beguiling buoyancy above the solid earth of human reality; and there is something at once discomfiting and exhilarating in Cowling's ruthless exposure of the banality, and of the immense intellectual amorphousness, of Toynbee's philosophy of history and "resentful, self-destructive, post-Christian Liberalism." And Collingwood, for all his obvious brilliance, comes across as perhaps a mite demented, a sometimes unhealthily self-important scholar who "allowed philosophy and history a quasi-religious authority which no sensible man will allow, except inadvertently, to any academic subject."

Nor are Cowling's most penetrating criticisms aimed only *à la gauche*. It is clear, for instance, that he finds Oakeshott's thought finally somewhat fruitless: for all the insight it provides into the "practical" ubiquity of religion, and of the irreducible richness of moral intercourse in human society, it cannot provide the thing most needful, and seems fatally contaminated by a powerful current of "Nietzschean or Hobbesian a-morality." And he is unsparingly honest about Churchill, a redoubtable champion of civilization, perhaps, but also as a man whose mind was shaped by materialism, Darwinism, and a semi-pagan and even nihilistic pessimism, to whom "Christian reactions ... should be ... mixed." Eliot's observations on the decay of Christian culture in England are presented as very accomplished expressions of suspicion, dismay, melancholy, or foreboding, but mostly devoid of concrete content; and even of Eliot's poetry Cowling predicts that "very little of it will be durable once the generations that have learnt to follow it have passed away. Eliot will not speak directly to the future."

With the second volume, *Assaults,* Cowling's project comes into focus, even as the number of subjects expands: Newman, Keble, Pusey, Gladstone, Manning, Ruskin, and Mill; George Eliot, Herbert Spencer, T. H. Huxley, and Leslie Stephen; Gilbert Murray, James Frazer, H. G. Wells, Belloc, Chesterton, and Shaw; W. H. Mallock, Winwood Read, Havelock Ellis, D. H. Lawrence, and Bertrand Russell ... (I could go on). It is in this volume that the case is most strikingly made that the nineteenth and twentieth centuries' struggle between Christian and anti-Christian thinkers for the moral and social future of England was not — as might be supposed — a struggle between religious and post-religious thought, but a war of creeds. The story begins with the Christian attack — by high-church Tractarians and reflective Protestants — upon the post-Christian mythologies of the eighteenth century, and its occasionally confused attempt to turn back the tide of unbelief. But the plot becomes most engrossing where Cowling turns to the tradition he calls "ethical earnestness": that is, the "progressive" assault on Christianity from the time of Mill, Eliot, and Spencer to that of Russell and Lawrence. It is here that Cowling begins, in scrupulous detail, to identify the sources of the religious consciousness of post-Christian England. "Ethical earnestness," as he recounts its development, consisted in a profound, often inchoate, but semi-mystical devotion to social improvement and rational morality as alternatives to the superstition, obscurantism, and tyranny of the old faith.

It was not, however, in any meaningful sense "post-religious," as it demanded of its votaries absolute and fervent devotion to a principle — social cohesion, human development, "Life" — that was itself not susceptible of doubt. In a sense, it was a new cosmology allied to a new moral metaphysics, constantly in ferment, producing movements and sects and new beginnings, but never straying beyond the boundaries of the world in which it believed: a universe of Darwinian struggle that, precisely in its savage economy of "nature red in tooth and claw," demanded of conscience that it assist evolution in its ascent towards higher ethical realizations of the human essence. In Cowling's account, one comes to see not only the broad unity of the school of "ethical earnestness," but the final incoherence of its ethos: the closed order of nature is at once merciless chaos and the source of our ethics; morality is both obedience to nature and rebellion against nature's implacable decrees; progress demands at once universal brotherhood and (especially among socialists) a ruthless eugenic purification of the race. What unifies this farrago into something like a moral vision is its most obviously religious element: complete devotion to the future, as an absolute imperative, requiring in consequence a renunciation of all faith in and charity towards the past — or, for that matter, the present.

This is both the most substantial and most diverting section of *Reli-*

gion and Public Doctrine, thronged as it is with sharply drawn portraits and bedizened with flashes of mordant wit. Cowling is extremely good at showing how, say, George Eliot's anti-Christian misunderstanding of Ruskin could so easily ally itself to her Feuerbachian ethical humanism, emanating its pale Dorotheas and paler creeds; but more enjoyable, and at the same time chilling, are the accounts of figures like Read (with his Malthusian, Darwinian, Comtean ideology and quaint utopianism of electricity, synthetic nutrition, and obedience to nature) or Ellis (with his worship of Art and Life, and his Nietzschean, Freudian, Frazerian dogmatism). Cowling's account of the turn of "ethical earnestness," in thinkers like Wells or Shaw or Lawrence, towards a grimmer social and sexual vision — less hospitable to liberal optimism, more marked by the influences of Schopenhauer, Wagner, Nietzsche, Ibsen, and Freud — reminds one that a certain cold, pervasive fanaticism in this tradition might have carried "ethical earnestness" towards a politics considerably less fond and feckless than the wan, sincere, liberal secularism of post-Christian Britain. (Indeed, one finds oneself wondering whether the failure of English progressivism to produce some suitably demonic thinker who could have caused the tradition to precipitate into conscious nihilism — more Byronic than Byron, with all the genius Lawrence lacked — can be attributed to anything other than the habitual British aversion to bombast and the cautionary example of Nazi Germany.)

In any event, volume II concludes with an examination of those Christian apologists who applied themselves to the task of thwarting the march of secularization to ultimate victory: Mallock, Coventry Patmore, Chesterton, Belloc, Christopher Dawson, etc. Sadly, however, Cowling finds little here to encourage or detain him; however sympathetic he may be to one or all of these figures, none of them to his mind provides a very substantial riposte to the forces of modernity. Chesterton, for instance, quickly exhausts Cowling's patience with his jollity and paradox and alternating appeals to common sense and to fairyland irrationality; of the much-revered *The Everlasting Man,* Cowling concludes that its attempts at a philosophy failed through its author's incapacity, and that all its virtues taken together "did not stop the structure of the book cracking under the strain of its own weightlessness."

Thus, if volume II chronicles the war waged for the future between Christian and post-Christian intellectuals, volume III, *Accommodations,* is a somber survey of the aftermath, and tells of one side's resigned retreat from the field of battle and of the other's consequent relaxation from a posture of arrogant triumphalism to one of mere contemptuous complacency. It is an immense volume, which takes a huge variety of figures into its capacious embrace — Carlyle, Kingsley, Burke, Disraeli, Darwin, Matthew Arnold, Dickens, Tennyson, Browning, Pater, Wilde, Macaulay, Acton, Inge, Shaftesbury, Tawney, Gore, Figgis, C. S. Lewis, Alasdair MacIntyre, Aldous Huxley, Elgar, Parry, Keynes, Hayek, Eagleton, Koestler, George Steiner . . . (to name a few) — but its form is fairly elementary: it addresses, in order, the accommodationism of English Christian latitudinarians, attempting to adjust themselves to the supremacy of secularist public doctrine; the reaction of more traditional Christian thinkers against the innumerable little apostasies and capitulations latitudinarianism entails; and the final victory of the public orthodoxy that now nourishes the imperturbable sanctimony, hectoring moralism, tender authoritarianism, and infinite dreariness of post-Christian Britain.

Cowling's account of the internecine, twilit struggle between accommodationism and a more defiant Christian orthodoxy begins with a trenchant treatment of Carlyle, makes its way through mires and over ridges of "sweetness and light," liberal race theory, social theologies, and many other halfway houses between the cultures of faith and of disenchantment, sojourns for a time with the last generation of Christian apologists who had any cause to hope for a public hearing, and concludes with an interlaced treatment of Alasdair MacIntyre's retrieval of the rationality of "tradition" and the aforementioned Milbank's militant, quixotic campaign to drive back all of modernity into its lair (except, notes Cowling, for socialism, which "stands out like a sanctified sore thumb"). But the book draws to its conclusion with an account of the concrescence of England's new religious consensus into its present form: the arrival of Darwinian science, the rise of the "science" of psychology, the ascendancy in literature and the arts of post-Christian theories and practices, the development of macro-economics, the evolution of British socialism and imbecile academic Marxism, the triumph of analytic philosophy, and many other of the broad currents that have subtly combined to replace faith in Christ with an (equally dogmatic) faith in sincerity, common sense, and social evolution.

IT WOULD BE dishonest to deny that the great (and palpably wicked) pleasure that *Religion and Public Doctrine* affords its reader comes from the

constantly flowing stream of caustic wit and surgically precise vitupera-
tion that runs through the entire work. The commentary rarely takes
leave of any subject without leaving saber scars behind. This is, as I have
said, part of Cowling's method; he sees the writing of history not as the
impassive recording of neutral facts, but as an act of interpretation that
speaks out of the preoccupations and experiences of the present by filtering the past through the prism of the historian's sensibility and reason.
Still, principled method or not, it makes for very entertaining reading.

At times, the invective is bruisingly terse. Macaulay tended "to
slobber over Bentham as a legal reformer"; "In his later years [Shaw]
became a bore, windbag and licensed clown"; "Orwell had a nasty
mind and, probably, a nasty body"; "[Anthony] Kenny's philosophy is
derivative, middle-rank and wanting in the higher creative power";
and so on.

At its best, however, it is an invective of anfractuous fullness, which
compresses large verdicts into small spaces. For example:

> [Raymond] Williams wrote at two levels — colloquially and self-
> confidently in confirming for audiences of his own persuasion the
> truths that they shared with him; opaquely and mistily in estab-
> lishing the truth and coherence of those persuasions.

Or:

> As a religious thinker, [Matthew] Arnold had an attractive sadness
> and resignation towards inevitabilities. . . . But there was an unat-
> tractive aspect to this as well — a fatalism which made a strategy
> out of testing the wind and blowing with it, and a bland, accom-
> modating, acquiescent Anglican grandeur which, while regretting
> the inevitability and lamenting the loss, was perfectly willing to
> accommodate away its own grandmother.

Or this uncomfortably accurate pastiche:

> [C. S.] Lewis bore the marks of Inkling-speak — the language of
> the pipe-smoking, beer-drinking 'jolly middle earth' whose idea it
> was that Christ had avoided 'idealistic gas', that mankind had got
> into a 'terrible fix', and that it had to avoid 'religious jaw' and 'cut

out' the 'soft soap' which had been 'talked about God for the last hundred years'.

Or (one more example) this:

> The courtroom scenes [in Forster's *Passage to India*] were . . . quintessentially Hollywood. . . . The Indian magistrate was a Hollywood hero, 'Esmiss Esmoore's' memory a Hollywood effect and Miss Quested's withdrawal of her allegations a vindication of Hollywood truth and right.

And then there is Cowling's trick of striking several targets at once. "[Ellis] was a bore, though less of a bore in socio-religious matters than Forster, say, or Auden"; "In reading Collingwood's later political ravings, one is reminded of Popper's *The Open Society* . . . which was written at the same time as *The New Leviathan,* and was subject to the same sort of hysteria"; and so on. Allied to this, moreover, is a talent for ambiguous praise: "[Owen Chadwick's] strength, like that of his brother, Henry, is that combination of blandness, dignity and learning which have been a special characteristic of the Anglican clergy."

The great strength of such writing is that it makes light reading out of sixteen hundred pages of close textual analyses; its only weakness is that it can produce so dominant an impression in the reader's mind as to obscure the prudent care and moral seriousness of the argument being advanced. And it is an argument that demands a hearing: nothing could be more important for an understanding of modernity (even if it is reached through a study only of the intelligentsia of England) than to recognize that we are not living in an age in which religious adherence has simply withered away before the parching wind of Enlightenment reason, but in one in which a new evangel has — over the course of a few centuries — displaced the old, and with it the cultural energy and rationale of Christian Europe: a new religion, whose most devout believers are as zealous, intolerant, and absolutist as any faith has ever produced, and whose vast silent constituency is as unreflective, passive, and pliant as any enfranchised clerisy could desire. It is probably good for Christians to grasp that, even in this hour, they struggle not simply with disillusion and demystification, but with strange gods.

However, Cowling's readers might protest, such knowledge is of little use if one does not — as Cowling refuses to do — lay out what the political and economic implications of Christian adherence should be. But, on this, Cowling is clear: he sees no legitimate liaison between Christian culture and a particular ideology; no less than the liberal religion that has captured the high ground of public doctrine, Christianity is a cultural and spiritual ecology, an impulse towards the ideal or ultimate that takes form in the bones and sinews (the cultural grammar) of a civilization, as well as a corporate and private habit of orientations, limits, practices, and possibilities — all of which allow for various social philosophies to arise and flourish, but which cannot be reduced to any of them. And this leads Cowling to make an assertion that, to idealistic Christians, might seem mildly perverse:

> A religion ought to be habitual and ought not to involve the self-consciousness inseparable from conversion. What Christianity requires is a second-generation sensibility in which . . . struggle has ceased to be of Christianity's essence. This is not a situation which can easily be achieved in the contemporary world; indeed, the religions which can most easily avoid self-consciousness in the contemporary world are the secular religions which are absorbed at the mother's knee or from the mother's television set.

In one sense, this might seem a counsel of hopelessness. Still, the burden of Cowling's argument is that, if indeed secularization is not what happens when religion withdraws, but is itself the positive artifact of an irrepressible religious agitation within human culture, then "it would be absurd to assume its permanence," because "the instinct for religion that lurks beneath the indifference of the public mind may yet surprise by its willingness to be led astray by Christianity."

Which leaves me, at least, with only one (unexpected) question: whether, despite Cowling's keen understanding of England's cultural quandary, his method of writing history has not led him towards something like faint and undue optimism. His only suggestion for how a second-generation Christian cultural sensibility might be recovered, apart from some cultural crisis that would spark a new generation of conversions, is "the slow influence which might be exerted by a Christian literature." At this point, though, I wonder whether Cowling's study might not profitably ballast itself with some element of material history; by all means, we should always be guilty of what Marx called ideology, and recognize that ideas shape culture *at least* as decisively as material conditions shape ideas, but one must ask whether, by confining his work to the rarefied atmosphere of intellectual discourse, Cowling does not allow himself to keep artificially alive debates that history has already decided.

At the level of general culture, England is post-Christian in ways that no one with a finite life should have the patience to enumerate — the deepening coarseness of popular culture, the spreading violence, Britain's pervasive malice towards its own cultural inheritance, demographic inanition, infantile politics, an almost total desiccation of a hunger for transcendence — and while it is commendable that Cowling denies himself the glamour of the unheeded Cassandra, or of the dour encomiast possessed of desolate omniscience, one must observe that an ancient and syphilitic demimondaine is unlikely to revert to virgin purity again. There is a qualitative difference between the savage energy of the pagan heart and the paralytic morbidity of the post-Christian. Each comprises in itself a kind of nihilism, but the former is frequently unconscious of this, moved as it is by the vitality of natural appetites, dreads, and elations that can carry it from the world of the gods into the Kingdom of God; the latter is not only conscious of its nihilism, but proud of it, and easily converts private despair into general resignation, incuriosity, sterility — both animal and spiritual — and the pitiable charade of a kind of wry, disabused urbanity.

And yet, no doubt, Cowling is right. Can these bones live? It would be impious to say they cannot, and Christianity has perhaps triumphed over crueler gods than these. Cowling understands quite well the magnitude of what has been lost to secularization, and the grim prospects for any attempt to rebuild the edifice of Christian culture on English soil. Nonetheless, he also understands that at the heart of secularity are a thousand arbitrary and fanatical cultural decisions masquerading as realism, ethics, or progress; and, by relentlessly exposing their arbitrariness, his history makes conceivable the ultimate collapse of the religion they sustain. Which suggests that — as my divinity school friends of old would never have credited — Cowling's very aloofness from the political enthusiasms of the moment, and his severe and solvent habit of critical suspicion, allow him to see the cultural situation around him not so much as a wasteland as, perhaps, a fallow field, and so to regard the present and the future with neither pessimism nor optimism, but with something like a wisely diffident charity.

4

Sheer Extravagant Violence:
Gogol's Taras Bulba

Nikolai Gogol, *Taras Bulba,* trans. Peter Constantine (Modern Library)

WHERE *Taras Bulba* should be ranked among the works of Nikolai Gogol (1809-1852) — or, for that matter, among the monuments of European literature — is by no means settled. Ernest Hemingway called it "one of the ten greatest books of all time," while Vladimir Nabokov, who adored the Gogol of the St. Petersburg stories and *Dead Souls,* dismissed it as a dull, melodramatic *juvenilium,* on a par with "rollicking yarns about lumberjacks." Of course, neither of these is an authority to be consulted too credulously; one can never be certain, when examining their critical verdicts, how deep the one was in his cups nor how high the other in his dudgeon. The truth is that *Taras Bulba* is a lesser achievement than the strange, brilliant, delirious works of Gogol's prime; but it is nevertheless colored throughout by the inspired exorbitances of his genuinely unquantifiable genius.

Originally published as a long short story in 1835, the tale had assumed the dimensions of a short novel by 1842. It is often described as a "prose epic," and Gogol certainly composed it in a Homeric key (blood-steeped battles, rudely eloquent perorations, a prose of studied naïveté, controlled torrents of parataxis, languidly involved similes, plentiful descriptions of insouciant brutality, and a narrative voice blessedly pure of psychological subtleties or moralism). But it also reflects the conventions of the historical romance, and owes as much to Sir Walter Scott and James Fenimore Cooper as to Homer. At its center, in fact, is a love story so implausible in its elements — an absurd coincidence, a girl apparently with the eyesight of a falcon, a maidservant able to find one sleeping soldier among thousands in the dead of night, a secret passage into a besieged town — that Anne Radcliffe might have recoiled from it as too fantastic.

The tale is set in the Ukraine, among the Cossacks of the great Zaporozhian Sech (a large fortified island encampment on the river Dnieper). In the new Modern Library edition, both Robert Kaplan's introduction and Peter Constantine's preface place the action "sometime between the mid-sixteenth and seventeenth century," but this is incorrect. The final chapter of the book recounts the Polish campaign of the Zaporozhian Cossacks under the Hetman Ostranitsa, which took place in 1637; and the preceding chapters are set not much earlier. The story concerns an old married Cossack — the book's eponymous hero — and his two sons, and how all three meet their deaths. By all rights, Bulba should command far less sympathy than he does. His sons have scarcely returned from their seminary training in Kiev when, indifferent to his wife's misery, he leads them off to the Sech. There, after a little while, he grows impatient for a war to try their mettle, and so intrigues to subvert the Sech's armistice with the Turkish Padishah — which proves needless when the Cossacks receive word of Polish outrages against the Russian faithful of the Ukraine and so decide to ride forth to fight for the "true Church." While Bulba lacks neither humanity nor courage, it is soon obvious that his sons' lives are of less account to him than that they acquit themselves honorably in battle; and, in the book's final pages, when moved to vengeance, he proves capable of the most implacable savagery. And yet such is his simplicity of character that he does compel us.

His sons are more uncomplicatedly attractive — especially the younger of them, Andri, who loses his heart to a Polish girl of fairly high degree. Gogol's portrayal of a young, warlike naïf vanquished in an instant by feminine beauty and grace is quite affecting, as is the heedlessness of Andri's surrender to his passion and renunciation of family, nation, and faith (though this will lead to the novel's most tragic moment). The elder son, Ostap, possesses none of his brother's complexities or susceptibilities; he is simply brave, adept at battle, a natural leader of men, and not given to the more barbarous proclivities of his fellows; and he dies well.

THE MOST INDELIBLE impression left by *Taras Bulba* is one of sheer extravagant violence. The book abounds in descriptions of the manic carnage of battle, starvation, murder, and torture; one reads of men entirely flayed below the knees, of women mutilated or burned alive at church altars, of infants speared, of Jews beaten and killed. And, while this violence is found on all sides, it is the unrelenting brutality of the Cossacks to which we are principally exposed. When, for instance, the Zaporozhians resolve to make war on the Poles, they first round up the Jewish merchants of the settlement (whom they see as allies of their enemies) and throw them into the Dnieper to drown (except for one whom Bulba rescues, in return for a favor once done his brother). The story is set in a sanguinary and sadistic age; but it leaves one with the sense that the Cossacks may ultimately have been unrivalled even in their time in their capacity for purely impulsive pitilessness, unlit by the faintest flickering of conscience.

And yet — and this gives the book much of its disturbing allure — Gogol clearly means in some sense to celebrate these men. However monstrous his Cossacks, they are not actually moved by malice, and somehow their cruelty is made to seem less appalling by its absolutely ingenuous spontaneity. It is as if Gogol sees a kind of animal innocence in their violence, a childlike boisterousness, of a piece with the recklessness that pervades all they do: they hoard treasure, but either forget where they have hidden it or squander it in mighty feats of dissipation; their appetites are titanic; they are generous to a degree, and to a greater degree merely profligate; they love heroic song; they slaughter their enemies with industrious gaiety.

Most importantly, Gogol sees his Zaporozhians not only as legendary heroes, but as knights of faith. He does not actually *approve* of their barbarity; but he sees them as having been created by centuries of religious and political crisis, as a reaction against forces threatening to destroy the Christian heritage of the Rus. Whereas other nations saw the Cossacks as something dark and terrible at the Asiatic periphery of Christian Europe, Gogol saw them as embodying something vast, invincible, and indomitably savage in the Russian soul: an unyielding spiritual bulwark against Orthodoxy's enemies.

It was in the south, after all, that Christianity established itself in Russia, in the late tenth century (which led to Kievan culture's brief flowering); but by 1240, all of Russia had fallen to the Tatars, who would rule the north for 250 years. The south was purged of its occupiers in the four-teenth century by the pagan Lithuanian Prince Gedimin, who permitted the Slavs the practice of their faith; but the conversion and marriage into the Polish royal family of the Lithuanian Prince Yagello in 1386 inaugu-rated the long history of Poland's attempt to absorb Lithuania and its possessions. In 1569, the Union of Lublin made "Little Russia" an appa-nage of the Polish crown, and the elaborate Polish culture of aristocratic privilege (including an absolute claim on property rights) was imposed upon a people accustomed to more spacious liberties. Then, with the "uniate" accommodation of 1595, the Ukraine's "official" Church became an Eastern rite of the Roman Church, which reduced the Orthodox to re-ligious outlaws in their own country.

The Cossacks appeared at the end of the thirteenth century. The vast open plains of southern Russia provided no natural brake against invad-ers from any quarter — Turk, Tatar, or Pole — and only these loosely or-ganized but formidable sodalities of "Christian warriors" secured for the Russians some measure of liberty on their own soil. By the time of the events recounted in *Taras Bulba,* the Ukraine's Orthodox Russians saw themselves as a disinherited people, whose oppressor despised their faith and coveted their lands. Hence the blazing ferocity of Gogol's Zaporozhians, and their ability to see their merciless rampages as "holy war." And hence, also, Gogol's strange sympathy for men of such bestial aptitudes.

I AM NOT wholly enamored of Peter Constantine's new translation. It suf-fers on occasion from a certain awkwardness of phrasing, and at times from a rather jarring incongruity of tone — as when the old, fairly rusti-cated Atamen of the Cossack horde assures his men that Catholic priests do nothing but "pontificate" — and on occasion from a ponderous literality. And solecisms such as calling the Orthodox liturgy a "mass" are mildly distracting. That said, Constantine does largely succeed at cap-turing the terse lyricism of Gogol's descriptions, and the unfaltering flow of the narrative. Perhaps more importantly, he is better than previous translators at conveying the novel's humor.

This is a considerable virtue, for the aspect of *Taras Bulba* that gen-erally goes unremarked is its willful absurdity. The book is an epic ro-mance, true; but Gogol was not a simple sentimentalist, and one need not be abnormally astute to notice that his admiration for the Cossacks contains an element of grave mockery. A certain removed and satirical tone pervades the book, and at times breaks forth with full brio. For instance, the entire scene in which Bulba attempts — with the assistance of the Jewish merchant he spared earlier — to visit his son on the eve of the latter's execution, but is thwarted by a guard with a "three-tiered mustache," is one of broad comedy. And when, the next day, the narrative drifts through the crowd assembled for the spectacle, and alights upon a butcher and the swordsmith he calls brother "because the two got drunk in the same tavern," one is not far from the surreally irrelevant detail of *Dead Souls*. And then there is the Polish aristocrat, delicately preparing his daughter for the day's events:

> "When [the executioner] puts the criminal on the wheel and starts torturing him the criminal is still alive, but when he chops his head off, my sweet, then the criminal is dead. At first you will see the criminal writhing and shouting, but once his head has been chopped off he won't be able to shout, or eat, or drink. This, my sweet, is because he won't have a head anymore."

Even at its most "epic," Gogol's voice is incapable of strict sobriety. When a girl's sorrow or a warrior's death is likened to a breeze playing in dry reeds or a hawk killing a quail, and the simile runs on long enough to acquire a brief life of its own, the tone is suitably Homeric; but what is one to make of this? —

> [Kukubenko's] young blood gushed like a rare wine brought in a crystal decanter by a careless servant, who stumbles, breaking the precious carafe, the wine spilling onto the floor, the master tearing his hair, for this was the wine he had been saving for the most important occasion of his life, the day when by God's grace he met once more the beloved comrades of his youth to reminisce of bygone times when men knew how to revel.

That is the Gogol of the St. Petersburg period — as is the brief parody of a mediaeval heroic tableau (Kukubenko's soul ascending to Christ's right hand) that follows.

For these passages alone, Constantine's can be embraced as the standard English translation. Properly to appreciate *Taras Bulba*, one must grasp what a promiscuous miscellany of styles and devices it comprises, and what a *tour de force* of intricate ambiguities it truly is. For this, finally, is why it can keep company with Gogol's more mature masterpieces: it, like them, is a strange, grim, whimsical, and fabulous tale, immersed in an aesthetic idiom unlike any other, and born from perhaps the most peculiar sensibility in the history of European letters.

5

Religion in America: Ancient and Modern

All culture arises out of religion. When religious faith decays, culture must decline, though often seeming to flourish for a space after the religion which has nourished it has sunk into disbelief.

Russell Kirk, *Eliot and His Age*

T he herdsman who comes to Pentheus from Mount Cithaeron in *The Bacchae* tells how the Theban women possessed by Dionysus (among other more fabulous and monstrous feats) take up serpents without being bitten and fire without being burned. It is not unlikely, given how common such phenomena are in "enthusiast" and "ecstatic" religion, that here and elsewhere Euripides grants us some glimpse of the actual dionysiac orgy, even long after its migration into Greece from Thrace, when the cult had been assumed into the soberer mysteries of the Olympians (that the revelers girded themselves with snakes, at least, bacchic iconography copiously attests). And other features of the rite, reported in various sources, follow the familiar enthusiast pattern. At the height of their devotions, the maenads were seized by violent raptures, to which they surrendered entirely; absorbed in the formless beauty of the god, and tormented by fitful intimations of his presence, they worshipped him with cries of longing and delight, desperate invocations, wild dithyrambs, delirious dance, inebriation, and the throbbing din of corybantic music; abandoning all sense of themselves, they suffered visions and uttered prophecies, fell ravished and writhing to the earth, or sank into insensibility. In short, it was all very — in a word — American.

At least, that is what I have been disposed to think ever since an epiphany visited itself upon me nearly twenty years ago, as I stood amid the pestilential squalor of an English railway station, awaiting my train, and deliberating on whether I should risk the ordeal of a British Rail sandwich. Generally one might prefer grander settings for one's moments of illumination — Wordsworth's lakes, Amiel's azure peaks — but it was, in this instance, the very dreariness of my surroundings that occasioned my awakening. The station's oblong pillars were blackly begrimed; shreds of posters in garish hues hung limply from the walls; in shallow depressions of the concrete floor opaque pools of oleaginous water glistened with a sinister opalescence; an astringent chemical odor of antiseptics vying with various organic purulences suffused the damp air; a scattering of gaunt torsos farther along the platform bore eloquent witness to the malaise of Britain's post-war gene pool; and nothing was out of the ordinary. But, all at once, two thoughts occurred to me simultaneously, and their wholly fortuitous conjunction amounted to a revelation. One was something like "Boredom is the death of civilization"; and the other something like "America has never been this modern."

Not that this place was conspicuously worse than — or even as wretched as — countless stops along the way in the United States; but anyone who has lived in Britain for some time should understand how such a place might, in a moment of calm clarity, seem like the gray glacial heart of a gray and glaciated universe. Somehow this place was adequate to its age — to that pervasive social atmosphere of resignation at which modern Britain is all but unsurpassed; it was disenchantment made palpable, the material manifestation of a national soul unstirred by extravagant expectations or exorbitant hopes. Admittedly, contemporary England's epic drabness makes everything seem worse; in the Mediterranean sun, culture's decay can be intoxicatingly charming (and Catholic decadence is so much richer than Protestant decadence). But really, anywhere throughout the autumnal world of old and dying Christendom, there are instants (however fleeting) when one cannot help but feel (however imprecisely) that something vital has perished, a cultural confidence or a spiritual aspiration; and it is obviously something inseparable from the faith that shaped and animated European civilization for nearly two millennia. Hence the almost prophetic "fittingness" of that rail station: once religious imagination and yearning have departed from a culture, the lowest, grimmest, most tedious level of material existence becomes not just one of reality's unpleasant aspects, but in some sense the limit that marks out the "truth" of things.

This is an inexcusably impressionistic way of thinking, I know, but it seems to me at least to suggest a larger cause for the remarkable willful infertility of the native European peoples: not simply general affluence, high taxes, sybaritism, working women, or historical exhaustion, but a vast metaphysical boredom. This is not to say that the American birthrate overall is particularly robust, hovering as it is just at or below "replacement level"; but it has not sunk to the European continental average of only 1.4 children per woman (so reports the United Nations), let alone to that of such extreme individual cases as Spain (1.07), Germany (1.3), or Italy (1.2). Britain, at almost 1.7 children per woman, is positively philoprogenitive by European standards. And the most important reason for the greater — if not spectacular — fecundity of the United States appears to be the relatively high rate of birth among its most religious families (the godless being also usually the most likely to be childless). It is fairly obvious that there is some direct, indissoluble bond between faith and the will to a future, or between the desire for a future and the imagination of eternity. And I think this is why post-Christian Europe seems to lack not only the moral and imaginative resources for sustaining its civilization, but even any good reason for continuing to reproduce. There are of course those few idealists who harbor some kind of unnatural attachment to that misbegotten abomination, the European Union — that grand project for forging an identity for post-Christian civilization out of the meager provisions of heroic humanism or liberal utopianism or ethical sincerity — but, apart from a bureaucratic super state, providently and tenderly totalitarian, one cannot say what there is to expect from that quarter: certainly nothing on the order of some great cultural renewal that might inspire a new zeal for having children. Unless one grants credence to the small but fashionable set that has of late been predicting a reviviscence of Christianity in Europe (in gay defiance of all tangible evidence), it seems certain that Europe will continue to sink into its demographic twilight, and increasingly to look like the land of the "last men" that Nietzsche prophesied would follow the "death of God": a realm of sanctimony, petty sensualisms, pettier rationalisms, and a vaguely euthanasiac addiction to comfort. For, stated simply, against the withering boredom that descends upon a culture no longer invaded by visions of eternal order, no civilization can endure.

However, as I say, this absolute degree of modernity has never quite reached America's shores. Obviously, in any number of ways, America is late modernity's avant-garde; in popular culture, especially, so prolific are we in forms of brutal vapidity and intellectual poverty that less enterprising savages can only marvel in impotent envy. Nevertheless, here alone among Western nations the total victory of the modern is not indubitable; there are whole regions of the country — geographical and social — where the sea of faith's melancholy, long, withdrawing roar is scarcely audible. There is in America something that, while not "Christendom," is not simply "post-Christian" either; it is (for want of a better term) a "new antiquity." In many ways, one might go so far as to say, the great difference between Europeans and Americans is that the former are moderns and the latter ancients (if sometimes of a still rather barbarous sort); and the reasons for this are religious.

Though really it would be truer to say that, as Americans, we know the extremes of both antiquity and modernity; what we have never yet possessed is the middle term — a native civilization, with religion as a staid and stable institution uniformly supporting the integrity of the greater culture — that might have allowed for a transition from the one to the other. Thus it is the tension between the two that makes America exceptional, and that lends a certain credibility both to those who contemn her for being so menacingly religious and to those who despise her for being so aggressively godless. In part because the United States broke from the old world at a fateful moment in history, in part because its immense geography preserves the restive peculiarities of various regions and social classes relatively inviolate, and so allows even the most exotic expressions of religious devotion to survive and flourish, it has never lost the impress of much of the seventeenth-century Protestantism — evangelistic, ecclesially deracinated, congregationalist, separatist — that provided it with its initial spiritual impulse. Hence Christendom could never die from within for us, as it has for the rest of the West; we fled from it long ago into an apocalyptic future, and so never quite suffered Europe's total descent into the penury of the present.

Instead the United States, to the consternation of *bien pensants* here and abroad, is saturated in religion as no other developed nation is. Not only do forty percent of its citizens claim to attend worship weekly, and sixty percent at least monthly (though those numbers have been disputed), but apparently — staggeringly — fewer than five percent are willing to call themselves atheists or even agnostics. And a very great number of the devout (at least in certain classes) are not merely pious, but God-haunted, apocalyptic, chiliastic, vulgarly religiose, and always living in the end times. Moreover, for most of us (even if we refuse to admit it), America itself is a kind of evangelical faith, a transcendent truth beyond the reach of historical contingency. Even our native secularism tends towards the fanatical. We remain believers. To some, of course, this American religiousness is simply the exasperatingly persistent residue of something obsolete, an alloy of which modernity has not yet entirely purged itself, and perhaps history will prove them right. But it is likely that such persons do not quite grasp the scale, potency, or creativity of the "ancient" aspect of America, and have little sense of its deepest wellsprings — which brings me back to the maenads of Dionysus.

In his account of Appalachian snake handling, *Salvation on Sand Mountain* (1995), Dennis Covington tells of worshippers taking up serpents without being bitten and fire without being burned; of a woman, seized by raptures, emitting ecstatic cries of pain and pleasure, which Covington himself involuntarily accompanies with a tambourine; of the "anointed" losing themselves in what could only be called an erotic torment; of wild clamors of glossolalia, fervent invocation, and the throbbing din of Pentecostalist music; of the faithful suffering visions and uttering prophecies; even of his own experience of handling a snake, and of his sense of world and self, in that moment, disappearing into an abyss of light. Nor is it unusual in many "Holiness" congregations for worshippers to fall to the ground writhing and "rolling" or — "slain in the Spirit" — to lapse into insensibility. Not that such forms of devotion are unknown in other parts of the developed world, but only here have they been so profuse, spontaneous, and genuinely indigenous. Take, for instance, the 1801 week-long revival at Cane Ridge, whose orgiastic rites were celebrated by as many as twenty-five thousand worshippers; or the 1906 "new outpouring" of the scriptural "gifts" or "charisms" of the Holy Spirit — prophecy, speaking in tongues, miraculous healings, the casting out of demons, and so forth — upon the Azusa Street Mission in Los Angeles, which gave birth to the "Pentecostalist" or "charismatic" spirituality that has spread throughout the global South more rapidly than any other form of Christianity in the modern world; examples are abundant.

And this is why I say Americans are "ancients": not simply because, throughout the breadth of their continental empire, as in the world of late antiquity, there exists a vague civic piety ramifying into a vast diversity of religious expressions, even of the most mysterious and disturbing kind; but because here there are those to whom the god — or rather God or his angel — still appears. That sort of religion is immune to disillusion, as it has never coalesced into an "illusion"; it moves at the level of vision. In a country where such things are possible, and even somewhat ordinary, the future cannot be predicted with any certitude.

ONE MUST AT LEAST say of the old Christendom that, if indeed it has died, it has nonetheless left behind plentiful and glorious evidence of its vanished majesty: its millennial growths of etherealized granite and filigreed marble, its exquisitely wrought silver, its vaults of gold: in all the arts miracles of immensity and delicacy. And the very desuetude of these remnants imbues them with a special charm. Just as the exuviae of cicadas acquire their milky translucence and poignant fragility only in being evacuated of anything living, so the misty, haunting glamor of the churches of France might be invisible but for the desolation in their pews. Similarly, countless traces of the old social accommodations — laws, institutions, customs, traditions of education, public calendars, moral prejudices, in short all those complex "mediating structures" by which the old religion united, permeated, shaped, and preserved a Christian civilization — linger on, ruined, barren, but very lovely.

There is nothing in the least majestic, poignant, or "exuvial" about American religion, and not only because it possessed very little by way of mediating structures to begin with. If the vestigial Christianity of the old world presents one with the pathetic spectacle of shape without energy, the quite robust Christianity of the new world often presents one with the disturbing spectacle of energy without shape. It is not particularly original to observe that, in the dissolution of Christendom, Europe retained the body while America inherited the spirit; but one sometimes wonders whether for "spirit" it would not be better to say "poltergeist." It is true that the majority of observant Christians and Jews in the United States are fairly conventional in their practices and observances, and the "mainstream" denominations are nothing if not reserved. But, at its most unrestrained and disembodied, the American religious imagination drifts with astonishing ease towards the fantastical and mantic, the messianic and hermetic. We are occasionally given shocking reminders of this — when a communitarian separatist sect in Guyana or a cult of comet-gazing castrati commits mass suicide, or when an encampment of deviant Adventists is incinerated by an inept Attorney General — but these are merely acute manifestations of a chronic condition. The special genius of American religion (if that is what it is) is an inchoate, irrepressibly fissiparous force, a peregrine spirit of beginnings and endings (always re-founding the church and preparing for Armageddon), without any middle in which to come to rest.

In part, this is explicable simply in light of colonial history. The founding myth of the English settlements, after all, was in large part that of an evangelical adventure (as can be confirmed from the first Charter of Virginia, or the Mayflower Compact, or the Fundamental Orders of Connecticut), marked indelibly by covenantal Puritanism. Even the Anglican establishments in the Deep South, Virginia, and Maryland (a criminal imposition, in this last case, upon an aboriginal Catholicism) were deeply influenced by Puritan piety, as were perhaps even the Presbyterian churches. Quakerism, principally in Pennsylvania, New Jersey, and Rhode Island, infused a mystical noncomformism into the colonies, while later immigrations of German Anabaptists — Mennonites, the Amish, Hutterites — imported a "free church" discipline of somewhat more rigorist variety, and perhaps something of radical Anabaptism's apocalyptic utopianism (it would be difficult, at any rate, to be unimpressed by the similarities between the tragic history of the 1535 "Kingdom of Münster" and that of the compound at Waco). In time even small Pietist communities added their distinctive colorations. And so on. Though the churches of the magisterial reformation, the Church of England, and Catholicism found America fertile soil (as every religion does), the atmosphere in which they flourished was one permeated by a religious consciousness little bound to tradition, creed, hierarchy, or historical memory, but certain of its spiritual liberty and special election.

Which is why one could argue that American religion found its first genuinely native expression during the great age of revivalism. The two Great Awakenings, early and late in the eighteenth century, the spread of evangelical Christianity throughout the southern states, the sporadic but powerful western revivals — all of these contributed to the larger synthesis by which contemporary American religion was fashioned. And from the revivalist impulse followed not only the broad main currents of

American evangelical Protestantism, but innumerable more heterodox and inventive forms of Christianity: millenarian sects like the Adventists or Jehovah's Witnesses, spiritual or enthusiast movements like Pentecostalism, perhaps even (in a way) "transcendentalist" schools like the quasi-Swedenborgian Christian Scientists. Nor, indeed, are the differences in sensibility as great as one might imagine between all of mainstream evangelicalism and its more outlandish offshoots. One need only consider the huge success of the ghastly *Left Behind* novels to realize that an appetite for luridly absurd chiliastic fantasies is by no means confined to marginal sects.

Certainly it is only in regard to this revivalist milieu that one might legitimately speak of "*the* American religion," as Harold Bloom did in his 1992 book of that title. Bloom, it should be noted, was scarcely the first to call it a "gnostic" religion, nor is his treatment of the matter exemplary in analytic precision; but he must be given credit for having grasped how deeply constitutive of America's normal religious temper the gnostic impulse is. If the pathos of ancient Gnosticism lay in a sense of cosmic alienation — in an intuition of the self's exile in a strange world, called in its loneliness to an identity and a salvation experienced only within the self's inmost core, and that by the agencies of a special spiritual election and a knowledge that elevate the self above the ignorance of the derelict — then it is a pathos readily discernible in any number of distinctively American religious movements and moments. At its most speculatively refined and eloquent, one finds it in Emerson and in the transcendentalism to which he gave voice; at its most risible and grotesque in Scientology and similar "schools"; and, as Bloom notes, nothing more perfectly fits the classic pattern of gnostic religion — fabulous mythologies, jealously guarded cryptadia, a collapse of the distinction between the divine and the human — than Mormonism. But it requires somewhat greater perspicacity to recognize this same pathos at work under more conventional guises.

Most of us, for instance, rarely have cause to reflect that some of the variants of America's indigenous evangelical Christianity, especially of the "fundamentalist" sort, would have to be reckoned — if judged in the full light of Christian history — positively bizarre. Yet many of its dominant and most reputable churches have — quite naturally and without any apparent attempt at novelty — evolved a Christianity so peculiar as to be practically without precedent: an entire theological and spiritual

world, internally consistent, deeply satisfying to many, and nearly impossible to ground in the scriptural texts its inhabitants incessantly invoke. And Bloom deserves some (reluctant) praise for having seen this,
and having seen why it should be: the American myth of salvation, at its
purest, is a myth of genuinely personal redemption, the escape of the
soul from everything that might confine and repress it — sin, the world,
and the devil, but also authority, tradition, and community — into an
eternal, immediate, and indefectible relation with God; and it is to this
myth, much more than the teachings of the New Testament, that some
forms of American evangelical Christianity, especially fundamentalism,
adhere. This is obvious if one merely considers the central (and some
might say only) spiritual event of fundamentalist faith and practice, that
of being "born again." In the third chapter of John's Gospel, where this
phrase is originally found, its context is mystagogical and clearly refers
to baptism; but so far removed has it become from its original significance in many evangelical circles that it is now taken to mean a purely
private conversion experience, occurring in that one unrepeatable authentic instant in which one accepts Jesus as one's "personal" Lord and
Savior. Some fundamentalists even profess a doctrine of "perpetual security," which says that this conversion experience, if genuine (and there-
from hangs, for some, an agonizing uncertainty), is irreversible; like the
initiation ceremonies of various ancient mystery cults, it is a magic
threshold, across which — once it has been passed — one can never
again retreat, no matter how wicked one may become. One could
scarcely conceive of a more "gnostic" concept of redemption: liberation
through private illumination, a spiritual security won only in the deepest
soundings of the soul, a moment of awakening that lifts the soul above
the darkness of this world into a realm of spiritual liberty beyond even
the reach of the moral law, and an immediate intimacy with the divine
whose medium is one of purest subjectivity.

THIS, AT ANY RATE, is one very plausible way of approaching the matter
of religion in America: to consider it primarily in its most distinctive of
autochthonous forms, as a new gnostic adventure allied to a new eschatological mythology, which has transformed the original Puritan impulse
of the upper English colonies into something like a genuinely new version of Christianity: one whose moderate expressions are, in the long historical view, amiably aberrant, but whose extreme expressions are fre-

quently apocalyptic, enthusiast, and even — again — dionysiac. One could argue, though, that it is an approach that, while not exactly unjust, is a mite perverse. After all, the exceptional nature of American piety consists not only in the opulence and prodigality of its innovations and deviations, but in the extraordinary tenacity (as compared, at least, to the situation in other developed nations) with which the more established and traditional communities hold on to their own, generation after generation, and in some cases attract new converts: Roman Catholicism, Lutheranism, Methodism, Presbyterianism, Eastern Orthodoxy, not to mention the various kinds of synagogical Judaism.

And surely one should note that — however widespread and dynamic the by no means uniform phenomenon of evangelical Christianity may be — the Roman Catholic Church constitutes the single largest denomination in the United States, and is growing at an impressive pace (in large part, obviously, because of Hispanic immigration). If fifty years hence, as demographic trends adumbrate, there are approximately 400 million Americans, fully a quarter may be Hispanic. Of these, one must immediately note, as many as a third may be evangelicals; but it seems clear that Catholicism will continue to increase not only in absolute numbers, but relative to other Christian denominations. And, despite Harold Bloom's quaint asseveration that "most" American Catholics are gnostics (rather than, as is true, "very many"), this might perhaps mean that the more extreme species of revivalist individualism may actually relinquish some slight measure of its dominance of the American religious consciousness.

And, then again, perhaps not. The institutional reality of American Christianity has always been too diverse for simple characterizations, but at present this much is certain: the churches most likely to prosper greatly are those that make an appeal to — and an attempt to adopt the style of — an emotive individualism. Whether this means seeking to provide a sort of chaplaincy for small communities of earnest, socially conscientious liberals (as do many mainstream Protestant parishes and many Catholic parishes that might as well be mainstream Protestant), or promoting a more traditional — if largely undemanding — popular moralism, or promising more extreme forms of spiritual experience, or supplying a sort of light spiritual therapy, what is ultimately important is that institutional authority and creedal tradition not interpose themselves between the believer and his God. And as a general, moderate, and respectable Christian piety has gradually lost its hold on the center of American society, this spiritual individualism has become more pronounced. Nothing is more suggestive of the immense institutional transformations that may lie ahead for American Christianity than the growth of the so-called "mega-churches," enormous urban "parishes" built more or less on the model of suburban shopping malls, accommodating sometimes more than twenty thousand congregants, and often featuring such amenities as bookstores, weight rooms, food courts, playing fields, coffee houses, even hostelries and credit unions. Worship in such churches often takes the form of mass entertainments — popular music, video spectaculars, sermons of a distinctly theatrical nature — and constitutes only one among a host of available services. Obviously, the scale of such enterprises is possible only because the spiritual life to which they give refuge is essentially private: each worshipper alone amid a crowd of other worshippers, finding Christ in the emotional release that only so generously shared a solitude permits. When Christ is one's personal Savior, sacramental mediation is unnecessary and pastoral authority nugatory; convenience, however, and social support remain vital. I do not mean to ridicule these churches, incidentally: I am not competent to say whether they represent merely a final disintegration of American Christianity into an absurd variety of consumerism, or whether they might be taken as — within the constraints of contemporary culture — a kind of new mediaevalism, an attempt to gather small cities into the precincts of the church and to retreat into them from a world increasingly inimical to spiritual longing. For me they do, however, occasion three reflections: first, that no other developed nation could produce such churches, because no other developed nation suffers from so unrelenting a hunger for God; second, that the social medium, the "middle," that I have claimed American religion has always largely lacked is perhaps more profoundly absent now than it has ever been, so much so that many Christians find themselves forced to create alternative societies to shelter their faith; and, third, that evangelical individualism may in fact be becoming even more thoroughly the standard form of American Christianity.

Prognostication is of course always perilous, especially when one is considering a matter as thronged with imponderables as America's religious future. My tendency, though, is to assume that for some years to come America will continue to be abnormally devout for an industrialized society; and in fact I suspect (for reasons that will presently become clear) that it might even become a great deal more devout. But there is also that "other America" that could scarcely be more energetically post-Christian, and it requires only a generation or two for a society to go from being generally pious to being all but ubiquitously infidel; in the age of mass-communication and inescapable "information," when an idea or habit of thought or fashionable depravity does not have to crawl from pen to pen or printing press to printing press, these cultural metabolisms occur far more quickly than they used to do. The ease with which an ever more flamboyant and temerarious sexual antinomianism has migrated through the general culture is instructive, at the very least, of how pliant even the most redoubtable of moral prejudices can prove before the blandishments of modern ideas when those ideas are conveyed, principally, by television. There is no reason to be confident that the rising and succeeding generations of Catholics and evangelicals, Hispanic or "Anglo," will not progressively yield to the attractions (whatever they are) of secularist modernity. Some estimates of the decline in church attendance over just the past dozen years put it as high as twenty percent (though neither the accuracy nor the meaning of that number is certain). And the young of college age profess markedly less faith than their elders, say some surveys (though this, if true, may be little more than callow defiance of parents or the affectation of intellectual and moral autonomy). The American habit of faith will probably run many of the new unbelievers to earth, of course, but the great age of disenchantment may yet dawn here as it has in other technologically and economically advanced societies.

What, however, I suspect will be the case is that — however playfully or balefully heathen the circumambient culture may continue to become — religion in America will remain at least as vigorous as it is now for at least a few decades. The two most influential and vital forms of Christianity, almost certainly, will be evangelical Protestantism and Roman Catholicism (between which even now, however irreconcilable their ecclesiological principles, one can observe certain areas of intellectual and cultural rapprochement taking shape). Pentecostalism, moreover, is growing everywhere in the Christian world, and it is reasonable to suppose that more "charismatic" forms of both Catholicism and Protestantism will increasingly flourish here as well. Around these two massive realities, smaller Protestant denominations of a markedly conservative complexion may remain relatively stable, I would imagine, so long as

they remain conservative. Eastern Orthodoxy — along with the other ancient Eastern Churches, the most intransigently immune of Christian
communities to the lure of change — has enjoyed something of a small
flood of conversions over the past three decades, especially from
Protestant denominations; though it has long been seen as a predominantly "ethnic preserve" for Greeks, Russians, Serbs, Arabs, etc., Orthodoxy will probably continue to grow from outside its "natural" constituency, and may in a few generations come to be dominated in this country
by communicants with no ethnic ties to the tradition.

Faiths other than Christianity will in all likelihood, even as their total numbers increase, decline in their percentage of the population (with
the possible exception of Mormonism). The cultural and even religious
influence of Judaism on America society will persist, one assumes, but in
this regard it will be practically unique. Certainly nothing like the constant and volatile growth of Islam in Europe is likely here in the near
term; despite occasional claims to the contrary, there are probably fewer
than two million American Muslims; the majority of American Arabs are
Christian, and our immigrants come principally from cultures where Islam is a small presence at best.

Where, among Christian congregations, it seems obvious to me that
there will be no conspicuous growth, and indeed a great deal of diminu-
tion, is among the more liberal of the mainstream Protestant denominations. As much attention as is given in the press to the "lively" debates
underway in many of the Protestant churches over such things as sexual
morality, or to the New Hampshire Episcopal church's elevation of the
adulterous and actively homosexual Gene Robinson to its episcopacy,
these remain matters of concern to communities so minuscule by comparison to the larger religious realities of American culture, and so
clearly destined for further fragmentation and tabescence, that it is inconceivable that they could be very relevant to the future shape of American religion. Things like the Gene Robinson affair may, of course, be
genuinely instructive regarding certain shifts in the larger society, especially in certain regions of the country. But, when one considers the most
liberal forms of mainstream American Protestantism, it is not even obvious that one is any longer dealing with religion at all, except in a formal
sense. Certainly they exhibit very few of the recognizable features of living faiths (such as a reluctance to make up their beliefs as they go along),
and it is difficult to see many of their "bolder" gestures of accommoda-

tion as amounting to anything more than judicious preparations for a final obsolescence. The future of American religion in the main, whatever it is, lies almost certainly elsewhere.

In saying this, I am not, I hasten to add, attempting to be either cavalier or contemptuous. My judgments are prompted simply by two immense sets of statistical fact: those concerning birth-rates and those concerning immigration. As for the former, I merely observe that theologically and morally conservative believers tend to have more children. Conservative American Christians reproduce at a greater rate than their liberal brethren, and at an enormously higher rate than secularized America; the extraordinary growth of traditionalist Christian communities in recent decades is something that has been accomplished not only by indefatigable evangelization, but by the ancient and infallible methods of lawful conjugation and due fruition.

More importantly, though, the form that American religion will take in coming years is increasingly dictated by the demographic influx from Latin America, Asia, and Africa. In his indispensable book, *The Next Christendom* (2002), Philip Jenkins remarks that the effect of mass immigration from the global South and Pacific East to the United States in recent years has been, in fact, to make America a more Christian nation. And the Christianity that is being imported from these parts of the world is, to a great extent, very conservative in its most basic moral precepts and metaphysical presuppositions. And, throughout the developing world, the Christianity that is growing most exuberantly (with, as Jenkins demonstrates, a rapidity that beggars the imagination) is in many cases marked by the New Testament charisms: prophecy, exorcisms, glossolalia, visions, miraculous healings. These are not things, one must make clear, confined only to small, sectarian communities. A Ugandan Catholic priest of my acquaintance has claimed to me — with obviously some hyperbole — that all African Christianity is charismatic to one degree or another. And the effect of Pentecostalism's success on the worship of Catholic congregations in places like the Philippines and Brazil is well documented.

All of which tends to make rather hilarious a figure like John Spong, the quondam Episcopal bishop of Newark. It was Spong who, in 1998, produced a hysterical screed of a book, pompously entitled *Why Christianity Must Change or Die,* that — in arguing for a "new Christianity," unburdened by such cumbrous appurtenances as, for instance, God — succeeded only in making audible the protracted death rattle of a moribund church. It was Spong also who, that same year, appalled that African bishops at the Lambeth Conference were about to defeat movements towards an official Anglican approbation of homosexuality, delivered himself of a fiercely petulant diatribe almost touching in its unreflective racism; these Africans, he declared (all of whom were far better scholars and linguists than he, as it happens), had only recently slouched their way out of animism, and so were susceptible to "religious extremism" and "very superstitious" forms of Christianity. Now, admittedly, Spong is a notorious simpleton, whose special combination of emotional instability and intellectual fatuity leaves him in a condition rather like a chronic *delirium tremens;* so it is not surprising that, on being somewhat unceremoniously roused from the parochial midden on which he had been contentedly reclining, his reaction should be puerile and vicious; but his perplexity and rage were genuine and understandable. Many within the languishing denominations of the affluent North, until they are similarly shaken from the slumber of their ignorance, are simply unprepared for the truth that, in the century ahead, Christianity will not only expand mightily, but will increasingly be dominated by believers whose understanding of engagement with the non-Christian or post-Christian world is likely to be one not of accommodation, compromise, or even necessarily coexistence, but of spiritual warfare. This is, in many ways, an "ancient" Christianity; and, as immigration from the developing world continues, it will almost certainly find itself most at home in "ancient" America. (But this suggests that my earlier approach to my topic was probably better after all.)

AN IRONY that attaches to these reflections is that many of the forms of Christianity entering America from the developing world are in a sense merely coming home. The Christian movements that have had the most prodigious success in Asia and the global South are arguably those that were born here and then sent abroad: revivalist evangelicalism, Pentecostalism, even the charismatic movement within Catholicism and certain of the mainstream Protestant churches. Indeed, when one considers the influence American Christianity has had on the evolution of Christianity in the wider world, and considers also the effect of America's popular culture on the evolution of secular culture everywhere, one might almost conclude that America's great central and defining tension —

between extreme forms of antiquity and modernity — has somehow reached out to draw the world into itself.

And it is a tension that — for want of that precious medium, civilization — looks likely to increase, for our extremes are becoming very extreme indeed: a modernity drained of any of the bright refinements and moral ambitions of Enlightenment reason or humanist idealism, reduced to a "high" culture of insipid ethical authoritarianism and a low culture consisting in dreary hedonism (without a hint of healthy Rabelaisian festivity), ever more explicit and repetitive celebrations of violence, sartorial and sexual slovenliness, atrocious music, and an idyllic emancipation from the fetters of literacy or (in fact) articulacy; and an antiquity of real and dynamic power, but largely uncontrolled by any mediating forces of order, stability, unity, or calm. To the dispassionate observer, there might be something exhilarating in the spectacle: the grand titanic struggle — within the very heart of their homeland — between a secular culture of militant vanity and incorruptible coarseness and a Christian culture of often purely experientialist ardor.

More prosaically speaking, though, a genuine civil religious struggle may well mark the coming decades, and how it will play out is hard to say. For the demographic reasons to which I have already adverted, as much as the social history of the United States, America is the one place in the Western world where one could conceivably see the inexorable advance of late modernity somewhat falter; or even the cultural power of the Christian global South establish something of a Northern redoubt. On the other hand, our strident secularity may ultimately triumph, and with it all the pathologies of cultural exhaustion; perhaps not only will the courts, and educational establishment, and American Civil Liberties Union, and all the other leal servants of a constitutional principle that does not actually exist, succeed in purging the last traces of Christian belief from our licit social grammar; but we may all finally, by forces of persuasion impossible to foresee, be conducted out of the darkness of our immemorial superstitions, nationalisms, moral prejudices, and retrograde loyalties into the radiant and pure universe of the International Criminal Court, reproductive choice, and the Turner Prize. Or some kind of uncomfortable but equable balance might continue to be struck between our extremes, under the sheltering pavilion of material satisfaction and narcissist individualism. But I tend to think otherwise, and not only because "spiritual warfare" is more interesting to write about than is bland social concord.

A culture — a civilization — is only as great as the religious ideas that animate it; the magnitude of a people's cultural achievements is determined by the height of its spiritual aspirations. One need only turn one's gaze back to the frozen mires and fetid marshes of modern Europe, where once the greatest of human civilizations resided, to grasp how devastating and omnivorous a power metaphysical boredom is. The eye of faith presumes to see something miraculous within the ordinariness of the moment, mysterious hints of an intelligible order calling out for translation into artifacts, institutions, ideas, and great deeds; but boredom's disenchantment renders the imagination inert and desire torpid. This claim is of course completely at variance with the Enlightenment mythology of modern secularism: that faith confined mankind within an incurious intellectual infancy, from which it has only lately been liberated to pursue the adult adventure of self-perfection; that the lineaments of all reality are clear and precise, and available to disinterested rationality and its powers of representation; that moral truth is not only something upon which all reasonable persons can agree, but something that, in being grasped, is immediately compelling; that human nature, when measured only by itself, will of course advance towards higher expressions of life rather than retreat into the vacuous self-indulgence of the last men or into mere brutish lawlessness; that reason can order society best only when all supernaturalism has been banished from its deliberations; and so on. In Wellington's words, if you believe that you will believe anything. Even if, however, one does not share my view that this entire mythology is an immense banality, and that modernity as a whole has resulted not in man's emergence into maturity, but in a degrading descent into a second childhood, still one must acknowledge that all the colossal creativity of modern culture taken together is manifestly unable to rise above a certain level of aesthetic or spiritual accomplishment, despite the greatness of certain individual achievements. And even if one has so little acquaintance with religious phenomena as to imagine that there are no moments of revelation; and that behind the surface of things there move no massive shapes that the religious consciousness dimly descries and imperfectly limns; and that in short religion is nothing but a gigantic feat of willful imagination; one must still grant that it is an engagement of, precisely, will and imagination, from which springs a magnificent profusion of cultural forms. Europe may now be its own mausoleum; but once, under the golden canopy of an infinite aspiration

— the God-man — the noblest of human worlds took shape: Hagia Sophia, Chartres, Rouen, and il Duomo; Giotto and Michelangelo; Palestrina and Bach; Dante and Shakespeare; Ronsard and Herbert; institutions that endured, economies that prospered, laws that worked justice, hypocrisies but also a cultural conscience that never forgot to hate them; and the elevation of charity above all other virtues.

As a person of reactionary temper, suffering from a romantic devotion to the vanished Christian order, and to all the marvels that flowed from its glorious synthesis of Judaic and Hellenic genius, I confess I often detest American religion (no doubt superciliously) as something formless, vulgar, saccharine, idolatrous, or — to intrude theology — heretical; and I continue to delude myself that Europe's spiritual patrimony need not have been squandered had it been more duly cherished and reverently guarded. At the same time, as something of an American chauvinist, I cannot help but see in our often absurd and sometimes barbarous spiritual and social ferment something infinitely preferable to the defatigation of vision, wisdom, and moral fortitude that is the evident condition of the post-Christian West. There may not be much hope that anything worth dignifying with the term "civilization" will ever emerge from American culture; but, then again, where religious life persists there are always possibilities.

And, if nothing else, there is such a thing as moral civilization; and that, I often think, is nowhere more advanced than among the sort of persons whose beliefs will always be a scandal to the John Spongs of the world. American religion is poor in palpable splendors, true; but it is often difficult not to be amazed at, say, the virtues that southern evangelical culture is able to instill and preserve amid the wreck of modern civility and conscience: the graciousness of true hospitality; the spontaneous generosity that prompts evangelicals, even those of small substance, to donate so great a portion of their wealth to charitable relief for the developing world; the haunting consciousness of sin, righteousness, and redemption that often even the most brutal of men cannot escape, and that can ennoble their lives with the dignity of repentance; a moral imagination capable of a belief in real "rebirth" (not merely "reform"), and the power frequently to bring it to pass. A culture capable of such things — and of the surrender of faith necessary to sustain them — is something rare and delightful, which cannot be recovered once it is lost.

If indeed American religion was born out of the exhaustion of one set of mediating cultural and institutional structures and has yet to find any to take their place; and if American secularism was born out of the decadence of European civilization and has so far succeeded only at producing a new kind of savagery; and if the two are destined to continue to struggle for the soul of the nation, it is obvious where the sympathies of anyone anxious about the survival or even recrudescence of Western civilization should lie. I am not always entirely convinced that irreligious cultural conservatives have an unquestioned right to lament the general decline around them, as in ungenerous moments I tend to see them as its tacit accomplices, whose devotion to the past I suspect of having the character of empty nostalgia; but I should think such persons would not be indifferent to religion. For, if we succumb to post-Christian modernity, and the limits of its vision, what then? Most of us will surrender to a passive decay of will and aspiration, perhaps, find fewer reasons to resist as government insinuates itself into the little liberties of the family, continue to seek out hitherto unsuspected insensitivities to denounce and prejudices to extirpate, allow morality to give way to sentimentality; the impetuous among us will attempt to enjoy Balzac, or take up herb gardening, or discover "issues"; a few dilettantish amoralists will conclude that everything is permitted and dabble in bestiality or cannibalism; the rest of us will mostly watch television; crime rates will rise more steeply and birth rates fall more precipitously; being the "last men," we shall think ourselves at the end of history; an occasional sense of the pointlessness of it all will induce in us a certain morose feeling of impotence (but what can one do?); and, in short, we shall become Europeans (but without the vestiges of the old civilization ranged about us to soothe our despondency). Surely we can hope for a nobler fate. Better the world of Appalachian snake handlers, mass revivals, Hispanic Pentecostals, charismatic Catholics, and millenarian evangelicals (even the Gnostics among them); better a disembodied, violent, and even dionysiac hunger for God than a dispirited and eviscerate capitulation before material reality; and much better a general atmosphere of earnest, if sometimes unsophisticated, faith.

My "epiphany" of twenty years ago, on the rail platform in England, was undoubtedly lacking in a certain balance, but the intuition that lay behind it was correct: that material circumstances (unless they are absolutely crushing) possess only such gravity or levity as one's interpretation of them; and how one interprets them is determined not merely by one's personal psychology, but by the cultural element in which they subsist. The almost luxuriant squalor of that railway station, had I found myself confronted by it in some corner of America, might have seemed a bleak disfigurement of the greater world in which I lived; it might even have struck me as depressingly emblematic of the profound hideousness of late industrial society and its inevitable utilitarian minimalism; but I do not believe it would have seemed to me the dark mystical epitome of a nation's soul. Allowing for all the peculiarities of personal temperament, and for the special pathos that homesickness can induce, my reaction to my miserable surroundings was a real — if inevitably subjective — awakening to a larger cultural and spiritual truth. Either the material order is the whole of being, wherein all transcendence is an illusion, or it is the phenomenal surface — mysterious, beautiful, terrible, harsh, and haunting — of a world of living spirits. That the former view is philosophically incoherent is something of which I am convinced; but, even if one cannot share that conviction, one should still be able to recognize that it is only the latter view that has ever had the power — over centuries and in every realm of human accomplishment — to summon desire beyond the boring limits marked by mortality, to endow the will with constancy and purpose, and to shape imagination towards ends that should not be possible within the narrow economies of the flesh.

In any event, whatever one makes of American religion — its genially odd individualism, or its often ponderous stolidity, or its lunatic extremism, or its prodigies of kitsch, or its sometimes unseemly servility to a national mythology, or simply its unostentatious pertinacity — it is as well to realize that it is far more in harmony with the general condition of humanity throughout history than are the preposterous superstitions of secular reason or the vile ephemeralities of post-Christian popular culture. And it is something alive and striving, which has the power to shelter innumerable natural virtues under its promises of supernatural grace. Most importantly, though, its strength and vitality portend something that might just survive the self-consuming culture of disenchantment; for, while it is possible that modernity may not have very much of a future, antiquity may very well prove deathless.

6

When the Going Was Bad:
On Evelyn Waugh's Travel Writings

Evelyn Waugh, *Waugh Abroad: Collected Travel Writing* (Knopf)

The year 2003 marked the centenary of the birth of Evelyn Waugh, which Knopf publishing has chosen to observe by reissuing all seven of his travel books in a single, handsome, inexpensive Everyman's Library edition. Most of these titles have been out of print, or only sporadically in print, since they were originally published. Waugh did make a selection from the first four of them in 1945, under the title *When the Going Was Good,* but that book omits too much material to serve either as a chronicle of the author's literary development or as a fully satisfying treatment of any of the events he recounts. And so this new collection is a considerable boon to the Waugh enthusiast.

It is not, however, a particularly notable contribution to the cause of travel books considered as a distinct genre. Such books have a rich tradition in Britain, and many occupy an honored place in the nation's literature. Many in fact preserve some of the more perdurable specimens of English prose: the dry picaresque of Robert Louis Stevenson's travel stories, the droll elegance of A. W. Kinglake's *Eothen,* the haunting beauty of C. M. Doughty's *Travels in Arabia Deserta,* the luminous austerity of Wilfred Thesiger's books, the crystalline perfection of Norman Douglas's, the fluent, faintly metaphysical lyricism of Freya Stark's. And, of course, towering above the entire field — serene and marmoreal — stand the works of Patrick Leigh Fermor. Judged alongside any of these, purely as literary excursions, Waugh's books fail almost absolutely.

But this is only to say that the pleasure they afford is of another sort. For the most part, these books are not really about travel at all. True travel writers work upon the assumption that their task is, primarily, to see and to describe, and where possible to enter into as profound a sympathy for their subjects as they can; Waugh proceeds upon the (subversive) assumption that his business is to evaluate and to comment, and to avoid sympathy as assiduously as circumstances and good taste permit. For all his considerable prowess as a stylist, in these books he rarely troubles to convey any images or experiences with appreciable vividness or pungency (except where the possibility of mockery presents itself). Any reader of his novels knows he was quite capable of painting pictures with words when necessary; but his genius lay elsewhere. His prose is urbane, unsentimental, and economical, hospitable to moments of purple abandon, but at its best when its controlled and even flow allows him to pass from delicacy to savagery and back again without any visible show of effort. It is, in short, a prose of personality, not of scenery; of irony, not of anecdotes. And so it is in these books.

And both the personality and the irony are ostentatiously those of Evelyn Waugh. The real "topic" of these works is his literary persona, which is an invention elaborate enough to sustain any reader's interest over long passages of vague description and uneventful narrative. Especially early on in this volume, when Waugh is still the *enfant terrible* of English letters, it is clear that the lands through which he passes and peoples among whom he sojourns are largely inconsequential to — except as occasions of — his writing; the more dreary the setting or ghastly the situation, the more he is at play in his native element. Where the surroundings are dull, the amenities frightful, the conversations insufferable, the flora withered, or the meals inedible, he is best able to fill in the portrait he wishes to paint of himself: acidulous, impassive, not vicious but mercilessly cognizant of unflattering details; mildly atrabilious but more typically phlegmatic, immune equally to alarm or enchantment, hewing to a fine medium between polished boredom and slightly macabre curiosity; passing overt judgment on nothing, but with such imperturbably sardonic detachment as in fact to pass judgment on everything; sagaciously callow, capable only of wan enthusiasms, already shaped by fixed — but not fanatical — prejudices, and entirely unsentimental regarding indigenous cultures.

THE MOST ENJOYABLE (indeed, hilarious) of these books is the first, *Labels* (1930). The putative subject of this work is the author's 1929 travels in the Mediterranean — including European, North African, and Near Eastern ports of call — but apart from exactingly observed instances of the absurd or the grotesque the prose souvenirs of his journey are cursory and gray. I came away from this book with no more vibrant images of Malta, Cairo, Naples, or Constantinople than when I began; but I vividly recalled Waugh's reflections on the travel snob's delight in the inconveniences visited on him by foreign customs officials, his proposals for a novel whose protagonist would be some item of women's clothing, his excursus on celibacy and the erotic reveries induced in affluent middle-aged widows by advertising copy, his distaste for Turkish decorative devices, and his devastatingly ambiguous "celebrations" of the architecture of Gaudi in Barcelona.

Between *Labels* and his second travel book, *Remote People* (1931), two immense events somewhat altered the course of Waugh's life: his first wife's adultery precipitated the collapse of his marriage and he was received into the Catholic Church. Of the first, one finds here no clue. For one thing, nowhere in *Labels* had Waugh even hinted that he had made his tour with his wife; instead he had transferred the travails of their journey (during which she was extremely ill) onto another, fictional English couple. His Catholicism, though, soon begins to make its effect felt: from this point on, a shift in Waugh's sympathies becomes ever more evident in these books, at least wherever he encounters Catholic piety; and it soon becomes obvious that there is one topic concerning which he is now incapable of jest.

Remote People, however, like its predecessor, is principally a burlesque. It recounts Waugh's travels in East Africa, first in Ethiopia (where he witnesses the events surrounding Haile Selassie's coronation), and then in and around the British colonial possessions — Kenya and Tanganyika, that is — to the south and the Belgian Congo. Waugh's Saxon hauteur before the pomp and pretense of the Ethiopian festivities is often parochial and small; he sees only tawdry vulgarity, casual cruelty, squalor, faded grandeur, and false glory; nothing of the ancient Christian civilization of the Amharic people even excites his attention. Still, one must admit, his reminiscences are extremely amusing (especially his description of the American professor, an "expert" in Coptic ritual, who is forever losing his place in the Ge'ez liturgies and making authoritative pronouncements that are promptly proved to be an entirely wrong). And the hellish narrative of his peregrinations through the colonial interior constitutes perhaps his best sustained assault on one's expectations of travel literature.

For Waugh's most irreverent treatment of the romantic conventions of the genre, however, one must read *Ninety-Two Days* (1934), which recounts his journeys through — and the very choice of setting bespeaks a certain perversity of temperament — the hinterlands of British Guiana. If there is any more unprepossessing expanse of earth upon the globe, one cannot imagine where. This book is an unremitting account of misery, privation, and pointlessness in a world of dun landscapes, tormenting insects, malnutrition, and cultural stagnancy. What makes it fascinating, though, is the almost demented composure of the author; it demonstrates with remarkable poignancy how, in its way, British equanimity can constitute a kind of emotional extremism. When Waugh describes *farine,* the practically inedible staple of the indigenous diet (which, in its unrefined form, is in fact toxic), or the nightly labor of extracting *djiggas* from the soles of his feet before they can lay their septicemial eggs, or his almost constant hunger or thirst, one is left with a sense not only of the sublime callousness of nature, but of the lunacy of choosing to confront it with a good will rather than fleeing from it with or without one's dignity intact. There are moments of brilliant comic portraiture here — for instance, the mad religious visionary Mr. Christie — but more striking perhaps is the way in which Waugh's Catholicism comes suddenly and soberly to the fore when he turns to his recollections of the St. Ignatius Mission, or when he ascribes to supernatural assistance a sequence of coincidences that saved him from becoming at one juncture irretrievably lost in the wilderness.

FOR READERS WHO SUFFER no excessive passion for completeness, *Waugh in Abyssinia* (1936) is the book in this collection most profitably skipped. Not only is it less diverting than those preceding it, it is an unsavory artifact of Waugh's mercifully brief infatuation with Mussolini, and is altogether deplorable. It recounts Waugh's impressions of Ethiopia before and during Italy's brutal invasion, which — through his positively incarnadine moral spectacles — he sees as a new advance of the Roman eagles into a land desirous (like ancient Britain) of the civilizing power they represent. He stalwartly refuses to believe stories of Italian atrocities. His distaste for Haile Selassie, while not unwarranted, leads him to describe the emperor's flight into exile, but not the emperor's direct part in the hopeless military campaigns of the Ethiopian military against a merciless and contemptible enemy. And his unfavorable comparison of the court ceremony of Ethiopia to that of mediaeval Europe is cretinous in its poverty of historical perspective.

Happily, Waugh had regained his sanity, and perhaps his soul, by the time he wrote *Robbery Under Law* (1939). This is not really a travel book (though it concerns a visit to Mexico), but an essay in political and moral philosophy, a meditation on the power of authoritarian ideology to desiccate and destroy even a rich and long-established civilization, and a frequently acute study of the strange liaison between autocracy and anarchy. He sees the Mexico of General Cardenas as a cautionary epitome of the fragility of all civilization, and of the peril that communism, or fascism, or Nazi ideology, or any other of the movements of "progressive" humanism represents for any people insufficiently jealous of its traditions, culture, and faith. It is, as well, rather touching to find Waugh defending the pieties of Mexican Indians (his fellow Catholics) against the disdain of more "advanced" nations, and heaping derision on racialist bigotries.

The final two volumes in this collection, *The Holy Places* (1952) and *A Tourist in Africa* (1960), emanate from a later, more fatigued period in Waugh's life. The former consists simply in two short, devout articles: one on St. Helena (protagonist of his most justly neglected novel), and another on the Holy Land (over which Britain's cession of authority displeases him mightily). The latter book is a diary of travel through British East Africa, marked by flashes of mordancy and moments of sincere sympathy for his African Christian brethren, but also by a certain intellectual lethargy: here alone in this collection his reliably pellucid prose becomes often flaccid and jejune. Again, he pours scorn on racialist mythology, but in his steadfastly conservative way refuses to become histrionically sanctimonious on the matter, preferring studied contempt to self-promoting outrage.

This volume is a substantial addition to Waugh's available literary remains. It begins better than it ends; but so, usually, does life, and this collection spans the entire creative life of its author. For all his well-deserved reputation as a caustic and irascible cynic, solicitous only of his prejudices, it is ultimately Waugh's skepticism towards any claims of cultural superiority on the part of modern civilization that constitutes the most continuous "moral" theme in these works (with one unfortunate interruption). Not that he does not exhibit his fair share of "Anglo-Saxon attitudes" (they are the mainstays of his humor), but when one reads through this volume from beginning to end — as I have just done — it is Waugh's increasingly Christian sense of a community of faith transcendent of race, culture, class, or country that leaves the most resonant impression. And for me, I must admit, that came as something of a revelation.

7

Freedom and Decency

Things could conceivably be far worse. The brief ebullition of indignation that followed Janet Jackson's rather pathetic exhibitionist display during the recent Superbowl's halftime was no doubt sincere, but surely was as nothing compared to the fury in Poland earlier this year after Polish state television aired a concert by a Norwegian "black metal" band in Krakow. The entertainment reportedly featured — among other whimsical conceits — naked women hanging from crosses (one of whom had to be hospitalized when she lost consciousness), a dozen sheep's heads impaled on stakes, perhaps a hundred liters of sheep's blood poured over the performers and their audience, a stage festooned with Satanist sigils, and songs of praise to the devil (I assume, also, that the music was not particularly good). Not that this concert was in any sense a departure for Norwegians: such bands are perhaps Norway's chief cultural export these days, and among their giddily irrepressible devotees they enjoy a celebrity of the sort once accorded to Paganini. Their performances invariably involve roughly equal measures of cruelty, obscenity, sacrilege, diabolism, and Norse paganism (thus accomplishing the difficult feat of simultaneously blaspheming both the Christian God and Odin). But it was certainly a departure for Polish television.

This, for me at least, places the episode of Miss Jackson's outraged bustier in a somewhat more forgiving light. Diversions and delights similar to the Krakow concert are not entirely unknown in America, but they appeal to a rather select and fugitive company; as yet, the nihilisms we allow to disport themselves at the center of our culture are more anodyne, or at least less explicit regarding their spiritual wellsprings. National television has not yet treated us to Satanists cavorting among dismembered animals and obscene mockeries of the crucifixion, and our "chief cultural export" — in terms of profits generated, at least — is not yet blasphemy (it remains, if one is curious, pornography). Measured against other degenerate cultures, we are still, in some respects, at the stage of a touchingly maladroit infancy.

Of course, it is always easy to flatter ourselves by reflecting upon the depths to which we have not yet descended, but we should resist the temptation to do so. In the nations of Scandinavia the Western European attempt to strike a happy balance between scrupulously amoral free-market consumerism and intrusively moralistic bureaucratic state socialism may have achieved something like a perfect synthesis: a sugar-soaked and narcotic totalitarianism so enveloping in its providence and so libertine in its materialism as to threaten to reduce its peoples to an almost brutish pliancy. It is not surprising then that many of Norway's young, when they choose to cast off the placidity of sheep, can imagine no better model for their rebellion than the pitilessness of wolves (this, at any rate, might explain the peculiar malice towards sheep exhibited in Krakow); when human existence has been winnowed down to an oscillation between ignoble complacency and shameless appetite, the golden mean between the ovine and the lupine can become somewhat elusive.

The question that interests me, however, is whether our cultural crisis here in America is really any less acute. For, while it is indeed true that things could be worse, it is also true that they probably will be very soon. It is heartening, naturally, to live in a country where so much righteous ire can be stirred by a fleeting glimpse of something the unarrested sight of which — on almost any summer day along certain sandy banks of the Seine — nourishes the tranquil noonday reveries of many a Parisian schoolboy. It attests to the persistence among us of the kind of social virtue — call it bourgeois respectability, or Puritanism, or simple decency — that is too often appreciated only in the aftermath of its disintegration. That said, however, there is still something odd in the symbolic importance this event has assumed for many, given that far worse evidences of the rapid coarsening of our culture surround us on every side all the time (examples are too numerous and obvious to cite). I suspect that among those who professed their dismay after the game there were many who as a rule are willing to tolerate most of the corrosive influences that invade family life — from advertising, films, popular music, the internet, video games, the language we have all become accustomed to hearing every day — so long as those influences continue unobtrusively to operate in their "proper" places.

THIS IS NOT TO SAY that there is not a real division in American society between those of devout and traditionalist temperament, who try to abide by some common standard of decency or courtesy, and those who regard any cultural resistance to vulgarity, or vicious fantasy, or explicit violence, or sexual degradation as an obstacle to be surmounted. Nor should one fail to deplore the sheer boorishness with which the latter class feels free to impose the refuse of its imagination on the former (what was truly appalling about the recent halftime show was probably simply its incivility). How deep our social division truly is, however, is difficult to ascertain. For it is one thing to lament the discourtesy of those who delight in giving offense, but another thing altogether to provide an effective remedy for it; and only when we honestly ask ourselves what remedy we are willing to contemplate will it become clear whether as a people we are truly engaged in a "culture war" (as we are often told we are) or are simply witnessing the effects of a genuine but transient tension between more refractory and more precipitate elements within a single cultural process.

I say this because my first impulse is to suggest that the simple (if not sufficient) answer to our cultural dilemma is probably censorship, against which almost every argument in the abstract is predictably fatuous. Upon this, it seems to me, any sane society should be able uncontentiously to agree. And yet ours cannot. That such a prescription should be either controversial or scandalous — as in fact it is — suggests that something is profoundly amiss in our culture, some defect that runs far deeper than any mere division between the pious and the profane, or between the puritanical and the hedonistic. Certainly there is nothing in the constitutional charter of free (political, religious, ideological) speech that obliges us to permit any product, no matter how depraved its content, to be created, sold, promulgated, procured, or kept. More importantly, though — and this should be obvious — a society that refuses all censorship is in some very crucial sense extremely unjust.

Every nation with any pretense to civilization, that is, must be governed by some regime of civic prudence, possessing the power to place certain restraints upon public transactions. But for such a regime, no society can assure its citizens any measure of genuinely *civil* freedom, by which I mean the freedom that only a rigidly observed social courtesy — necessarily confining and somewhat artificially ceremonious — provides: freedom from other persons' bad taste. There is almost no such thing as purely private expression under the best of circumstances; in the age of mass communication, when every venture into a public space quickly becomes complete immersion in a world of jarring noise and garish pomps and shrill distraction, it is folly to imagine that one can if one chooses simply "turn things off" and go unmolested by the worst elements of popular culture. It is folly also to believe that the cause of freedom is advanced when a society's citizens cannot demand — with the full force of law and custom on their side — that others not be given license to subject them constantly to offensive materials or to corrupt their children with impunity.

This is, one could argue, the simplest matter of moral stewardship. The forces of barbarism that are always eager to assail civilization — from without and within — are, if not tireless, at least remarkably resilient. Where no codes of civil conduct govern cultural production, it is inevitable that those who are coarsest and least constrained by conscience — those who are most wanting in shame, restraint, imagination, modesty, consideration, or charity — will prevail. What then of everyone else whose peace and dignity a just political order should be concerned to protect? I think it safe to say there has never been a society where the lewd, the dissolute, or the perverted have not been able to find some place for their recreation, and this is a reality to which we are wise to be in some degree resigned. But we live now in an age in which crudity refuses to be confined within its own sphere, but rather forces itself upon us, and indeed demands (almost sanctimoniously) that it be embraced and granted social legitimacy, and that it be subject to no strictures other than those of the free market. Anyone so quaintly retrograde as to want to escape the deluge must retreat to some jealously insulated domestic realm, guarded with almost martial vigilance against any intrusion by the encircling culture.

Frankly, I find it somewhat difficult to make much sense of many of the conventional objections to censorship. The one that in my experience tends to be adduced most promptly (and with the greatest degree of hysteria) whenever the subject is broached is that of the "slippery slope":

but grant some agency the legal power of censure, the argument goes, and before long political speech will be suppressed, privacy invaded, legal protections eroded, republican liberties abridged, schools taken over by fundamentalists from Alabama, women reduced to chattels, and the demonic ferment of fascism lying always just below the surface of American life loosed upon the world. This, at any rate, is more or less the case that was once made to me by a depressingly earnest civil liberties attorney in North Carolina, with just enough of an air of catechetical exactitude to make it obvious to me that she was merely giving voice to a deeply entrenched professional orthodoxy. It was plainly inconceivable to her that a humane regime of censorship could be evolved in such a way as to make abuse of its authority all but legally impossible. Apparently, as a society, we are poised precariously and vertiginously upon the narrowest precipice of a sheer escarpment as smooth as glass, overlooking a vast chasm of totalitarian tyranny; so much as a single step towards censorship will send us hurtling into the abyss, and nothing will be able to stay our fall.

This is, of course, nonsense. In the days when the US Post Office had the authority to bring prosecution against those who delivered obscene materials through the mails, and cinema was subject to the Hayes Office, and communities were permitted to ban books, there were certainly cases of excessive zeal in the application of these powers, and instances when provincialism triumphed over art, and perhaps many miscarriages of justice; but, *mirabile dictu,* we were not at the mercy of a secret police; warrantless incarceration in nameless prisons, torture, murdered journalists, the cult of the Great Leader, the rule of clandestine tribunals, the bullet in the back of the head in the nacreous light of dawn — all of these things remained miraculously absent from our society. Indeed, were there any historical example of republican freedom weakened or subverted by public and commercial codes of decency, this line of argument might command some force. As it is, it seems to me that any people that honestly believes political despotism to be the inevitable consequence of any constraints being placed upon the dissemination of popular artifacts — say, forbidding the sale of recordings made by some sullen, talentless thug fantasizing about raping his girlfriend's daughter — is a people that has elevated the cult of personal liberty to a new and oppressive fanaticism.

A somewhat more plausible objection is that a public censor will as often as not turn out to be some well-intentioned philistine who cannot distinguish artistically or conceptually accomplished treatments of delicate themes from simple pornography; and this, in turn, will have a stifling effect on artists and thinkers. Here, one must acknowledge, there is enough historical evidence to render this anxiety credible. It does require a fairly perceptive and finely discriminating eye to judge intelligently the intrinsic qualities of any work of art. It is somewhat embarrassing to recall the legal perils that delayed production of an American edition of *Lolita,* which is really — quite apart from its extraordinary aesthetic merit — a rather moral and even slightly sentimentalist work (though Nabokov would bristle at those words). That *Ulysses* ever had to appear before an American bar of justice now rightly seems ridiculous. Of course, we would all have been better off to have been spared the intellectually arthritic and incompetently written melodrama of *Lady Chatterley's Lover,* but it is not the business of the courts to protect society from bad prose or adolescent philosophy.

Even here, however, I think I am still largely unconvinced. For one thing, great art endures, and over time distinguishes itself from all the lesser accomplishments with which it might initially have been confused; and it is not necessarily a bad thing for the artist who wishes to treat of things usually left decently veiled to have to submit his work to the ordeal of prevailing moral prejudice: it is likely, for one thing, to inspire more ingenious art, as well as to test the mettle of the artist. There were many inconveniences suffered by the "urbane" bibliophile in the days when the unexpurgated Aretino or Rochester was available only in private editions, and Burton's complete *Thousand Nights and a Night* existed only in limited printings, and volumes of Pierre Louÿs were sold exclusively out of back rooms and in borrowed dust-jackets by booksellers of dubious character, and Frederick Rolfe's Venetian letters could bring fines and imprisonment to their purveyors; but I am not convinced that the cause of civilization was grievously impaired by such inconveniences. Nor does it seem plausible to me to suggest that our national literature has noticeably improved since these fetters were struck off. There is, after all, a kind of philistinism on either side of this issue. Is good art suppressed more by rules of public decency (even when applied with a heavy hand) or by the barbarism of a culture whose sensibilities have become so debauched by constant exposure to the scabrous or the vile as to have become incapable of any discrimination, or of any due appreciation of subtlety or craft?

Consider one of the more obvious cases of commercial standards abandoned, that of cinema. For all the ponderous parochialism of the old motion picture code, it did at the very least demand of screen writers the kind of delicate technique necessary to communicate certain things to mature viewers without giving any hint of their meaning to the children also watching. Thus films had to be written by adults, and the best films required writers of some considerable skill. After all, everyone of a certain age in the audience was well aware of what things occurred between men and women in private. They understood, therefore, what may have happened between Humphrey Bogart and Ingrid Bergman when the camera cut away to the watchtower's revolving beam of light; what had failed to happen when Spencer Tracy quietly slipped out of Katharine Hepburn's apartment, neglecting to take his hat with him; what it was that Katharine Hepburn was both relieved and offended to discover had not happened when, on the previous evening, her inebriation had required Jimmy Stewart to carry her to her bed; what Bogart and Bacall were really discussing under the veil of their equestrian metaphors; why Glenn Ford was treating Rita Hayworth with at once such tenderness and such malice; and what (and I fear one needs to be something of a Preston Sturges aficionado to catch this reference) Barbara Stanwyck was implying when she wrapped her arms around Fred MacMurray's neck and murmured, "But, darling, we *are* at Niagara Falls."

Well, nostalgia can be a particularly dangerous opiate. Obviously many extraordinary films have been produced since the Hayes Office vanished — there was even a brief golden age of sorts in the early '70s — and among them have been many that could never have appeared under the old code. Even now, one is occasionally astonished by a gleam of gold amid the dross. Nevertheless, the current state of cinema seems to suggest that where good or at least clever writing is not a commercial necessity, and where there are no artificially imposed limits within which writers must work, the general intellectual quality of the medium cannot help but decline, and do considerable cultural damage as it descends. It would certainly be hard, if nothing else, to argue credibly that artistic expression has been well served by the revolution in standards that has made script-writing an occupation dominated by sadistic adolescents, or that the art has exactly flourished in an era in which it has been proved that immense profits can be generated from minimal dialogue but plenteous bloodshed, and in which practically nothing is considered too degraded or degrading for popular tastes.

All my bitter musings aside, however, let me stipulate that, in an ideal situation, the practice of censorship would be undertaken only by persons properly educated and formed, whose decisions would be under some form of collective review. But, precisely at this point (alas), I discover an obstacle to censorship that makes a creditable regime of public standards seem so unlikely as to be, for all intents and purposes, a utopian fantasy. For, while it really is not that difficult to recognize irredeemable obscenity when one encounters it, as things now stand it is difficult to say whom — what class of persons — one would care to entrust with a censor's authority. We live at a time, after all, when even the humanities departments in our universities are frequently populated by scholars of really rather exiguous learning, who think that "*épater les bourgeois*" is a significant cultural and moral achievement, and who — in their insatiable craving for ever greater *frissons* of the subversive — can make an "artist," "philosopher," and "martyr" out of an ineffably tedious mediocrity like the Marquis de Sade. Censors drawn from those ranks might prove eager and indefatigable in searching out and suppressing every form of "hate speech" (that is, anything you are likely to find in a Papal encyclical), but little else. I do not believe that, if we were to create some sort of board of censors, we would be likely to suffer the reign of the American equivalent of Soviet realist art; but this is in part because the persons we would choose for the office might not be sufficiently sophisticated to rise to so plausible a level of philistinism. Simply said, it may be that we no longer have enough civilization left to save.

At least, in my darker moments (which are frequent), that is what I think. At the end of the day, however, it does not matter whether I am right to do so; all of these considerations have about them something of the fabulous and absurd. Obviously no new laws of censorship will be passed in America; even among those who sincerely wish that the circumambient culture could be purged of its ever more aggressive coarseness, there are many who would see such laws as somehow contrary to the principles of their democracy and a threat to liberty in general. This is why I suspect — as I hinted above — that the real malady afflicting our culture lies not primarily in the division between those who would prefer and those who would resent more rigid social standards of decency, but far deeper down, in many of the premises that both parties share. As it happens, by far the worst argument against censorship is the one likely to carry most weight with persons on both sides of the cultural divide: that, were certain cultural products legally proscribed, we would be denying people things they want, denying them the right to choose for themselves, putting limits upon expressive freedom, refusing to trust in the law of supply and demand — all of which is of course quite true. But to find this a compelling argument, obviously, one must already be convinced of the inalienable sanctity of choice, over against every other social good, and convinced moreover that freedom and choice are more or less synonymous. It is indeed true that many of us manifestly do want unimpeded access to explicit depictions of sex and violence, and to mindlessly brutal forms of entertainment, and to artifacts born solely from the basest impulses of the imagination; but surely, in point of fact, no society that simply concedes the prior right of its citizens to have whatever they want can ever really be free.

THIS IS THE CRUCIAL ISSUE, I think: not what we understand decency to be, but what we mean when we speak of freedom. It is a curious condition of late Western modernity that, for so many of us, the highest ideal of the good society is simply democracy as such, and then within democracy varying alloys of capitalism, the welfare state, regionalism, federalism, individualism, and so on. And what we habitually understand democratic liberty to be — what we take, that is, as our most exalted model of freedom — is merely the unobstructed power of choice. The consequence of this, manifestly, is that we moderns tend to elevate what should at best be regarded as the moral life's minimal condition to the status of its highest expression, and in the process reduce the very concept of freedom to one of purely libertarian or voluntarist spontaneity. We have come to believe — more or less unreflectively — that the will necessarily becomes more free the more it is emancipated from whatever constraints it suffers; which means that, over the course of time, even our most revered moral traditions can come to seem like onerous nuisances, which we must shed if we are to secure our "rights." At the very last, any constraint at all comes to seem an intolerable bondage. But it was not ever thus.

Obviously any sane organism is predisposed to resist subjugation to forces outside itself — which is to say, forces related to it only by their power over it — and every healthy soul has a natural prejudice in favor of

77

its own autonomy. Moreover, any rational person naturally prefers the local to the general, the familiar to the abstract, the intimate to the universal, and so resents the intrusion of any alien or usurpatious power (the state, or large corporations, or heartless bureaucracies, or unjust laws) upon the independence or integrity of his person, or family, or native heath, or culture, or faith. But this is to say no more than that it is natural to rebel against purely arbitrary or extrinsic constraints, either upon oneself or upon what one loves. What distinguishes the specifically modern conception of freedom from earlier models, however, especially in its most extreme expressions, is that it seems often to presume that all constraints are arbitrary and extrinsic, and that there is no such thing as a natural or intrinsic constraint at all.

And yet — and I would not even go so far as to call this a paradox — freedom is possible only through constraints. That "sane organism" of which I spoke above can be solicitous of its autonomy only because it is some particular thing; and for anything to be anything at all — to possess, that is, a concrete form — it must acquire and cultivate useful, defining, shaping limits. True freedom, at least according to one venerable definition, is the realization of a complex nature in its proper good (that is, in both its natural and supernatural ends); it is the freedom of a thing to flourish, to become ever more fully what it is. An absolutely "negative liberty" — the absence of any religious, cultural, or social restrictions upon the exercise of the will — may often seem desirable (at least for oneself) but ultimately offers only the "freedom" of chaos, of formless potential. This is enough, admittedly, if one's highest model of life is protoplasm; but if one suspects that, as rational beings, we are called to a somewhat more elevated existence than that, one must begin to ask which impulses within us should be suppressed, both by ourselves and by the cultural rules that we all must share.

For instance, if one wishes to become "honorable" (a word so quaint and antique as now to have the power to charm but not to compel), one must accede to any number of elaborate restrictions upon one's actions and even thoughts; and these restrictions unquestionably confine and inhibit desire and volition, and are themselves often more a matter of ritual comity and factitious grace and painful reserve than of practical necessity. And yet, as one learns to consent to a common and demanding set of conventions and duties, one also progressively acquires an ever greater purity of character, a stability and hence identity, a unified "self";

one emerges from the inchoate turmoil of mere emotion, and is liberated from the momentary impulses and vain promptings of the will, and arrives at what can truly be called one's essence. The form, as Michelangelo liked to say, is liberated from the marble. In this way, precisely through accepting freely the constraints of a larger social and moral tradition and community, one gives shape to a character that can endure from moment to moment, rather than dissolving in each instant into whichever new inclination of appetite or curiosity rises up within one. One ceases to be governed by caprice, or to be the slave of one's own liberty.

This understanding of freedom, however, requires not only a belief that we possess an actual nature, which must flourish to be free, but a belief in the transcendent Good towards which that nature is oriented. This Christians, Jews, and virtuous pagans have always understood: that which can endure in us is sustained by that which lies beyond us, in the eternity of its own plenitude. To be fully free is to be joined to that end for which our natures were originally framed, and for which — in the deepest reaches of our souls — we ceaselessly yearn. And whatever separates us from that end — even if it be our own power of choice within us — is a form of bondage. We are free not because we can choose, but only when we have chosen well. And to choose well we must ever more clearly see the "sun of the Good" (to employ the lovely Platonic metaphor), and yet to see more clearly we must choose well; and the more we are emancipated from illusion and caprice, and the more our will is informed by and responds to the Good, the more perfect our vision becomes, and the less there is really to choose. The consummation for which we should long, if we are wise, is that ultimately we shall, in St. Augustine's language, achieve not only the liberty enjoyed by Adam and Eve — who were merely "able not to sin" *(posse non peccare)* — but the truest freedom of all, that of being entirely "unable to sin" *(non posse peccare),* because God's will works perfectly in ours.

Which is why it is not only perplexing but deeply disturbing that so many Christians and Jews in the modern world unthinkingly embrace and defend a purely libertarian understanding of freedom, even as they decry the constant gravitation of modern society towards ever more arbitrary, decadent, and extreme expressions of just this kind of freedom. Nor can they be acquitted on the grounds that the cultivation of virtue is the work of individual souls, not of society at large; there is no such thing as private virtue, any more than there is such a thing as private language, and fallen creatures vary enormously in their capacity for obedience to the Good. Though this might make me seem like an unregenerate Christian Platonist (which is not too dreadful a fate, since that is precisely what I am), a society is *just* precisely to the degree that it makes true freedom possible; to do this it must leave certain areas of moral existence to govern themselves, but it must also in many cases seek to defeat the most vicious aspects of fallen nature, and to aid as far as possible in the elevation in each soul of right reason over mere appetite and impulse — which necessarily involves denying certain persons the things they want most. A just social order, that is to say, would be one devoted to a "paedagogy of the Good," and would recognize that there can be no simple partition between the polity of the soul and the polity of the people, and that there is in fact a reciprocal spiritual relation — a harmony — between them. When appetite seizes the reins of the soul or the city, it drives the chariot towards ruin; so it is the very art of sound governance to seek to perfect the intricate and delicate choreography of moral and legal custom that will best promote the sway of reverent reason in city and soul alike.

Democracy is not an intrinsic good, after all. Where the moral formation of a people is deficient, the general will malign, or historical circumstance unpropitious, it is quite unambiguously wicked in its results. All of Plato's warnings against "ochlocracy" have been proved prophetic often enough, even within the confines of duly constituted republics, and even he could not foresee the magnitude of the evil that can be born from a popular franchise (the Third Reich leaps here rather nimbly to mind). The only sound premise for a people's self-governance is a culture of common virtue directed towards the one Good. And a society that can no longer conceive of freedom as anything more than limitless choice and uninhibited self-expression must of necessity progressively conclude that all things should be permitted, that all values are relative, that desire fashions its own truth, that there is no such thing as "nature," that we are our own creatures. The ultimate consequence of a purely libertarian political ethos, if it could be taken to its logical end, would be a world in which we would no longer even remember that we should want to choose the good, as we would have learned to deem things good solely because they have been chosen. This would in truth be absolute slavery to the momentary, the final eclipse of rational dignity, the triumph within us of the bestial over the spiritual, and so of death over life.

WHEN ALL IS SAID AND DONE, however, as I have already more or less acknowledged, I am trading here not merely in speculation, but in extravagant fantasy. We are very far removed indeed from a culture capable of such paedagogy — perhaps farther now than at almost any other point in Western history. And, in the age of the omnicompetent liberal state, when government is at once more intimately pervasive of and more airily abstracted from the concrete reality of communities and families, even to speak of moral paedagogy is likely to invite any number of pernicious authoritarianisms. Moreover, we are very near to a consensus as a society not only that choice and self-expression are values in and of themselves, but that they are perhaps the highest values of all; and no society can believe such nonsense unless it has forsaken almost every substantial good.

This is why, as I say, I am not convinced that we are in any very meaningful sense in the midst of a "culture war"; I think it might at best be described as a fracas. I do not say that such a war would not be worth waging. At the moment, however, most of us have already unconsciously surrendered to the more insidious aspects of modernity long before we even contemplate drawing our swords from their scabbards and inspecting them for rust. This is not to say there are no practical measures for those who wish in earnest for the battle to be joined: home-schooling, perhaps, or private "trivium" academies; forbidding one's children video games and attempting to instill a love of good music in them; Greek and Latin; great books; remote places; archaic enthusiasms. It is generally wise to seek to be separate, to be in the world but not of it, to be no more engaged with modernity than were the ancient Christians with the culture of pagan antiquity; and wise also to cultivate in our hearts a generous hatred towards the secular order, and a charitable contempt. Probably the most subversive and effective strategy traditionalists might undertake would be one of militant fecundity: abundant, relentless, exuberant, and defiant child-bearing. Given the reluctance of modern men and women to be fruitful and multiply, it would not be difficult, surely, for the devout to accomplish — in no more than a generation or two — a demographic revolution. Such a course is quite radical, admittedly, and contrary to the spirit of the age, but that is rather the point, after all. It would mean often forgoing certain material advantages, and forfeiting a great deal of our leisure; it would often prove difficult to sustain a two-career family or be certain of a lavish retirement. But if it is a war they want, they should not recoil from sacrifice.

In the end, however, no matter how much we might want to win back the culture around us, we can hope for no "victory" at all — no matter what practical measures we take — if we are not resolved first and foremost to extirpate the habits and presuppositions of secular modernity from ourselves. What we call the "culture war" is, after all, only one outward manifestation of a spiritual war that is being waged at all times and in all places, but whose first battleground is the heart. We have become all of us so accustomed to thinking like modern men and women, to believing that it is the power of the arbitrary in ourselves and in others that defines for us at once our dignity and our political freedom, that we often lack the moral resources necessary to alter the course of our culture, or even to frame intelligible arguments for wishing to do so. If we are serious Christians, or Jews, or even virtuous pagans (assuming any still exist), we should know that mere libertarian license is as often as not quite nefarious in its employment and its effects, and that our political rights are the products of a charter agreed upon for the common good (nothing more or less), and that we have no rights at all not wedded to responsibilities and to the moral claim of our neighbors upon us. Even when we know all this, we probably do not know it deeply enough. And if we insist on being moderns, or Americans, or democrats, or consumers first, rather than Christians, Jews, and virtuous pagans above all, whose spiritual loyalties transcend all other associations, and allow ourselves to believe that true freedom is anything other than the liberation and perfection of a definite nature in conformity with the highest Good — with God himself, that is — we will always be divided against ourselves, and to some degree accomplices of those very forces whose defeat we think we desire. Indeed, we cannot really affect the course of our society at all, or even properly imagine what kind of political or social future we should want, so long as we fail to remember (and to fashion our lives according to the knowledge) that we exist only because there is One who has called us from nothingness to be what he desires us to be, not simply what we would like to make ourselves, and that we shall truly be free — and know what freedom is — only when we have no choices left.

8

The Pornography Culture

Writing not *(Deo gratias)* as a lawyer, but simply as a person of somewhat reactionary temperament, with a mind formed by certain Christian moral prejudices, I am able to address the Supreme Court's recent decision regarding the Child Online Protection Act (or, rather, regarding the stay a lower court placed upon this act) only somewhat obliquely. Concerning the legal merits of the case, certainly, I have little to say. This is not necessarily because I believe one must be a lawyer to understand the court's decision, but because I am largely indifferent to the legal arguments contained within it, and am convinced that even the question of whether or not it was dictated by genuine constitutional concerns deserves very little attention (as I shall presently argue).

I can begin, however, by confessing the perplexity my untutored mind feels at some of the *reasoning* behind the court's majority ruling, most especially the curious contention that COPA might prove to be unconstitutional on the grounds that there exists filtering software that provides a "less restrictive means" of preventing access to pornography on the internet and that, moreover, does not involve "criminalizing" any particular category of speech. Surely, if we are to be guided by logic, the existence or nonexistence of such software (which is, after all, merely a commercial product that parents may purchase and use if they are so inclined and have the money) cannot possibly make any difference regarding the question of whether the act violates constitutional protections. If a law is constitutional under any conditions, one would think, then it is constitutional under all, as all conditions are — strictly speaking — adventitious to the principles by which the law is judged (else they are not *principles* in any meaningful sense).

By the same token, it is difficult to grasp why the court thinks it necessary to act upon the premise that whatever means is employed to prevent children from gaining access to pornography on the worldwide web should involve the barest minimum imposition possible upon the free expression of pornographers, and that the availability of alternative means must therefore render the law invalid. Either the use of the internet to disseminate pornographic images and texts constitutes a form of protected "speech" or it does not; and, if it does not, by what authority does the court presume to assay any opinion regarding how onerous the legal restrictions upon it should be? (This, needless to say, is a facetious question.) As for the matter of "criminalizing" certain forms of "speech," that — one would have thought — was precisely the idea behind COPA; it rather begs the question then to adduce this as a compelling argument against the constitutionality of the act.

Again, I have no legal training, so I have no idea what shadowy precedents might be slouching about in the background of such apparently feeble reasoning; I am aware, moreover, that the alliance between law and logic is as often as not a tenuous one. And I can even appreciate something of the court's anxiety concerning the scope of the government's control over "free expression," given that the modern liberal democratic state — with its formidable apparatus of surveillance and legal coercion, and its inhuman magnitude, and its bureaucratic procedural callousness, and its powers of confiscation, taxation, and crippling prosecution, and its immense technological resources — is among the most intrusive, sanctimonious, and irresistible forms of political authority yet devised by man. Allow the government even the smallest advance past the bulwark of the first amendment, one might justly conclude, and before long we will find ourselves subject to some variant of "hate speech" legislation, of the sort that holds sway in the insect societies of Canada and Northern Europe. We have, as a culture, long accepted the legal fiction that we are incapable of even that minimal prudential wisdom necessary to distinguish speech or art worthy of protection from the most debased products of the imagination, and so have become content to rely upon the abstract promise of free speech as our only sure defense against the lure of authoritarianism. And perhaps, at this juncture in cultural history, it is no longer really a fiction.

In a larger sense, however, all human law is a fiction, especially law of the sort adjudicated by the Supreme Court. As much as jurists might be inclined to regard constitutional questions as falling entirely within the province of their art, the constitution is not in fact a legal document; it is a philosophical and political charter, and law is only one (and, in isolation, a deficient) approach to it. Constitutional jurisprudence, moreover, is essentially a hermeneutical tradition; it is not the inexorable unfolding of irrefragable conclusions from unambiguous principles, but a history of willful and often arbitrary interpretation, and as such primarily reflects cultural decisions made well before any legal deliberation has begun. And since legal principles — as opposed to exact ordinances — are remarkable chiefly for their plasticity, it requires only a little hermeneutical audacity to make them say what we wish them to say (one never knows, after all, what emanations may be lurking in what penumbras). Just as the non-establishment clause might well have been taken — had our society evolved in a more civilized direction — as no more than a prohibition upon any federal legislation for *or against* the establishment of religion at the state level, so the promise of freedom of speech might have been taken as a defense of (quite precisely) *speech* — which is to say, principled political or religious discourse, and nothing more. There is certainly no good reason why "free speech" should have come to mean an authorization of every conceivable form of expression, or should have been understood to encompass not only words but images and artifacts, or should have been seen as assuring either purveyors or consumers of such things a right of access to all available media or technologies of communication. We interpret it thus because of who we are as a society, or who we have chosen to be; we elect to understand "liberty" as "license." How we construe the explicit premises enshrined in the constitution is determined by a host of unspoken premises that we merely presume, but that also define us. This is why I profess so little interest in the question of the constitutionality of COPA; the more interesting question, it seems to me, concerns what sort of society we have succeeded in creating if the conclusions we draw from the fundamental principles of our republic oblige us to defend pornographers' access to a medium as pervasive, porous, intricate, and malleable as the internet against laws intended to protect children.

THE DAMAGE that pornography can do — to minds or cultures — is not by any means negligible. Especially in our modern age of ubiquitous and passive entertainment, saturated as we are by an unending storm of noises and images and barren prattle, portrayals of violence or of sexual degradation possess a remarkable power to permeate, shape, and deprave the imagination; and the imagination is, after all, the wellspring of desire, of personality, of character. Anyone who would claim that constant or even regular exposure to pornography does not affect a person at the profoundest level of consciousness is either singularly stupid or singularly vicious. Nor has the availability and profusion of pornography in modern Western culture any historical precedent. And the internet has provided a means of distribution whose potentials we have scarcely begun to grasp. It is a medium of communication at once transnational and private, worldwide and discreet, universal and immediate. It is, as nothing else before it, the technology of what Gianni Vattimo calls the "transparent society," the technology of global instantaneity, which allows images to be acquired in a moment from almost anywhere, conversations of extraordinary intimacy to be conducted with faceless strangers across continents, relations to be forged and compacts struck in almost total secrecy, silently, in a virtual realm into which no one — certainly no parent — can intrude. I doubt that even the most technologically avant-garde among us can quite conceive how rapidly and how insidiously such a medium can alter the culture around us.

We are already, as it happens, a casually and chronically pornographic society. We dress little girls in clothes so scant and meretricious that honest harlots are all but bereft of any distinctive method for catching a lonely man's eye. The popular songs and musical spectacles we allow our children to listen to and watch have transformed many of the classic *divertissements* of the bordello — sexually precocious gamines, frolicsome tribades, erotic spanking, Oedipal fantasy, very bad "exotic" dance — into the staples of light entertainment. The spectrum of wit explored by television comedy runs almost exclusively between the pre- and the post-coital. In consequence, a great deal of the diabolistic mystique that once clung to pornography — say, in the days when even Aubrey Beardsley's scarcely adolescent nudes still suggested to most persons a somewhat diseased sensibility — has now been more or less dissipated by the solvent of familiarity. But the internet offers something more disturbing yet: an "interactive" medium for pornography, a parallel world both fluid and labyrinthine, where the most extreme forms of depravity can be cheaply produced and then propagated on a global scale, where consumers (of almost any age) can be cultivated and groomed, and where a restless mind sheltered by an idle body can explore whole empires of vice in untroubled quiet for hours on end. Even if filtering software were as effective as it is supposed to be (and, as yet, it is not), the spiritually corrosive nature of the very worst pornography is such that — one would think — any additional legal or financial burden placed upon the backs of pornographers would be welcome.

I am obviously being willfully naïve. I know perfectly well that, as a culture, we value our "liberties" above almost every other good; indeed, it is questionable at times whether we have the capacity to recognize any rival good at all. The price of these liberties, however, is occasionally worth considering. For instance: I may be revealing just how quaintly re-actionary I am in admitting that nothing about our pornographic society bothers me more than the degraded and barbarized vision of the female body and soul it has so successfully promoted, and in admitting also (perhaps more damningly) that I pine rather pathetically for the days of a somewhat more chivalrous image of woman. One of the high achievements of Christian civilization, after all, was in finding so many ways to celebrate, elevate, and admire the feminine; while remaining hierarchical and protective in its understanding of women, admittedly, Christendom also cultivated — as perhaps no other civilization ever has — a solicitude for and a deference towards women born out of a genuine reverence for their natural and supernatural dignity. It may seem absurd even to speak of such things at present, after a century of Western culture's sedulous effort to drain the masculine and the feminine of anything like cosmic or spiritual mystery, and now that vulgarity and aggressiveness are the common property of both sexes and often provide the chief milieu for their interactions; but it is sobering to reflect how far a culture of sexual "frankness" has gone in reducing men and women alike to a level of habitual brutishness that would appall us beyond rescue were we not, as a people, so blessedly protected by our own bad taste. The brief flourishing of the 1970s' ideal of masculinity — the epicene ectomorph, sensitive, nurturing, flaccid — soon spawned a renaissance among the young of the contrary ideal of conscienceless and predatory virility, one somehow (almost magically) fitted to the political and social pieties of our time of course, but no less rapacious and cynical for all that. Not to wax too apocalyptic, but it is difficult not to wonder — as imaginations continue to be shaped by our pornographic society —

what sorts of husbands or fathers are being bred. And how will women continue to conform themselves — as surely they must — to our cultural expectations of them? To judge from popular entertainment, our favored images of women fall into two complementary, if rather antithetical, classes: on the one hand, sullen, coarse, quasi-masculine belligerence, on the other, pliant and wanton availability — viragoes or odalisques. I am fairly sure that, if I had a daughter, I should want her society to provide her with a sentimental education of richer possibilities than that.

My backwardness aside, however, it is more than empty nostalgia or neurotic anxiety to ask what virtues men and women living in an ever more pervasively pornographic culture can hope to nourish in themselves or in their children. Sane societies, at any rate, care about such things — more, I would argue, than they care about the "imperative" of placing as few constraints as possible upon individual expression. But we have made the decision as a society that unfettered personal volition is (almost) always to be prized, in principle, above the object towards which volition is directed. It is in the will — in the liberty of choice — that we place primary value, which means that we must as a society strive, as far as possible, to recognize as few objective goods outside the self as we possibly can. Of course, we are prepared to set certain objective social and legal limits to the exercise of the will, but these are by their very nature flexible and frail, and the great interminable task of human "liberation" — as we tend to understand it — is over time to erase as many of these limits as we safely can. What is irreducibly "the good" for us is subjective desire, self-expression, self-creation; the very notion that the society we share could be an organically moral realm, devoted as a whole to the formation of the mind or the soul, or that unconstrained personal license might actually serve to make society as a whole less free by making others powerless against the consequences of the "rights" we choose to exercise, runs contrary to all our moral and (dare one say?) metaphysical prejudices. We are devoted to — indeed, in a sense, we worship — the will; and we are hardly the first people willing to offer up our children to our god.

THIS IS FAIRLY EXTREME rhetoric, I know, but really I am saying nothing more than that our society is a product of late Western modernity. The history of modern political and social doctrine is, to a large degree, the history of Western culture's long, laborious departure from classical and

Christian models of freedom, and the history in consequence of the ascendancy of the language of "rights" over every other possible grammar of the good. It has become something of a commonplace among scholars to note that — from at least the time of Plato through the high Middle Ages — the Western understanding of human freedom was inseparable from an understanding of human nature: to be free was to be able to flourish as the kind of being one was, so as to attain the *ontological* good towards which one's nature was oriented (human excellence, charity, the contemplation of God . . .). For this reason, the movement of the will was always regarded as posterior to the object of its intentions, as something wakened and moved by a desire for rational life's proper *telos,* and as something truly free only insofar as it achieved that end towards which it was called. To choose awry, then — through ignorance or malfeasance or corrupt longing — was not considered a manifestation of freedom, but of slavery to the imperfect, the deficient, the privative, the (literally) subhuman. Liberty of choice was only the possibility of freedom, not its realization, and a society could be considered just only insofar as it allowed for and aided in the cultivation of virtue. Not that we can return to antique models of freedom as a culture (would that we could); but it is worthwhile to reflect how entirely we have taken leave of that world in which God could be conceived of as infinitely free because — in the fullness of his nature — he was "incapable" of evil.

There would be little purpose here in rehearsing the story of how late Mediaeval "voluntarism" altered the understanding of freedom — both divine and human — in the direction of the self-moved will, and subtly elevated will in the sense of sheer spontaneity of choice *(arbitrium)* over will in the sense of a rational nature's orientation towards the good *(voluntas);* or of how later moral and political theory evolved from this one strange and vital apostasy, until freedom came to be conceived not as the liberation of one's nature, but as power over it. What is worth noting, however — at least from my perspective — is that the modern understanding of freedom is essentially incompatible with the classical or Christian understanding of man, the world, or society. Freedom, as we now conceive of it, presumes — and must ever more consciously pursue — an irreducible nihilism: for there must literally be *nothing* transcendent of the will that might command it towards ends it would not choose for itself, no value higher than those the will imposes upon its world, no nature but what the will elects for itself. It is also worth noting, somewhat in passing, that only a society ordered towards the transcendental structure of being — towards, that is, the true, the good, and the beautiful — is capable of anything we might meaningfully describe as civilization, as it is only in the interval between the good and the desire wakened by it that the greatest cultural achievements are possible. Of a society no longer animated by any aspiration nobler than the self's perpetual odyssey of liberation of itself, the best that can be expected is a comfortable banality. Perhaps, indeed, a casually and chronically pornographic society is the inevitable form late modern liberal democratic order must take, since it probably lacks the capacity for anything better.

All of which yields two conclusions, with which I shall draw to a close. The first is that the gradual erosion — throughout the history of modernity — of any concept of society as a moral and spiritual association governed by useful ethical prejudices, immemorial reverences, and subsidiary structures of authority (Church, community, family) has led inevitably to a constant expansion of the power of the state. In fact, it is ever more the case that there are no significant social realities other than the state and the individual (collective will and personal will, that is); in the absence of a shared culture of virtue, of an agreed grammar of the good, and of social structures of authority possessing some recognized power to invigilate and protect particular communities, the modern liberal state must function — even if benignly — as a police state, making what use it may of the very technologies that COPA was intended somewhat to control. And that may be the truly important implication of a decision such as the Supreme Court's judgment on COPA: whether we are considering the power of the federal government to penalize pornographers or the power of the federal court to shelter them against such penalties, it is a power that has no immediate or necessary connection to the culture over which it holds sway. We call upon the state to shield us from vice or to set our vices free, because we do not have a culture devoted to the good, or dedicated to virtue, or capable of creating a civil society that is hospitable to any freedom more substantial than that of subjective will. This is simply what it is to be modern.

And the second conclusion concerns only persons who continue to harbor certain Christian convictions: that every time a decision like that regarding COPA is handed down by the high court, it should serve to remind them that between the Christian and the liberal democratic traditions there must always be some element of enmity. What either understands as freedom the other must view as a form of bondage. This particular decision is not especially dramatic in this regard — it is certainly nowhere near as apocalyptic in its implications as *Roe v. Wade* — and no doubt there are plausible legal and even ethical arguments to be made on either side of the issue, within the terms our society can recognize. All that I would hope devout Christians (and Jews, and others with similarly pre-modern allegiances) should feel when confronted by such a decision, and the sort of reasoning informing it, is a profound sense of alienation. It is good to be reminded from time to time — good for Christians, that is — that their relations with the liberal democratic order can be cordial to a degree, but are at best provisional and fleeting, and can never constitute a firm alliance; that here they have no continuing city; that they belong to a kingdom not of this world; and that, while they are bound to love their country, they are forbidden to regard it as their true home.

9

The Laughter of the Philosophers

Thomas C. Oden, *The Humor of Kierkegaard* (Princeton University Press

My favorite "whimsical" anecdote about a philosopher goes like this: Arthur Schopenhauer once threw an old woman down a flight of stairs (note how the first line immediately seizes one's attention). He claimed it was an accident, of course, but I for one prefer to believe that it was nothing of the sort, and that in fact he took the defenseless crone by her wizened weasand and — with full malice aforethought — flung her over the balustrade to the landing below, uttering a curse as he did so; it better accords with my general impression of the man. Not that he acted without cause. The old lady was a cleaning woman who had made too great a clamor outside his rooms, a transgression than which (as anyone familiar with his essay on noise should know) nothing could have vexed him more; and it was only when his rebukes were met by intolerable impudence that he resorted to force. Curiously, however, the magistrate failed to see the justice in his actions, and sentenced him to pay the woman a monthly pension for the rest of her life, which somewhat straitened his finances. When she was finally considerate enough to die, and Schopenhauer saw the notice in the morning obituary, his only reaction was to reach for his pen and write in the margin: *"Anus obit, onus abit"* (the old woman dies, the debt departs).

The reason this grim little tale so amuses me (quite apart from the magnificent play on words, which one hopes was purely extemporaneous), is that the lives of philosophers are so often oppressively, obtundently dreary that any diverting story — even one as macabre as the ordeal of Schopenhauer's poor old *Putzfrau* — comes to the scholar as a cherished respite. And, for the most part, the works of philosophers mirror the shapes of their lives. The sublime spiritual sterility of the texts of Kant's philosophical maturity, for instance, could scarcely provide a more perspicuous glimpse into the personality of perhaps the single most boring man ever to darken a wigmaker's doorway. The leaden, caliginous bombast of Hegel's prose was a pure emanation of his grindingly pompous soul. The turgidity of Derrida's attempts at playfulness are little more than clinical specimens of his insufferable self-infatuation. As a general rule, to put it simply, if one wanders into one's library in search of mirth, good fellowship, or wit, one does well not to seek out the company of the philosophers.

There are exceptions, however, and none more notable than Søren Kierkegaard. In some sense, Kierkegaard's whole life could be written as a kind of dark comedy; despite his premature death, and a great number of sadnesses that afflicted him along the way, there was something enchantingly absurd about his character, a certain benign perversity that prompted him to make himself willfully ridiculous, and a touching quality of the ludicrous that clung to him all the way to his early grave. Few philosophers' lives can boast comic (or, for that matter, tragic) material comparable to Kierkegaard's aborted engagement to Regine Olsen, the bizarrely exaggerated symbolic significance he attached to it, his firm expectation of death before the age of thirty-four on account of some unnamed sin of his father's, his intentional provocation of a feud with the satirical review *The Corsair,* or his splenetic quarrels with the Danish Lutheran church (and so on).

And he had wit. It is said that once, for instance, as he came to a stream spanned by a bridge so narrow that two men could not cross it abreast, nor pass one another upon it, a belligerent burger arrived at the bridge's other end and — recognizing Kierkegaard — promptly announced that he would not stand aside for an infamous buffoon. "Ah, yes"; replied Kierkegaard, unperturbed, stepping back with a ceremonious sweep of his arm, "I, however, shall." And, of all the diverting tales that can be told about Kierkegaard, none is really any more terrible than that: if he was ever cruel, it was principally to himself, and he managed to live out his brief but prolific philosophical career without once (if you can credit it) feeling the need to heave an elderly charwoman into a stairwell. Moreover, happily, he was possessed not only of wit, but of literary genius; and for this reason he is one of that blessed and select company of modern philosophers whose writings can be read purely for the pleasure they afford.

THOMAS ODEN's generous anthology, *The Humor of Kierkegaard,* is a sequel to his deservedly popular collection of 1978, *Parables of Kierkegaard.* Unlike its predecessor, though, it is — in Oden's own words — intended "as entertainment with no noble purpose." But it is also, in a sense, a compilation of evidences, offered in support of a very large claim. In his introduction, Oden throws down a "gauntlet": he challenges the reader to assemble a collection of passages from any ten major philosophers as diverting as those he has compiled from Kierkegaard's writings; furthermore, he makes bold provisionally — until this challenge is met — to declare Kierkegaard "as, among philosophers, the most amusing." Now, as I have intimated already, I am prone to regard this as a distinction rather like that of owning "the finest restaurant in South Bend, Indiana": the quality of the competition renders the achievement somewhat ambiguous. Despite which, I am not entirely convinced that Oden makes an incontrovertible case. He does, I think it safe to say, prove that Kierkegaard was probably among the most amusing of Danes, but (again) the quality of competition must be taken into account.

In truth, Oden advances his claim with such vigor and so many proleptic cautions that one might be pardoned for suspecting that he is trying to compensate for some deficiency in the material. While he acknowledges that there is something absurd about offering a theoretical rationalization or justification of humor, he does nevertheless — more as a concession, apparently, to editorial pressure than out of personal inclination — provide a long treatment of the Kierkegaardian theory of comedy. Oden himself urges the impatient reader to skip these pages, and I am almost tempted to recommend impatience to the reader, lest all good will be defeated long before Kierkegaard's voice has been heard. Oden proceeds here at a very deliberate pace, as no doubt a scholar must, and this often obliges him to illustrate a point by quoting some amusing passage from Kierkegaard's work only then to offer an inevitably ponderous explanation of the joke. This sort of thing, in sufficient quantity, can quickly ruin one's appreciation of what follows.

This is not to say — I hasten to add — that Oden says nothing of interest at this point. He offers much to think upon. What I gleaned from these pages, in part, is that for Kierkegaard the roots of the comic lie in the inherent contradictoriness of human nature: soul and body, freedom and necessity, the angelic and the bestial, eternity and temporality, and so on. Moreover, I learned how profound a difference Kierkegaard saw between genuine humor and mere irony. Certainly the ironist can recognize that the incongruities that throng human experience typically frustrate the quest for truth; but, having seen as much, he is then impotent to do anything more than unveil failure and vanquish pretense. Humor, on the other hand, is born from an altogether higher recognition: that tragic contradiction is not absolute, that finitude is not only pain and folly, and that the absurdity of our human contradictions can even be a cause for joy. Humor is able to receive finitude as a gift, conscious of the suffering intrinsic to human existence, but capable of transcending despair through jest. And this is why the power of humor is most intense in the "religious" sphere: Christianity, seeing all things from the perspective of the Incarnation (the most unexpected of peripeties), is the "most comic" vision of things: it encompasses the greatest "contradictions" and "tragedies" of all, but does so in such a way as to take the suffering of existence into the unanticipated absurdity of our redemption. Which yields the somewhat gratifying conclusion that, to be both a "lover of wisdom" and an accomplished humorist, one must almost certainly be a Christian; or, rather, that only a Christian philosophy can be truly "comic."

Again, though, there are times when theory should be touched upon only very lightly. Kierkegaard's writings — taken in themselves — provide Oden with wonderfully rich sources of plunder, especially the early pseudonymous works, with their thickets of prefaces, interludes, interjections, postscripts, and appendices, and with their multiple voices, and preposterous authorial names, and sinuous coils of indirection. And Oden displays a keen eye for the comic and lyric *trouvailles* to be reaped from them. He is clearly a man whose long acquaintance with these texts has given him an enviable knowledge of their riches, and a deep enthusiasm for their complexities and subtleties. *Either/Or* emerges as the most fertile and delightful of Kierkegaard's literary achievements in this regard, though almost all the early books abound in comic invention. And, as a whole, this collection can be recommended, for light or serious reading alike. That said, while I enjoyed this anthology thoroughly, I nevertheless came away from it still somewhat unconvinced regarding Oden's high claims for Kierkegaard; and I find myself still inclined to ask whether Kierkegaard was really the nonpareil humorist that Oden makes him out to be.

FOR ME, this is a question with a special significance. I am one of that minority of readers who admire Kierkegaard more for his literary and satiric gifts than for his contribution to philosophy — which I regard as dubious — or his understanding of Christianity — which I regard as, in many significant respects, disastrously misguided. While I acknowledge his importance as an inspiration to later thinkers, and am conscious of how eagerly he was absorbed, midway through the last century, into the genealogy of "Existentialism" (perhaps the most annoying philosophical movement to arrive on the continental scene before the advent of post-structuralism), I cannot honestly profess immense admiration for his speculative powers. I think his critiques of Hegel, for instance, obvious at best, monotonously superficial at worst. As for his place among Christian thinkers, I think it a fairly minor one. As much as I approve of his contempt for polite, liberal, rationalized, and innocuous faith, his actual critique of "Christendom" often seems surprisingly barren and unsubtle. And, for all the initial appeal exercised by his talk of Christian "paradox," I think it a meretricious and misleading appeal in the end. For such as me, Kierkegaard the humorist — or novelist, or aphorist, or ironist — possesses an unquestioned eminence, whereas Kierkegaard the philosopher — or theologian, or pietist, or polemicist — cuts a far more equivocal figure. This might dispose me happily to accede to the claim Oden wishes to make did it not also dispose me to judge the evidence he presents somewhat variably, depending on which aspect of Kierkegaard's mind is reflected in any given selection. And, as it happens, my verdict on the material collected here is distinctly mixed; but I do not think it a verdict dictated solely by personal predilections.

Simply said, this anthology is too long. None of it lacks literary charm, that is certain; but much of it lacks any actual comic element. Oden does rightly caution the reader against imposing contemporary standards of humor on Kierkegaard, and I would add that it would be a mistake to impose upon him any of one's customary expectations of a humorist from any period; the reader who takes up this volume anticipating something on the order of Jonathan Swift, Charles Lamb, Max Beerbohm, or S. J. Perelman will unquestionably be disappointed. All this granted, though, in too many instances Oden is attempting to wring water out of stones.

This is not, certainly, to deny the comic brilliance of many of the passages gathered here. There is, for instance, a genuinely hilarious reflection on how embarrassing it is that there is so marked an absence of the Chinese in the Hegelian system, while not a single German assistant professor is excluded. And there is a wonderful passage where Kierkegaard likens the prospect of his imminent excommunication from the Danish church to the discovery that, though he is in Copenhagen, he is being given a thrashing in the distant town of Aarhus. Elsewhere he likens a pastor gesticulating vehemently over a mundane matter to a man proclaiming he would give his life for the fatherland and then adding, with full pathos, "Indeed I would do it for ten rix-dollars!" And there is one passage I especially liked (though it comes from a period in Kierkegaard's authorship of which I am not overly fond):

> [I]n modern drama the bad is always represented by the most brilliantly gifted characters, whereas the good, the upright, is represented by the grocer's apprentice. The spectators find this entirely appropriate and learn from the play what they already knew, that it is far beneath their dignity to be classed with a grocer's apprentice.

A somewhat greater number of passages, however, could be described only as mild witticisms:

> So let the history books tell of kings who introduced Christianity — I am of the opinion that a king can introduce an improved breed of sheep and railroads etc., but not Christianity.

This is vaguely amusing, perhaps (even though the sentiment it expresses is entirely false), but is it worthy of anthologization? And there are other passages that might perhaps — and then only if one were desperate to justify their inclusion in this volume — be described as "wry," such as one long and splendid (though not really humorous) portrayal of the boredom that afflicts the ironist. And there are still other passages that are so earnest, however charming they may be, that I cannot believe that any humor was intended at all.

Somewhat too often, Oden includes excerpts whose only distinction is that they contain somewhat involved metaphors — a journey from Peking to Canton, one thief accusing another to the police, a merchant momentarily given false hope as he watches his ship founder at sea, an emperor choosing a day-laborer as his son-in-law, the difference in value between a pound of gold and a pound of feathers, a corpse still able to perform some of the functions of a living body — as if such metaphors were intrinsically humorous. Perhaps the most enchanting metaphorical passage in the entire collection concerns a young seamstress — I lingered over it for some time — but there is nothing amusing about it in the least.

The most dispensable selections are drawn largely from the late polemical writings, particularly the *Attack upon Christendom.* Here, even where an attempt has been made to amuse, the humor is so often irascibly joyless that it comes across not as Christian mirth, but simply as irony embittered with sanctimony; and much of it is written in a voice so strident, vitriolic, and ulcerated that it seems not so much prophetic as petulant.

> The result of the Christianity of "Christendom" is that everything ... has remained as it was, only everything has assumed the name "Christian." ... The change is ... that the whorehouse remains exactly what it was in paganism, lewdness in the same proportion, but it has become a "Christian" whorehouse. A whoremonger is a "Christian" whoremonger. ...

This is shrill and tiresome. Yes, in fact there *are* "Christian" whorehouses, and whoremongers, and whores, and they are nothing like their pagan predecessors, because the formation of conscience within even a defectively Christian culture is something altogether unprecedented; the whorehouse is now full of sinners, whose memories necessarily bear the impress of moral grammars and spiritual promises that the pagan order never knew, and who in consequence may yet awaken to their sin, and who may even find themselves at unexpected moments haunted by charity or tormented by grace. And it is the repeated failure of Kierkegaard to understand just this that makes his treatment of the whole question of Christendom finally so boring — and so humorless.

WHAT THEN of Oden's gauntlet? Clearly I think that he has been a mite too avid in searching out passages to corroborate his argument, and that he would have done better to produce a volume of perhaps a hundred pages. Still, though, he may have proved his point. Who, after all, are Kierkegaard's rivals? Plato had as ready a wit as Kierkegaard's, and probably a healthier nature, and certainly Aristophanes's speech in *The Symposium* is a work of comic genius. Schopenhauer was a more agile epigrammatist, despite his streak of pubescent gloom ("Never a rose without a thorn; yet many a thorn without a rose"). Nietzsche was perhaps a greater satirist, even if the savagery of his wit confined his voice to a single comic register. One might, if one is no slave to occidental prejudice, suggest Chuang-Tzu, who was more adept at the droll and the fantastic. But none of these poses any credible challenge to Kierkegaard's supremacy. There are, of course, philosophers who are unintentionally amusing. I find Kant's *Critique of Practical Reason* nearly as fanciful, silly, and diverting as *Alice in Wonderland*. Almost everything of Daniel Dennett's has the power to reduce me to tears of jollity. Heidegger, at his worst, both invites and defies parody. But, in these cases, the temperament of the reader provides the better part of the jest. And certainly it would be cheating to adduce even more entertaining works of "occasional" philosophy, like Poe's *Eureka* or D. H. Lawrence's *Fantasia on the Unconscious*.

There are, it seems to me — after some reflection — only two figures who might credibly displace Kierkegaard from his throne: Voltaire and J. G. Hamann. The former, without question, was a greater and more versatile humorist than Kierkegaard, and in those terms alone there could scarcely be any comparison. The question worth asking, however, is whether Voltaire was in any real sense a philosopher, rather than a mere *philosophe;* and I would say he was not. I tend to take the view expressed by Baudelaire in his *Journaux intimes:* Voltaire was a man with no speculative capacity whatsoever, oblivious to mystery, mentally lethargic, a "pastor to the concierges," whose entire method of reflection consisted in a kind of systematic intellectual philistinism. So that leaves only Hamann; and here, I think, Kierkegaard simply is not equal to the contest.

Johann Georg Hamann (1730-88) is, by any measure, an obscure figure, little known outside the exclusive circles of a certain very rarefied kind of scholarship, hardly read at all even in his native Germany, and perhaps truly understood by next to no one. And yet it would be difficult to exaggerate not only the immensity of his influence upon all the great European intellectual and cultural movements of his age, but his continued significance for philosophers and theologians. A friend (and antagonist) of Kant's, an inspiration to Herder and Jacobi, read and admired by the likes of Goethe, Schelling, Jean Paul, and Kierkegaard, he is the only figure to whom Hegel felt it necessary to devote a long monograph. Today, however, his importance is scarcely a rumor even to the very literate, and the best known book about him in English is a ghastly and imbecile portrait in crayon by that most indefatigably fraudulent of modern intellectuals, Isaiah Berlin. John R. Betz, of Loyola College in Baltimore, is due soon to produce what promises to be the definitive appreciation of Hamann in English, which may go some small way towards reviving interest in this miraculous man; but, as of yet, that book has not appeared.

That Hamann suffers so much neglect, one must concede, is largely the result of the willfully hermetic impenetrability of his most important works. His humor is not, to say the least, immediately accessible: his style is often reminiscent of Laurence Sterne's or James Joyce's, and is full of eccentric, perverse, and somewhat demented textual games; his prose is almost always intentionally obscure, overflowing with classical references, cryptic metaphors, and convoluted pranks. It is no hyperbole to say that Hamann's writings constitute the most difficult body of literature in the German language: they are brief, compressed, manic, irrepressibly inventive, at once diffuse and piercing, and almost occult in their impregnability. Consider this, for example, from his *New Apology for the Letter 'h'* (written as a protest against orthographical reforms introduced under Frederick the Great):

> To be sure, I would ten times rather lose my breath in the wind talking to a blind man about the *first* and *fourth* days of the Mosaic creation story, or to a deaf man about the harmony of a little nightingale or Italian castrato than submit myself any longer to an opponent who is not even capable of seeing that a universal, sound, practical language, reason, and religion without *arbitrary* axioms is his own *oven of ice.*

And that is by no means Hamann at his most forbidding. At its most unrestrained, his voice is not merely mercurial, but Heracleitean, vatic, sibylline; even in his own day he was called "enigmatical," "dark," the "Magus in the North." He claimed he could not help but speak "the language of Sophists, of puns, of Cretans and Arabians, of wise men and Moors and Creoles" and "babble a confusion of criticism, mythology, rebuses, and axioms." To Hamann, it was obvious that the Age of Reason — which, to his mind, was an age of deepest darkness — required a prose of almost insoluble opacity. It was to his masterpiece, the *Aesthetica in Nuce,* that Hamann gave the subtitle "A Rhapsody in Kabbalistic Prose," but he might have attached it to almost everything he wrote. And yet he was never a wanton irrationalist; Kierkegaard spoke entirely in earnest when he ranked Hamann and Socrates together as "perhaps two of the most brilliant minds of all time."

Admittedly, it would be all but impossible to assemble an anthology of Hamann's wit and wisdom like the one Oden has created for Kierkegaard. Hamann's humor consists so much in ludicrous involutions of thought and language, and in the cumulative effect of one absurdity heaped atop another, and in the sweetly earnest obliviousness of a holy fool's voice that one must simply immerse oneself in his imaginative world in order to grasp his comic genius. One need only attempt to describe the lunatic intricacies of Hamann's prose to realize how impossible it is adequately to convey any sense of its frenzied ingenuity. For instance, one of Hamann's works written in French is a sardonically fawning open letter to Frederick the Great (whose superstitious servility to the mythology of Enlightenment reason Hamann particularly detested) called *To the Solomon of Prussia,* a text so savage and unrestrained in its mockery that no one would publish it when it was first written for fear of the state censor. Hamann's last attempt to get it printed was through C. F. Nicolai in Berlin; and when Nicolai failed to respond to his request, Hamann published an exquisitely deranged feuilleton called *Monologue of an Author* under the ridiculous "Chinese" pseudonym Mien-Man-Hoam. This at least prompted Nicolai to send Hamann an official rejection. But this rejection, in turn, inspired Hamann to compose and publish a piece called *To the Witch at Kadmanbor,* a "letter" supposedly written by Nicolai to an old sorceress, asking her to translate Hamann's *Monologue* from the Chinese of the "Mandarin" who wrote it: a letter that, midway through its course, suddenly becomes a delirious monologue of its own (in which the witch now appears as the Fury Alecto, but with two faces, "a calf's eye like Juno's, and the watery eye of an owl") before concluding with the recommendation that Hamann be forced like his illustrious ancestor Haman — from the book of Esther — to mount the scaffold. Honestly, works like these, when hastily read, merely seem like the ravings of a Bedlamite; to understand them, one must descend deep into their depths; and to appreciate their humor properly, one must take them in their totality.

Oden, to his credit, briefly mentions Kierkegaard's estimation of Hamann as "the greatest humorist in Christianity" (actually — Oden neglects to mention — "the greatest humorist in the world"), but pursues it no further; and this is a pity, because in many ways Hamann provided Kierkegaard with the model for his own authorship; and it is arguable that Kierkegaard's entire career as a Christian thinker and humorist was a somewhat failed attempt to achieve the clarity of insight and wealth of mirth that were simply natural and unforced elements of Hamann's mind and idiom. It was from Hamann that Kierkegaard learned the power of "indirect communication" and the impossibility of making the passion of faith conform to any recognized standards of "responsible" discourse. It was from Hamann too that Kierkegaard acquired his taste for outlandish pseudonyms (though Kierkegaard's were never quite as wild or surreal as some of Hamann's — Vettius Epagathus Regiomonticolae, An Apocryphal Sibyl, Ahasuerus Lazarus, Abelard Viterbius, Aristobulus, An Angry Prophet from the Brook Kerith, and so on). Kierkegaard even once remarked that, had he known earlier the tale of Hamann's marriage to the serving-girl Regina Schumacher (Hamann called her his "hamadryad"), he himself might have married Regine Olsen after all.

One could, I suppose, argue that Hamann was not a philosopher in the proper sense; but, if Kierkegaard was a philosopher, so was Hamann, and probably a more important one. In fact, Kierkegaard's own struggle with the legacy of Hegel was, to a great degree, a conscious reprise of Hamann's agon with Kant and his disciples. In either case, the great *moral* labor of the critic was to shelter particularity against the all-consuming abstractions of (transcendental or absolute) idealism, and to raise a protest on behalf of the concrete against the ghostly universalisms of modern rationality. In later years, in attempting to disentangle the significance of his authorship from that of Hamann's, Kierkegaard liked to assert that he had given theoretical depth to insights that, in Hamann, had only the quality of aphoristic lightning bolts; and, increasingly, Kierkegaard came to judge Hamann as too irresponsibly playful, ill-controlled, self-indulgent, and flippant — perhaps even blasphemous. (Certainly some of Hamann's contemporaries had felt that way about the man, especially after he had adorned the title-page of his *Crusades of a Philologian* with the leering visage of a satyr.)

It is true, one must concede, that Hamann eschewed systematic expositions of theory to the end; he never abandoned pseudonymy or indirection, never attempted to bring the passion of faith within the securer enclosure of any sort of psychological or speculative science, never condescended to the soberer disciplines of "direct communication." Indeed, his opinion of philosophical method as practiced in his day was almost entirely dismissive; when, after his powerful conversion experience in London, Hamann was met by Kant, who had been sent by friends to rescue him from his newfound "enthusiasm," his reaction was one of polite amusement: "I must laugh at the choice of a *philosopher* to bring about my conversion. I view the finest demonstration as a sensible girl views a love letter, and view a Baumgartian explication as a diverting *fleurette.*" Hamann's most devastating assault upon Kant's *Critique of Pure Reason* (the manuscript of which the "Magus in the North" actually stole from the printer before it was published) is an intricate and inspissated satire, a mere seven or so pages long, entitled the *Metacritique of the Purism of Reason,* in which Hamann — in a series of brilliant and parodic strokes — exposes all the ineradicable impurities upon which Kant's "pure reason" depends. And yet Hamann's critique of Kant, though it is written as a kind of burlesque, is far more original and startling — and a far more penetrating assault upon modernity — than is Kierkegaard's critique of Hegel (despite the latter's satiric excellence). The *Metacritique,* when its implications are grasped, retains a power to disturb and provoke that nothing of Kierkegaard's possesses.

This is not to diminish Kierkegaard's accomplishments, but only to recognize Hamann's genius. And it is worth noting that Kierkegaard's theory of comedy — at least, as Oden has explicated it — is far easier to reconcile with Hamann's writings than Kierkegaard's own. The special logic of this theory, after all, is that the *Christian* philosopher — having surmounted the "aesthetic," "ethical," and even in a sense "religious" stages of human existence — is uniquely able to enact a return, back to the things of earth, back to finitude, back to the aesthetic; having found the highest rationality of being in God's *kenosis* in the Incarnation, the

Christian philosopher is reconciled to the particularity of flesh and form, recognizes all of creation as a purely gratuitous gift of a God of infinite love, and is able to rejoice in the levity of a world created and redeemed purely out of God's pleasure. Of no philosopher could this be truer than Hamann. He was a man of the deepest, most fervent piety, and yet of an almost Nietzschean irreverence, of a kind that has lost little of its power to scandalize ("My unrefined imagination has never been able to conceive a Creative Spirit without *genitalia*"); he was practically a Christian mystic, and yet he delighted in the world of the senses, especially in the joys of sexual love (his repeated and most disdainful accusation of the apostles of Enlightenment was that they were spiritual eunuchs piping their dreary abstractions in shrill falsetto voices). This was so because in the Christian evangel he had encountered a God whose creatures are the work of delight, who is pleased to reveal his majesty in total abasement, and who is himself always "the Poet in the beginning of days." For Hamann, the return to finitude was unreserved and utterly charitable; everything he wrote or did was touched with a spirit of festivity; his humor contained no lingering residue of fatalism, irony, or rancor.

Of Kierkegaard, this is not true. For him, until the end, the return to finitude was a return only to the singular and terrible enigma of the incarnate God in time. There is always a tragic, "dialectical," even Gnostic tension in his thought: the Incarnation remains a "paradox" rather than a delightful "surprise," an invasion of worldly time that time cannot comprehend, and that thus forbids any real reconciliation with the world. For Hamann, by contrast, the *kenosis* of God illuminates and transfigures everything, grace transfuses all of nature, culture, and cult, and so his humor has a wealth, an overwhelming hilarity, and a truly Christian mirthfulness that Kierkegaard's does not. Where Kierkegaard was most inclined to become severe and saturnine, Hamann was most reckless in his rejoicing. Hamann would have looked, certainly, with a more tender regard upon the absurdity of a "Christian whorehouse"; the idea would probably have moved him more to reflect upon the prodigality of divine love than to indulge in caustic complaint.

This, then, is why I would want to deny Kierkegaard the laurels Oden has so diligently plaited for him: because Kierkegaard fell short, at the last, of his own high vision of the Christian humorist, while Hamann realized it. I might just qualify my judgment by saying that Kierkegaard remains perhaps the greatest human humorist among philosophers, since

I suspect that — at least at some spiritual level — Hamann was actually the miscegenate offspring of a satyr and an angel. But, taken without qualifications, the title of "most amusing" philosopher must be accorded to Hamann, and Hamann alone. And, as it happens, I suspect that Kierkegaard (at least in his better moments) would entirely agree.

Appendix: Letters to the Editor

As a rule, letters written to an editor in response to a particular article, as well as any answers the author of the original article might wish to make to those letters, are of marginal interest at most, and ought to be treated as ephemera. Occasionally, though, the exchanges that take place on the letters pages succeed in substantially clarifying, deepening, and extending the reflections found in the original essay, and to that degree are worth reproducing. And no other article of mine has ever provoked so great or so indignant a response from so many readers. I was rather unprepared for this, to be honest. I had thought this article little more than a journalistic bagatelle, prompted by a light confection of a book. In fact, in its first form, it was a mere twelve-hundred-word review of that book, and its chief complaint was that the critical introduction with which Oden had burdened his anthology — under editorial pressure, admittedly — was so disproportionate in size and style to the entertainments that followed that the ultimate effect was rather like that of affixing a solemn prolegomenon to a sorbet. The editor at *First Things* who had asked for my review, however, kept asking me to expand it — no fewer than four times, in fact — until it had become an article in its own right, and the single sentence on Hamann in the original had become a small essay. Even in its final form, however, it seemed to me little more than a good-naturedly whimsical — if finally earnest — piece, and I could not have anticipated the reaction it would elicit. But, as I remarked in my reply to several of these letters on the editor's pages in *First Things*, "The reason it is dangerous to write an ostentatiously opinionated piece, and to use flippancy as a means for securing a few cheap laughs, is that the objects of one's irreverence are often the objects of others' sincerest devotion. That said, I remain largely impenitent regarding this article, principally because I do not believe — nor do I think it legitimate to conclude — that every unflattering remark made about some aspect of a philosopher's work or personality is equivalent to a complete rejection of that philosopher. Of many of the figures I mock, I am both an admirer and a student."

I shall not reproduce those letters here, of course, nor all of my answers to them. One letter in particular, however, prompted me to expand upon a remark I had made in my articles regarding Kant's ethical philosophy, and for that I am grateful. A Mr. Ben Carter of Texas, in a brief but pointed missive, merely recited a few of my remarks on Kant, Hegel, Kierkegaard, Derrida, and Isaiah Berlin — though he got the one on Kant rather badly wrong — and suggested that I was floundering in "deep waters," and asked why *First Things* would publish "such tripe." My reply was as follows:

> While I am of course entirely disarmed by the richness, complexity, and subtlety of Mr. Carter's argument, I am not confident he can properly assess the degree of my intellectual buoyancy or determine whether I am indeed "floundering in deep waters" (and, surely, in the cases of Derrida and Berlin, the metaphor should have been something more like "thrashing in the shallows"). I suspect (or at least hope) that *First Things* publishes my tripe because the editors believe that my judgments, however misguided, at least proceed from some measure of scholarly competence. It is, I like to think, a very high quality tripe.
>
> I must add, though, that Mr. Carter has attributed to me a remark I did not and would not make; it was the *Critique of Practical Reason* — not *Pure Reason* — about which I was so rude (let's make the charitable, though perhaps unwarranted, assumption that Mr. Carter is aware of the difference), and my remark was anything but frivolous. Frankly, the second *Critique* has been so often and so devastatingly taken apart (Hegel's attack on Kantian ethics, for instance, is a *tour de force*) that it is a wonder that the poor beast has not long since slouched off to some secluded grotto to expire peacefully from its wounds. Let me point to just one notorious defect of Kant's ethical thought, identified originally by such contemporaries of Kant as Tittel and Pistorius: that the categorical imperative's universality cannot be demonstrated apart from an examination of consequences. Hence Kant's infamous appeal (in the *Grundlegung*) to the trustworthiness of money lending, which all at once renders what is supposed to be

an austerely deontological ethics indistinguishable from pure utilitarianism.

This is not a momentary wobble: at this point the acrobat has slipped off the high wire altogether and brought the show to a tragic halt. Simply said, it is manifestly false that the moral law can be grounded in the transcendental subject; reason — at least as Kant understands it — cannot establish the categorical imperative in itself: either it must submit to some calculation of consequences or it must degenerate into sheer assertion, premised upon a transcendental feat of will. This latter course, in fact, is already adumbrated at certain junctures in the *Opus Postumum*. This is one reason why the transcendental project could not help but gravitate towards the metaphysics of the will in Fichte and even in Schopenhauer (who correctly viewed himself as a child of Kant) and Nietzsche (as Heidegger so acutely recognized). It is also one reason why I (personally) find the second *Critique* fanciful, silly, and diverting. . . .

. . . Mr. Carter would do well to remember . . . that irreverence is not the same thing as contempt. Occasionally it is a sign of long familiarity and perhaps an absence of misplaced piety.

10

Tremors of Doubt

O n November 1, 1755, a great earthquake struck offshore of Lisbon. In that city alone, some sixty thousand perished, first from the tremors, then from the massive tsunami that struck half an hour later. Fires consumed much of what remained of the city. The tidal waves spread death along the coasts of Iberia and North Africa.

Voltaire's *Poëme sur le désastre de Lisbonne* of the following year was an exquisitely savage — though sober — assault upon the theodicies prevalent in his time. For those who would argue that "all is good" and "all is necessary," that the universe is an elaborately calibrated harmony of pain and pleasure, or that this is the best of all *possible* worlds, Voltaire's scorn was boundless: by what calculus of universal good can one reckon the value of "infants crushed upon their mothers' breasts," the dying "sad inhabitants of desolate shores," the whole "fatal chaos of individual miseries"?

Perhaps the most disturbing argument against submission to "the will of God" in human suffering — especially the suffering of children — was placed in the mouth of Ivan Karamazov by Dostoyevsky; but the evils Ivan enumerates are all acts of human cruelty, for which one can at least assign a clear culpability. Natural calamities usually seem a greater challenge to the certitudes of believers in a just and beneficent God than the sorrows induced by human iniquity. Considered dispassionately, though, man is part of the natural order, and his propensity for malice should be no less a scandal to the conscience of the metaphysical optimist than the most violent convulsions of the physical world. The same ancient question is apposite to the horrors of history and nature alike: whence comes evil? And as Voltaire so elegantly apostrophizes, it is useless to invoke the balances of the great chain of being, for that chain is held in God's hand, and he is not enchained.

I cannot really imagine any answer to the question of evil likely to satisfy an unbeliever; I can note though that — for all its urgency — Voltaire's version of the question is not in any proper sense "theological." The God of Voltaire's poem is a particular kind of "deist" God, who has shaped and ordered the world just as it now is, in accord with his exact intentions, and who presides over all its eventualities austerely attentive to a precise equilibrium between felicity and morality. Not that reckless Christians have not occasionally spoken in such terms; but this is not the Christian God.

The Christian understanding of evil has always been more radical and fantastic than that of any theodicist; for it denies from the outset that suffering, death, and evil have any ultimate meaning at all. Perhaps no doctrine is more insufferably fabulous to non-Christians than the claim that we exist in the long melancholy aftermath of a primordial catastrophe, that this is a broken and wounded world, that cosmic time is the shadow of true time, and that the universe languishes in bondage to "powers" and "principalities" — spiritual and terrestrial — alien to God. In the Gospel of John, especially, the incarnate God enters a world at once his own and yet hostile to him — "He was in the world, and he made the world, and the world knew him not" — and his appearance within "this cosmos" is both an act of judgment and a rescue of the beauties of creation from the torments of fallen nature.

Whatever one makes of this story, it is no bland cosmic optimism. Yes, at the heart of the gospel is an ineradicable triumphalism, a conviction that the victory over evil and death has been won; but it is also a victory yet to come. As Paul says, all creation groans in anguished anticipation of the day when God's glory will transfigure all things. For now, we live amid a strife of darkness and light. When confronted by the sheer savage immensity of worldly suffering — when we see the entire littoral rim of the Indian Ocean strewn with tens of thousands of corpses, a third of them children — no Christian is licensed to utter odious banalities about God's inscrutable counsels or blasphemous suggestions that all this mysteriously serves God's good ends. We are permitted only to hate death and waste and the imbecile forces of chance that shatter living souls, to believe that creation is in agony in its bonds, to see this world as divided between two kingdoms — knowing all the while that it is only charity that can sustain us against "fate," and that it must do so until the end of days.

11

Tsunami and Theodicy

No one, no matter how great the scope of his imagination, should be able easily to absorb the immensity of the catastrophe that struck the Asian rim of the Indian Ocean on the second day of Christmas this past year; nor would it be quite human to fail, in its wake, to feel some measure of spontaneous resentment towards God, fate, *natura naturans,* or whatever other force one imagines governs the intricate web of cosmic causality. But, once one's indignation at the callousness of the universe begins to subside, it is worth recalling that nothing that occurred that day or in the days that followed told us anything about the nature of finite existence of which we were not already entirely aware.

Not that one should be cavalier in the face of misery on so gigantic a scale, or should dismiss the spiritual perplexity it occasions. But, at least for Christians, it is prudent to prepare as quickly and decorously as possible for the mixed choir of secular moralists whose clamor will soon — inevitably — swell about their ears, gravely informing them that here at last their faith must surely founder upon the rocks of empirical horrors too vast to be reconciled with any system of belief in a God of justice or mercy. It is of course somewhat petty to care overly much about captious atheists at such a time, but it is difficult not to be annoyed when a zealous skeptic, eager to be the first to deliver God his long overdue *coup de grâce,* begins confidently to speak as if believers have never until this moment considered the problem of evil or confronted despair or suffering or death. Perhaps they did not notice the Black Death, the Great War, the Holocaust, or every instance of famine, pestilence, flood, fire, or earthquake in the whole of the human past; perhaps every Christian who has ever had to bury a child has somehow remained insensible to the depth of his own bereavement. For sheer fatuity, on this score, it would be difficult to surpass Martin Kettle's pompous and platitudinous reflections in *The Guardian,* appearing two days after the earthquake: surely, he argues, the arbitrariness of the destruction visited upon so many and such diverse victims must pose an insoluble conundrum for "creationists" everywhere — although he wonders, in concluding, whether we are "too cowed" even to ask "if the God can exist that can do such things" (as if a public avowal of unbelief required any great reserves of fortitude in modern Britain). It would be courteous, one would think, if secular moralists would make more than a perfunctory effort to ascertain what religious persons actually do believe before presuming to instruct them on what they cannot.

In truth, though, confronted by such enormous suffering, Christians have less to fear from the piercing dialectical sallies of the village atheist than they do from the earnestness of certain believers, and from the clouds of cloying incense wafting upward from the open thuribles of their hearts. As irksome as Kettle's argument is, it is merely insipid; more troubling are the attempts of well-meaning Christians to rationalize this catastrophe in ways that, however inadvertently, make that argument all at once seem profound. And these attempts can span almost the entire spectrum of religious sensibility: they can be cold with Stoical austerity, moist with lachrymose piety, wanly roseate with sickly metaphysical optimism. Grimly instructive to me were some remarks sent to a Christian web page discussing a *Wall Street Journal* column of mine from the Friday following the earthquake. A stern if somewhat excitable Calvinist, intoxicated with God's sovereignty, asserted that in the — let us grant this chimaera a moment's life — "Augustinian-Thomistic-Calvinist tradition," and particularly in Reformed thought, suffering and death possess "epistemic significance" insofar as they manifest divine attributes that "might not otherwise be displayed." A scholar whose work I admire contributed an eloquent expostulation invoking the Holy Innocents, praising our glorious privilege (not shared by the angels) of bearing scars like those of Christ, and advancing the venerable heresy that our salvation from sin will result in a greater good than could have evolved from an innocence untouched by death. A man manifestly good and devout, but unable to distinguish providence from karma, argued that all are guilty through original sin but some more than others, that our "sense of jus-

tice" requires us to believe that "punishments and rewards [are] distrib-
uted according to our just desserts," that God is the "balancer of accounts," and that we must suppose that the suffering of these innocents
will bear "spiritual fruit for themselves and for all mankind."

All three wished to justify the ways of God to man, to affirm God's
benevolence, to see meaning in the seemingly monstrous randomness of
nature's violence, and to find solace in God's guiding hand. None seemed
to worry that he might be making a compelling case for a rejection of
God, or of faith in divine goodness. But, simply said, there is no more liberating knowledge given us by the gospel — and none in which we
should find more comfort — than the knowledge that suffering and
death, considered in themselves, have no ultimate meaning at all.

THE *locus classicus* of modern disenchantment with "nature's God" is
probably Voltaire's *Poëme sur le désastre de Lisbonne,* written in response
to the great earthquake that — on All Saints' Day, 1755 — struck just offshore of what was then the resplendent capital of the Portuguese empire.
Lisbon was home to a quarter million, at least sixty thousand of whom
perished, both from the initial tremor (reckoned now, like the Sumatran
earthquake, at a Richter force of around 9.0) and from the tsunami that it
cast up on shore half an hour later (especially murderous to those who
had retreated to boats in the mouth of the river Tagus to escape the destruction on land). An enormous fire soon began to consume the ruined
city. Tens of thousands were drowned along the coasts of the Algarve,
southern Spain, and Morocco.

For Voltaire, a catastrophe of such indiscriminate vastitude was incontrovertible evidence against the bland optimism of popular theodicy.
His poem — for all the mellifluousness of its alexandrines — was a lacer-
ating attack on anyone who would assert that "*Tout est bien.*" Would you
dare argue, he asks, that you see the necessary effect of eternal laws de-
creed by a God both free and just as you contemplate

Ces femmes, ces enfants l'un sur l'autre entassés,
Sous ces marbres rompus ces membres dispersés . . .

"These women, these infants heaped one upon the other, these limbs
scattered beneath shattered marbles . . ."? Or would you argue that all of
this is but God's just vengeance upon human iniquity?

Quel crime, quelle faute ont commis ces enfants
Sur le sein maternel écrasés et sanglants?

"What crime and what sin have been committed by these infants crushed and bleeding on their mothers' breasts?" Or would you comfort those dying in torment on desolate shores by assuring them that others will profit from their demise and that they are discharging the parts assigned them by universal law? Do not, says Voltaire, speak of the great chain of being, for that chain is held in the hand of a God who is himself enchained by nothing.

For all its power, however, Voltaire's poem is a very feeble thing compared to the case for "rebellion" against "the will of God" in human suffering placed in the mouth of Ivan Karamazov by the fervently Christian novelist Dostoyevsky; for, while the evils Ivan recounts to his brother Alexey are acts not of impersonal nature but of men, Dostoyevsky's treatment of innocent suffering possesses a profundity of which Voltaire was never even remotely capable. Famously, Dostoyevsky collected accounts of children tortured and murdered with which to supply Ivan: Turks tearing babies from their mothers' wombs, impaling infants on bayonets, firing pistols into their mouths; parents savagely flogging their children; a five-year-old girl tortured by her mother and father, her mouth filled with excrement, locked at night in an outhouse, weeping her supplications to "dear kind God" in the darkness; an eight-year-old serf child torn to pieces by his master's dogs for a small accidental transgression. But what makes Ivan's argument so disturbing is not that he accuses God of failing to save the innocent; rather, he rejects salvation itself, insofar as he understands it, and on moral grounds. He grants that one day there may be an eternal harmony established, one that we will discover somehow necessitated the suffering of children, and perhaps mothers will forgive the murderers of their babies, and all will praise God's justice; but Ivan wants neither harmony — "for love of man I reject it," "it is not worth the tears of that one tortured child" — nor forgiveness; and so, not denying there is a God, he simply chooses to return his ticket of admission to God's Kingdom. After all, Ivan asks, if you could bring about a universal and final beatitude for all beings by torturing one small creature to death, would you think the price acceptable?

Voltaire's poem is not a challenge to Christian faith; it inveighs against a "deist" God who has simply ordered the world exactly as it now is, and who balances out all its eventualities in a precise equilibrium between felicity and morality. Nowhere does it address the Christian belief in an ancient alienation from God that has wounded creation in its uttermost depths, and reduced cosmic time to a shadowy remnant of the world God intends, and enslaved creation to spiritual and terrestrial powers hostile to God. But Ivan's rebellion is something altogether different. Voltaire sees only the terrible truth that the actual history of suffering and death is not morally intelligible; Dostoyevsky sees — and this bespeaks both his moral genius and his Christian view of reality — that it would be far more terrible if it were.

CHRISTIANS OFTEN find it hard to adopt the spiritual idiom of the New Testament — to think in terms, that is, of a cosmic struggle between good and evil, of Christ's triumph over the principalities of this world, of the overthrow of hell. All Christians know, of course, that it is through God's self-outpouring upon the cross that they are saved, and that they are made able by grace to participate in Christ's suffering; but this should never be allowed to obscure what is revealed at Easter: that the incarnate God enters "this cosmos" not simply to disclose its immanent rationality, but to break the boundaries of fallen nature asunder, and to refashion creation after its ancient beauty — wherein neither sin nor death had any place. Christian thought has traditionally, of necessity, defined evil as a privation of the good, possessing no essence or nature of its own, a purely parasitic corruption of reality; hence it can have no *positive* role to play in God's determination of himself or purpose for his creatures (even if by economy God can bring good from evil); it can in no way supply any imagined deficiency in God's or creation's goodness. Being infinitely sufficient in himself, God had no need of a passage through sin and death to manifest his glory in his creatures or to join them perfectly to himself. This is why it is misleading even to say, as did the scholar mentioned above, that the drama of fall and redemption will make the final state of things more glorious than it might otherwise have been. No less metaphysically incoherent — though immeasurably more vile — is the suggestion of that Calvinist that God requires suffering and death to reveal certain of his attributes (capricious cruelty, perhaps? injustice? a depraved sense of humor?); it is precisely sin, suffering, and death that blind us to God's true nature.

There is, of course, some comfort to be derived from the thought that everything that occurs at the level of what Aquinas calls secondary causality — in nature or history — is governed not only by a transcendent providence, but by a universal teleology that makes every instance of pain and loss an indispensable moment in a grand scheme whose ultimate synthesis will justify all things. But consider the price at which that comfort is purchased: it requires us to believe in and love a God whose good ends will be realized not only in spite of — but entirely by way of — every cruelty, every fortuitous misery, every catastrophe, every betrayal, every sin the world has ever known; it requires us to believe in the eternal spiritual necessity of a child dying an agonizing death from diphtheria, of a young mother ravaged by cancer, of tens of thousands of Asians swallowed in an instant by the sea, of millions murdered in death camps and gulags and forced famines (and so on). It seems a strange thing to find peace in a universe rendered morally intelligible at the cost of a God rendered morally loathsome. Better, it seems to me, the view of the ancient Gnostics: however ludicrous their beliefs, they at least, when they concluded that suffering and death were essential aspects of the creator's design, had the good sense to yearn to know a higher God.

I do not believe Christians are obliged — or even allowed — to look upon the devastation visited upon the coasts of the Indian Ocean and to console themselves with vacuous cant about the mysterious course taken by God's goodness in this world, or to assure others that some ultimate meaning or purpose resides in so much misery. Theirs is, after all, a religion of salvation; their faith is in a God who has come to rescue his creation from the absurdity of sin and the emptiness of death, and so they are permitted to hate these things with a perfect hatred. For while Christ takes the suffering of his creatures up into his own, it is not because he or they had need of suffering, but because he would not abandon his creatures to the grave. And while we know that the victory over evil and death has been won, we know also that it is a victory yet to come, and that creation therefore, as Paul says, groans in expectation of the glory that will one day be revealed. Until then, the world remains a place of struggle between light and darkness, truth and falsehood, life and death; and, in such a world, our portion is charity.

As for comfort, when we seek it, I can imagine none greater than the happy knowledge that when I see the death of a child I do not see the face of God, but the face of his enemy. It is not a faith that would necessarily satisfy Ivan Karamazov, but neither is it one that his arguments can defeat: for it has set us free from optimism, and taught us hope instead. We can rejoice that we are saved not through the immanent mechanisms of history and nature, but by grace; that God will not unite all of history's many strands in one great synthesis, but will judge much of history false and damnable; that he will not simply reveal the sublime logic of fallen nature, but will strike off the fetters in which creation languishes; and that, rather than showing us how the tears of a small girl suffering in the dark were necessary for the building of the Kingdom, he will instead raise her up and wipe away all tears from her eyes — and there shall be *REV. 21: 4-5* no more death, nor sorrow, nor crying, nor any more pain, for the former things will have passed away, and he that sits upon the throne will say, "Behold, I make all things new."

12

Where Was God?
An Interview with David Bentley Hart
by The Christian Century

Christian Century: It's often said that three claims of the Christian tradition — "God is omnipotent," "God is love," and "Evil exists" — present a logical contradiction. One of the claims has to be revised. Do you agree?

If by "evil exists" you mean that evil possesses a real substance of its own, and that it therefore exists in the way goodness exists (or, for that matter, a tree, a rabbit, an idea or a dream exists), in point of fact Christian tradition has usually denied this quite forcibly. Patristic and medieval thought (drawing, admittedly, on Platonic precedent) defined evil as a privation of the good: a purely parasitic and shadowy reality, a contamination or disease or absence, but not a real thing in itself. This, incidentally, is a logically necessary claim if one understands goodness and being as flowing alike from the very nature of God and coinciding in him as one infinite life.

That said, there surely is no contradiction between God's omnipotent goodness and the reality of evil. It may seem somewhat trite to invoke the freedom of creation as part of the works and ends of divine love, or to argue that the highest good of the creature — divinizing union with God in love — requires a realm of "secondary causality" in which the rational wills of God's creatures are at liberty; nonetheless, whether the traditional explanations of how sin and death have been set loose in the world satisfy one or not, they certainly render the claim that an omnipotent and good God would never allow unjust suffering simply vacuous. By what criterion could one render such a judgment? For Christians, one must look to the cross of Christ to take the measure of God's love, and of its worth in comparison to the sufferings of a fallen world. And one must look to the risen Christ to grasp the glory for which we are intended, and take one's understanding of the majesty and tragedy of creation's freedom from that.

CC: In Dostoevsky's novel *The Brothers Karamazov,* Ivan Karamazov famously points to the brutal killing of children and proclaims that he refuses to believe in any God who has arranged the world in such a way that it entails such suffering — regardless of what "meaning" can be attached to it. What does a Christian say to Karamazov's protest?

Actually, what Ivan ultimately refuses is not belief but consent: he will not acknowledge that there is any justice, any glory, any truth that is worth the suffering of a child. If he were merely a truculent atheist, he would be a boring figure. Instead, he is a rebel against the divine order, and intends to remain a rebel even if that order should — in some way transcending his finite understanding — prove to be perfectly just. One might very well read his protest not as a brief for atheism, but as a kind of demythologized Gnostic manifesto, an accusation flung in the face of the demiurge.

Still, the pathos of his protest is, to my mind, exquisitely Christian — though he himself seems not to be aware of this: a rage against explanation, a refusal to grant that the cruelty or brute natural misfortune or evil of any variety can ever be justified by some "happy ending" that makes sense of all our misery and mischance.

In a sense the whole of *The Doors of the Sea* was a response to Ivan's "rebellion" — and indeed a kind of endorsement of it. What I would say here is that it is important to understand the terms of the argument clearly: Ivan assumes — in good late-19th-century fashion — that the eschatological horizon of history and nature is, in a very direct way, the consummation of a process wherein all the apparent contingencies of history and nature have an indispensable part to play. For him, the Christian promise of the kingdom of God is the promise, as well, of a final justification not only of those who have suffered, but of their suffering, and of the part suffering plays in bringing the final kingdom of love and knowledge to pass. This is what he finds intolerable: the notion that the suffering of children will prove to have been meaningful, to have had a purpose, to have been in some sense a good and necessary thing; for him, the suffering of children is an infinite scandal, and his conscience could never allow it to sink to the level of some provisional passage through darkness on the way to some radiant future.

My contention is that this places Ivan's sensibility much nearer to the authentic vision of the New Testament than are many of the more pious and conventional forms of Christian conviction today. The gospel of the ancient church was always one of rebellion against those principalities and powers — death chief among them — that enslave and torment creation; nowhere does the New Testament rationalize evil or accord it necessity or treat it as part of the necessary fabric of God's world. All that Christian Scripture asserts is that evil cannot defeat God's purposes or thwart the coming of his kingdom. Divine providence, of course, will always bring about God's good ends despite — and in a sense through — the evils of this world; but that is not the same thing as saying that evil has a necessary part to play in God's plans, and that God required evil to bring about the kingdom. As the empty tomb of Christ above all reveals, the verdict of God that rescues and redeems creation also overturns the order of the fallen world, and shatters the powers of historical and natural necessity that the fallen world comprises.

CC: Christians often try to distinguish between what God wills and what God permits or allows. But does this distinction really help? If God allows something, or creates a world in which evil is allowed, then in some sense isn't it part of God's will?

Unless one thinks that God's act of creation is purely arbitrary — and it would be incoherent to attribute arbitrariness of any kind to a God of infinite goodness (an argument for another time) — then one must understand creation as a direct expression of God's own Logos. God does not create like an omnipotent consumer choosing one world out of an infinity of possibilities that somehow stand outside of and apart from his own nature. Here's one without cancer, there's one without Bach, over there's one with a higher infant mortality rate, and so on; this is the worst sort of anthropomorphism.

God creates the world of Jesus, the world conformed to his infinite love for his Son in the joy and light of the Spirit; he thereby also wills his goodness in all his creatures infinitely, which is to say he wills this world for eternal union with him in love, and he wills that we should become partakers of the divine nature.

There is no other world that God might have created, not because he is bound by necessity, but because he is infinitely free, and so nothing can hinder him from expressing his essential and infinite goodness perfectly, in and through the freedom of creatures created to be the fellows of his eternal Son.

That may seem obscurely phrased — it is, I know — but if one thinks through what it means to understand God as the transcendent source of all being, one must abandon the notion that God chooses to create in the way that I choose to buy blue drapes rather than red. God creates a realm of rational freedom that allows for a union between Creator and creature that is properly analogous to the Trinity's eternal union of love; or, stated otherwise, God creates his own image in his creatures, with all that that may entail.

CC: Followers of Calvin have been particularly concerned to defend God's sovereignty. Do you think that tradition presents a particular problem for Christian thinking today?

Yes — and not only today. I quite explicitly admit in my writing that I think the traditional Calvinist understanding of divine sovereignty to be deeply defective, and destructively so. One cannot, as with Luther, trace out a direct genealogy from late medieval voluntarism to the Calvinist understanding of divine freedom; nevertheless, the way in which Calvin himself describes divine sovereignty is profoundly modern: it frequently seems to require an element of *pure* arbitrariness, of *pure* spontaneity, and this alone separates it from more traditional (and I would say more coherent) understandings of freedom, whether divine or human.

This idea of a God who can be called omnipotent only if his will is the *direct* efficient cause of every aspect of created reality immediately makes all the inept cavils of the village atheist seem profound: one still should not ask if God could create a stone he could not lift, perhaps, but one might legitimately ask if a God of infinite voluntaristic sovereignty and power could create a creature free to resist the divine will. The question is no cruder than the conception of God it is meant to mock, and the paradox thus produced merely reflects the deficiencies of that conception.

Frankly, any understanding of divine sovereignty so unsubtle that it requires the theologian to assert (as Calvin did) that God foreordained the fall of humanity so that his glory might be revealed in the predestined damnation of the derelict is obviously problematic, and probably far more blasphemous than anything represented by the heresies that the ancient ecumenical councils confronted.

CC: Is universal salvation a corollary of your view of the absurdity of evil?

Probably not; but Gregory of Nyssa would say otherwise. The preferred Eastern Orthodox understanding of hell, one with profound patristic pedigrees, defines hell as something self-imposed, a condition of the soul that freely refuses to open itself in love to God and neighbor, and that thereby seals itself against the deifying love of God, thereby experiencing divine glory as an external chastisement. That hell I believe in, inasmuch as all of us from time to time have tasted it in this world. The refusal of love makes love a torment to us.

CC: Does your understanding of evil have implications for pastoral practice in the face of evil?

I honestly don't know. I haven't a pastoral bone in my body. But I would implore pastors never to utter banal consolations concerning God's "greater plan" or the mystery of his will. The first proclamation of the gospel is that death is God's ancient enemy, whom God has defeated and will ultimately destroy. I would hope that no Christian pastor would fail to recognize that that completely shameless triumphalism — and with it an utterly sincere and unrestrained hatred of suffering and death — is the surest foundation of Christian hope, and the proper Christian response to grief.

CC: So where was God in the tsunami?

Where was God? In and beyond all things, nearer to the essence of every creature than that creature itself, and infinitely outside the grasp of all finite things.

Almost all the reviews of *The Doors of the Sea* that I have read have recognized that, at the heart of the book, is a resolute insistence upon

and adoration of the imperishable goodness of creation, an almost willfully naive assertion that it is the beauty and peace of the created world
that truly reveal its original and ultimate nature, while the suffering and
alienation and horror of mortal existence are, in an ultimate sense, fictions of fallen time, chains and veils and shadows and distortions, but no
part of God's will for his creatures. This is why, at one point in the book, I
grant the Gnostics of old the validity of their questions, though I go on to
revile the answers at which they arrived.

BUT NOT UNREAL; MERELY A NAR- RATIVE W/NO TELOS.

To see the world in the Christian way — which, as I say in the book,
requires the eye of charity and a faith in Easter — is in some sense to venture everything upon an absurd impracticality (I almost sound Kierkegaardian when I say it that way). But, as I was writing the book, I found
myself thinking again and again of a photograph I had seen in the *Baltimore Sun*. The story concerned the Akhdam, the lowest social caste in
Yemen, supposedly descended from Ethiopians left behind when the ancient Ethiopian empire was driven out of Arabia in the sixth century, who
live in the most unimaginable squalor. In the background of the photo
was a scattering of huts constructed from crates and shreds of canvas,
and on all sides barren earth; but in the foreground was a little girl, extremely pretty, dressed in tatters, but with her arms outspread, a look of
delight upon her face, dancing. To me that was a heartbreaking picture,
of course, but it was also an image of something amazing and glorious:
the sheer ecstasy of innocence, the happiness of a child who can dance
amid despair and desolation because her joy came with her into the
world and prompts her to dance as if she were in the midst of paradise.

She became for me the perfect image of the deep indwelling truth of
creation, the divine Wisdom or Sophia who resides in the very heart of
the world, the stainless image of God, the unfallen. I'm waxing quite
Eastern here, I know. But that, I would say, is the nature of God's presence in the fallen world: his image, his bride, the deep joy and longing of
creation, called from nothingness to be joined to him. That child's dance
is nothing less than the eternal dance of divine Wisdom before God's
throne, the dance of David and the angels and saints before his glory; it is
the true face of creation, which God came to restore and which he will
not suffer to see corruption.

13

Roland Redivivus

Matteo Maria Boiardo, *Orlando Innamorato (Orlando in Love)*, trans. Charles Stanley Ross (Parlor Press)

Orlando (or Roland, in the French of his earliest exploits), the greatest paladin of the mythic court of Charlemagne, once loomed in the consciousness of Western culture at least as large as any of King Arthur's knights. He began his (extant) literary adventures perhaps in the late tenth century, in the *Chanson de Roland*, as a gallant, formidable, intrepid, rash, and guileless chevalier who is betrayed by his stepfather Ganelon and — along with the whole rearguard of Charlemagne's retreat from Spain — dies in an ambush by Muslim "paynims" in a pass of the Eastern Pyrenees, at Roncevaux (Roncesvalles). Behind that story, it seems, stands a real historical personage: we know that a certain Count Rotholandus was among the courtiers of Charlemagne in the year 772, and in Einhard's *Vita Karoli* the story of the death of "Hruolandus" is recounted for the first time. If nothing else, the ambuscade at Roncesvalles — traditionally dated August 15, 778 — did take place, though it was perpetrated by Basques, not Moors.

In later *chansons de geste,* however — such as *Les Quatre Filz Aymon, Enfances Roland,* and *Entrée en Espagne* — the details of Roland's earlier life were filled in, with ever more fanciful elements entering the narrative, and it was not long before the real Roland (such as he was) had all but disappeared behind the more resplendent figure of the hero of legend. And as the adventures of this hero grew in number and improbability, he was joined along the way by other Carolingian peers who would, in time, acquire legends of their own (Renaus, for instance — or Renaud, Ranaldo, Rinaldo, etc. — ultimately went on to rival Roland not only in martial proficiency, but in literary popularity). And Roland and his fellow paladins soon migrated into other tongues: into the German of the *Ruolandes Liet,* into Spanish tales of the exploits of "Roldan," into the English of romances such as *Sir Ferumbras* and *Roland and Ferragus,* and (most crucially) into Italian.

This last of these proved a language especially hospitable to Orlando (as he was now known); in no other would his fortunes fare quite so magnificently well. Dante, for instance, not only placed Ganelon — or Ganellone — in the lowest circle of hell, but in the *Paradiso* counted Orlando among eight great warrior martyrs who shine with a ruby incandescence in the sphere of Mars. And it was in Italian that Orlando ultimately achieved his apotheosis as the supreme hero of chivalric fiction, in the three great Italian romances of the late fifteenth and early sixteenth centuries: the *Morgante* of Luigi Pulci, the *Orlando Innamorato* of Matteo Boiardo, and the *Orlando Furioso* of Ludovico Ariosto. In these immense, fantastic, intricate, and bizarre epics, the figure of Orlando came at last to assume literary dimensions that no other warrior of Christendom could ever hope to equal.

Today, however, Orlando's fame seems to have sunk to its lowest ebb. The legends of the Carolingian peers certainly do not generate popular literature and cinema in the way that the stories of Camelot do. Perhaps this is simply because the court of Charlemagne, even in fable, occupies too specific a place in history. Orlando is, unambiguously, a champion of an imperiled Christendom; his stories cannot be resituated (in the manner of contemporary Arthuriana) in a realm of fatuous new age pantheism. Whatever the cause, however, Orlando — especially in the English-speaking world — is all but forgotten. Of the three great epics, only Ariosto's tends to enjoy a distinct presence in the minds of even the most literate among us, and then usually only as a book lurking unread upon some rarely visited shelf.

It was not ever thus. Once these works were part of the common heritage of European culture and exercised an immense literary influence. Without the great Italian romances, Spenser's *Faerie Queene,* for instance, would not have been written. Milton mentions the siege of

Albraca — described in the *Innamorato* — in *Paradise Lost*. It would be difficult to exaggerate how deeply these epics entered into the imaginative world of English literature (especially in the Romantic period). In Bulfinch's *Legends of Charlemagne,* published in 1867, the author uncontentiously numbers these works "among the most cherished creations of human genius," some knowledge of which "is expected of every well-educated young person." And yet by 1936 C. S. Lewis could only lament that these "masterpieces" were now so neglected and that all of us had been robbed of the enjoyment of "one of the great trophies of the European genius."

This, though, may be a propitious moment for a revival of interest in these works, at least among Anglophone readers. For the first time ever, complete translations of all three of the Orlando epics are available, and at reasonable prices. The *Furioso* has been rendered into English on a number of occasions, but by far the most delightful modern version is that of Barbara Reynolds. The first complete translation of the *Morgante,* by Joseph Tusiani, appeared in 1998. And now, with this release of Charles Stanley Ross's translation of the *Innamorato* (revising an earlier version, in a limited and very expensive critical edition), the entire Orlando cycle lies at our fingertips. And, given that the *Furioso* is the completion of the *Innamorato* (left unfinished at Boiardo's death), readers who have not mastered the dialects of Renaissance Italy can now enjoy the whole narrative arc of these two linked epics without resorting to abridgments.

THERE IS SOMETHING slightly subversive in the title of Boiardo's epic. The early *chansons de geste* were works notorious for their martial austerity, and were largely devoid of whimsy, extravagant invention, or any trace of romantic love (as Boiardo at one point coyly notes). Pulci had introduced certain vaguely "Arthurian" elements into the Carolingian mythos; but it was Boiardo who first explicitly united the two streams of lore, importing into his poem not only one of the relics of Merlin, and various dimensions of the magical and the "fay," but the Arthurian emphasis upon human love.

To someone unacquainted with the conventions of Italian romance, the first encounter with any of these epics might be somewhat jarring. They are far and away the most wildly farraginous and gloriously irresponsible masterpieces in Western literature, at once heroic, comic, allegorical, lyrical, satirical, fabulous, and (occasionally) dark; they move with alarming ease between the metaphysical and the ribald, the figural and the brutal, the exalted and the grotesque. The *Innamorato* might almost seem formless, but for the ingenuity with which Boiardo continually weaves the many strands of his story together into ever more diverting designs and elaborate choreographies. At any moment in the story, a paladin might find himself confronted by a giant Saracen astride a galloping giraffe, or trapped in a magic castle, or beset by an army of demons, or challenged by an ogre, or lost amid the exquisite enchantments of the fairy realm, or at the mercy of a sorcerer. And Boiardo — even more than Ariosto — is so irrepressibly inventive a fabulist that one often has the feeling that, but for the author's mortality, the story need never come to an end.

There is, however, a larger plot to the poem, in which all of its disparate elements and wild divarications have a place. It begins at a Pentecost tournament convoked by Charlemagne, for Christian and Muslim knights alike, which is interrupted by the arrival of Angelica, a woman of astonishing beauty who offers herself as the prize to any knight who can defeat her brother upon the field of battle. (She is, we later learn, daughter of the King of Cathay, mistress of the magic arts, sent to bring ruin upon the emperor's court.) The assembled warriors are smitten with her at once, none more hopelessly than Orlando, and are willing to venture anything to win her. Thus when she is forced to flee back to Asia, Orlando follows her, and he is followed by other of the paladins.

An additional comic twist is given to the tale when, wandering in the forest of Arden, Ranaldo — also pursuing Angelica — drinks from Merlin's well (upon which the wizard long ago cast a spell, in order that Tristan, in drinking from its waters, might cease to love Isolde). All at once, his love for Angelica is turned to hatred. But then Angelica drinks from the Stream of Love and falls slavishly in love with Ranaldo, and — when she has returned home — contrives to have him spirited away to the Far East upon a magic ship. Finally — by way of innumerable detours — a host of players, Christian and "pagan," are brought together at the city of Albraca, where Angelica is besieged by her jealous suitor Agricane of Tartary, and where Orlando and Ranaldo find themselves fighting on opposite sides.

In the second book of the epic, however, the action shifts back towards the West. Albraca falls and Angelica escapes with Orlando. Meanwhile, the Muslim kings of North Africa launch an assault on Charlemagne's empire. The earlier comic twist is twisted again when Angelica and Ranaldo drink from (respectively) Merlin's well and the Stream of Love, and so exchange the spells that bind them. And, if anything, the involutions of plot become more elaborate than in the first half of the poem. The Muslim invasion of France and siege of Paris occupy the rest of the epic, and are still in progress when it abruptly terminates. Among the new characters are Rodamonte (Rodomonte in Ariosto, whence the word "rodomontade"), the fierce, godless, and all but invincible Saracen king of Sarza, and Rugiero, the mythical progenitor of the House of Este. The former, it is arguable, provided one of the models for Milton's Satan. The latter was of special significance for Boiardo because the poet was a gentleman of Ferrara and a beneficiary of the Estensi. Ariosto was dependent on the same House's patronage, incidentally, and so in his epic he explicitly transformed "Ruggiero" into a Ferraran Aeneas, and Rodomonte into a new Turnus (which gives Rodomonte the privilege of bringing the epic to its sudden conclusion by dying under Ruggiero's blade).

BOIARDO HAS OFTEN been dismissed as Ariosto's inferior, and in many respects he is (though not in fertility of imagination). One charge too often laid against him, though, is that his characters are not consistently developed. It is true that he does not provide much in the way of "psychological" portraiture; but one of the astonishing things about the *Innamorato* is how clearly its characters linger in one's imagination. Despite the mythic scale of their prowess, the human dimensions of their personalities are almost always poignantly visible. It is difficult to convey how touching, for instance, the character of Orlando is in some respects: especially his utter naïveté regarding — and childlike faith in — women (the very characteristic that will lead, in Ariosto's epic, to the madness that gives the poem its title). And certain characters — like Astolfo, the impossibly brave and somewhat inept English paladin, or the "pagan" (later Christian) paramours Brandimarte and Fiordelisa — are rendered as vividly as any figures in epic fiction.

All the Orlando epics are marvelous works, and the whole cycle is like nothing else in the Western canon. Though Ariosto's poem introduces undeniably tragic themes into the story, and though Pulci retells the story of Roncesvalles, none of these poems is tragic in the classical sense; and they certainly display little of the grave grandeur of classical epic. They are the imaginative product of late Christendom at the threshold of modernity, an exorbitant flourishing of the riches of a fully formed and complex civilization. Like Elizabethan drama, they are so heterogeneous in form — such promiscuous mixtures of intense pathos and high comedy, stateliness and farce, heroic magnificence and nursery fantasy — that they practically constitute a rebellion against classical restraints. These are joyous books, festive, pervaded by a spirit of carnival and of rude happiness; they contain no hint of morbid fatalism; they cannot conceal their mirth. Even the bloodshed is somehow lighthearted. If Dante's *Commedia* is the consummation of the high culture of developed Christendom, these works represent the final triumph of the sort of worldly imagination incubated by the Christian order (which is so often more fanciful than the pagan).

Ross's translation of the *Innamorato* is not always exemplary. Boiardo was a "rougher" poet than Ariosto, true, but Ross is sometimes far too colloquial; and often the delicate glitter of Boiardo's few genuinely lyric passages is rendered by Ross in a pale gray wash. He confines himself, for some reason, to a tetrameter line that is needlessly curt. But his is a scrupulous and readable translation, and (most importantly) it is complete. For this we must be grateful. Only a sensibility in some part stillborn could fail to delight in these books. One does not so much read them as feast upon them; and it is our very great good fortune that now, for the first time in the history of our language, the feast has been laid for us in full.

14

The Soul of a Controversy

In the past several days, as Terri Schiavo has been slowly fading from our world, I have heard three persons speculate publicly on the present whereabouts of her "soul." One opined that, where consciousness has sunk below a certain minimally responsive level, the soul has already departed the body; the other two thought that the soul remains, but as a dormant prisoner of the ruined flesh, awaiting release. Their arguments, being entirely intuitive, were of little interest; what caught my attention was the unreflective dualism to which all three clearly subscribed: the soul, they all assumed, is a kind of magical rational essence haunting the body, a ghost in a machine.

This is in fact a peculiarly modern view of the matter, not much older than the seventeenth-century philosophy of Descartes. While it is now the model to which most of us habitually revert when talking about the soul — whether we believe in such things or not — it has scant basis in either Christian or Jewish tradition. The "living soul" of scripture is the whole corporeal and spiritual totality of a person whom the breath of God has wakened to life. Thomas Aquinas, interpreting centuries of Christian and pagan metaphysics, defined the soul as the "form of the body," the vital power animating, pervading, shaping one from the moment of conception, drawing all the energies of life into a living unity.

The soul, one might almost say, is the event — and mystery — of a life in its fullness. In it all the multiplicity of experience is knit into a single continuous and developing identity. It encompasses all the dimensions of human existence: animal functions and abstract intellect, sensation and reason, emotion and reflection, flesh and spirit, natural aptitude and supernatural longing. As such, it grants us an openness to the world of which no other creature is capable, allowing us to take in reality through feeling and thought, recognition and surprise, will and desire, memory and anticipation, imagination and curiosity, delight and sorrow, invention and art.

The fourth-century theologian Gregory of Nyssa calls the soul a "living mirror" in which all things shine, so immense in its capacity that it can, when turned towards the light of God, grow eternally in an ever greater embrace of divine beauty. For the seventh-century theologian Maximus the Confessor, the human soul is the "boundary" between material and spiritual reality — heaven and earth — and so constitutes a microcosm that joins together, in itself, all the spheres of being.

Such language would not impress the dogmatic materialist. But nothing can diminish this miraculous oddity that in the midst of organic nature there exists a creature so exorbitantly in excess of what all the other grandeurs of material causality could possibly adumbrate, a living mirror where all splendors gather, an animal who is also a creative and interpretive being with a longing for eternity. Whether one is willing to speak of a "rational soul" or not, there is obviously an irreducible mystery here, one that commands our reverence.

It is easy, of course, to sense this mystery when gazing at the Sistine Chapel's ceiling or listening to *The Art of Fugue;* but — for Christians at least — it should be evident even when everything glorious and prodigious in our nature has been stripped away, and all that remains is frailty, brokenness, and dependency, or when a person we love has been largely lost to us in the labyrinth of a damaged brain. Even among such ravages — for those with the eyes to see it — a terrible dignity still shines out.

I do not understand why there is such urgency, for those who want Terri Schiavo's life to end, that she die now. If they believe her to be as "vegetative" as they claim, what harm would it have done, I wonder, to surrender her to the care (however fruitless) of her parents? I cannot, of course, pretend to know all the details, or even very many of them. Of this I am certain, though: Christians who understand their faith are obliged to believe that she is still, as she has always been, a living soul. It is true that, in some sense, it is her soul that those who love her cannot now reach, but it is also her soul that they touch with their hands and speak to and grieve over and adore. Thus it is also, in a sense, her soul that we have, as a society, abandoned to starvation and death — and that, at the very least, should cause us to wonder what else we may have abandoned along the way.

15

Beyond Disbelief:
On Alister McGrath's The Twilight of Atheism

Alister McGrath, *The Twilight of Atheism: The Rise and Fall of Disbelief in the Modern World* (Doubleday)

In *The Daily Telegraph* not long ago, A. N. Wilson produced one of those short but seemingly interminable opinion columns at which he so often excels, this one putatively in praise of the present Archbishop of Canterbury. The panegyric, however, was somewhat overwhelmed by the comical dolorousness of the prose. No fewer than sixteen-hundred times (at least, if the impression lingering in my memory is to be believed), Wilson departed from his theme to inform us that we are living in the waning days of the Christian religion, that it will not be long before the last church is closed, and that hence we may not see the likes of the good Archbishop very often again. Surely, I thought as I was reading, this is a man in whom parochialism has metastasized into a psychosis. Here we are living in an age when Christianity is spreading more rapidly and more widely than at any other point in the two millennia of its history — throughout the global South and East — and yet, because the Church languishes in the senile cultures of a small geological apophysis (with a few appertinent isles) at the western edge of continental Asia, Wilson concludes that the faith is in its death throes. Of course, being morbidly tiresome is part of Wilson's special post-Christian style: the air of weary, sage solemnity and flaccid resignation, the boring declarations of religious disenchantment, the bleak glimpses he affords us into the empty closets of his soul, the oracular intimations of the fate he has suffered for all of us in advance. But sometimes one really must wonder how he can remain so blissfully unaware that the great spiritual drama he is intent upon living out in print is roughly a century out of date (as far as I can tell, his heroic dash towards our common future is just now bringing him up hard on the heels of Havelock Ellis).

In any event, that column kept resurfacing in my mind as I read Alister McGrath's *The Twilight of Atheism,* which I suppose is why the principal thought I took away from the book was how very quaint predictions of religion's eventual demise now seem. McGrath himself, as it happens, in the days of his youthful Marxism, believed that one day faith would wither away, along with all the other venerable structures of alienation supporting the decaying edifice of the capitalist social order. Now though, looking back from his perch as professor of historical theology at Oxford, he finds the convictions of his youth amazingly drab and implausible.

Not that, in his earlier days, he was out of step with his times. More than midway through the last century, it still seemed inevitable to many that atheism would one day triumph. The majority of mankind lived under nominally atheist rule; the occasionally convulsive but more typically incremental advance of western secularization seemed inexorable, the desacralization of the world a *fait accompli;* even in America, despite the obstinate credulity of the folk, intellectual fashion tended in the direction of a confident liberal laicism; and only a very small number of prescient observers doubted that Islam was a spent force in the history of the world. As McGrath notes, the modern period alone has known a movement of ideological and passionate atheism, with ambitions comparable to the great evangelical creed it sought to displace, and there was a point not very far in the past when one could still honestly believe in its eventual victory.

How swiftly the fashion of the world changes. Idiot apologists for blood-steeped tyrannies like Jean-Paul Sartre and Eric Hobsbawm may still not be held in sufficient contempt, but the systems of butchery they so slobberingly adored have been discredited beyond revision. Pope John Paul II required only a decade to demonstrate how much more powerful is religious faith than the banalities of dialectical materialism. The forces of demography, we find, preponderantly favor the devout: rather than a bright idyll of rational humanism, secularism creates a culture of almost mystical triviality, and *homo secularis* turns out to be a creature so devoid of any sense of purpose that he can scarcely be stirred to reproduce. And what only a generation or two ago looked like imminent triumph now has about it the suspicious appearance of intellectual exhaustion.

THE FIRST HALF of McGrath's book is his brief history of modern dogmatic atheism, which follows the pattern one might expect. A series of colorful French vignettes (La Mettrie, Holbach, the Marquis de Sade, the merry sanguinary frolics of the Jacobins and *armées révolutionnaires* and *colonnes infernales,* the Panthéon, the "Cult of Reason") is followed by a few grim German etchings (Feuerbach, Marx, and Freud) and a whole assortment of English pastels, aquarelles, and oils (John William Draper, the rise of Darwinism, Godwin's asinine *Political Justice,* Keats and Shelley, Arnold and Hardy, George Eliot's dreary, dispiriting moralism, Swinburne's sickly, sadistic, dainty paganism, and so on). And, of course, Nietzsche, and Camus, and the lesser heralds of the "death of God" get a chapter to themselves.

Much of this, frankly, reads like a dutiful collation of atheism's greatest hits. Original argumentation is sparse and too often tends towards the needlessly tentative. Still, as a whole, these pages provide a sound and instructive treatment of their topic. The best moments come, though, when McGrath allows himself the odd passage of sly *ad hominem* abuse, such as his treatment of Swinburne's enthusiasm for flagellation. This is, after all, an entirely legitimate mode of argument: since Swinburne chose to proclaim himself a prophet of heathen health, sexual vitality, and spiritual exuberance, nothing could be more probative of his credibility than the discovery that the erotic license he longed to recover from the cold despotism of the "pale Galilaean" consisted principally in groveling at the boots of Madame Rosalind of Verbena Lodge with his naked hindquarters thrust in the air. How perfect a symbol, really, for the vast chasm separating the "liberating" rhetoric of the modern atheist's revolt against God from the debased squalor of post-Christian culture; and how very soothing to recall that behind the loping, pitilessly unvarying pulse of all that strident, sticky doggerel lurked only a frail, nervous flagellomane with a weak mouth and unruly hair.

The second half of the book attempts to describe and account for the ebbing of the atheist project, and it occasionally feels somewhat diffuse and uninspired. It has its moments, definitely, but it could perhaps be more daring. McGrath points out certain of the obvious causes of doctrinaire atheism's declining fortunes: the sheer imaginative sterility of the materialist perspective on reality; the historical evidence of the twentieth century, which clearly demonstrates that atheist ideology — far from bringing an end to intolerance and cruelty — is capable of incubating social evils more monstrously brutal, heartless, and violent than any hitherto imagined; the success of Christian movements — such as Pentecostalism — that no one in possession of his senses could possibly see as tainted by association with the *ancien régime;* and the postmodern collapse of confidence in the Enlightenment project. (In this last instance, McGrath may be insufficiently attentive to the ways in which the intellectual fashions we call postmodern have, for the most part, followed quite naturally from certain principles intrinsic to Enlightenment rationality, but that is a minor point at most.)

At the end, McGrath's is a very good book, but is not perhaps as profound as it might have been. He skirts near but never addresses certain large questions that seem to pose themselves in the course of his narrative — why, for instance, modern atheism is the product uniquely of Christian culture; and whether, then, ideological atheism (as opposed to simple, unpretentious unbelief) is not in some sense just another Christian heresy, an exaggeration of the gospel's ancient rebellion against the spiritual or divine "principalities and powers" that rule "this age." The one point at which McGrath tangentially touches upon such matters is where he argues that magisterial Protestantism, on account of its divorce between the sacred and the secular and its parching desacralization of the natural order, is in large part to blame for the rise of modern atheism. Here McGrath's treatment of his subject is acute and convincing (so much so, in fact, that one is tempted to ask by its end why McGrath himself remains a Protestant). Too often, though, McGrath is less ambitious, and seems content simply to reiterate that atheism is uninspiring and wanting in emotional succor, and that the disagreement between belief and unbelief is simply philosophically inadjudicable (which, as it is probably false, is a concession that need not be made). As a result, it is hard to say whether indeed he has quite penetrated to the real sources of modern atheism's apparent retreat.

LET ME (quite inappropriately) propose a simpler — if perhaps more conjectural — explanation of the present crepuscular situation of the atheist revolution.

As McGrath notes, now that the initial, delirious raptures of eighteenth- and nineteenth-century atheism have long since subsided, and a sober survey of the landscape left behind by God's departure has become possible, only the most ardently self-deluding secularist could possibly fail to see how much of the moral, imaginative, creative, and speculative glory of humanity seems to have vanished from the earth. Far from draining the world of any intrinsic meaning, as many of the critics of religion are wont to claim, faith in the divine source and end of all reality had charged every moment of time with an eternal significance, with possibilities of transcendence, with a reason for moral striving and artistry and dreams of future generations. Materialism, by contrast, when its boring mechanistic reductionism takes hold of a culture, can make even the immeasurable wonders of matter seem tedious and life seem largely pointless.

As for why this should be, it is surely not enough to say merely that atheism fails to divert our thoughts from our mortality as religion supposedly used to do; television does that much better. It seems more correct to say that religion, far from suppressing the vitality of human reason and will, opens up a dimension coterminous with rational consciousness as such. In purely theoretical terms, the question of the transcendent source of reality is an ontological — not a causal — question: not how things have come to be what they are, but how it is that things exist at all. And none of the customary post-Christian attempts to make the question of being disappear can possibly succeed: even if physics can trace all of time and space back to a single self-sufficient set of laws, that those laws exist at all must remain an imponderable problem for materialist thought (for possibility, no less than actuality, must first of all *be*); all the brave efforts of analytic philosophy to conjure the ontological question away as a fallacy of grammar have failed and always will; continental philosophy's attempts at a non-metaphysical ontology are notable chiefly for their lack of explanatory power. In the terms of Thomas Aquinas, there is simply an obvious incommensurability between the essence and the existence of things, and hence finite reality cannot account for its own being. And if this incommensurability is considered with adequate probity and clarity, it cannot fail but lead reflection towards something like what Thomas calls the *actus essendi subsistens* — the subsistent act of being — which is one of his most beautiful names for God.

Of course, very few persons ever have an occasion to think of reality in terms so abstract. But I would argue that this recognition of the sheer fortuity of being — the sheer impossibility of anything's essence ever being adequate to its existence — is what a certain sort of phenomenologist would call a "primordial intuition." Though we may not all have concepts available to us to understand it, all of us experience from time to time that kind of wonder that for Plato and Aristotle is the beginning of all philosophy, that sudden immediate knowledge that existence is something in excess of everything that is, something not intrinsic to it, something strange in its familiarity and transcendent in its immanence. This is an awareness so obvious that there may never be a theoretical language sufficiently limpid and innocent to express it properly, but in it is a wisdom basic to all reflective thought. To fail to see it requires either an irredeemably brutish mind or a willful obtuseness of the sort that only years of higher education can induce. And this, I venture to say, is why atheism cannot win out in the end: it requires a moral and intellectual coarseness — a blindness to the obvious — too immense for the majority of mankind.

These are claims too large to defend here, and I have strayed far from McGrath's argument. Simply said, *The Twilight of Atheism* is a lucid and suggestive historical survey of its topic. Had McGrath advanced his own arguments more audaciously, though, and been more merciless in his treatment of the logical inadequacies of materialism, and shown more confidence in the Christian philosophical tradition's power to reveal those inadequacies, the book would probably have been better. If indeed the atheist revolution has begun to flag, as McGrath believes, some measure of counterrevolutionary boldness is surely appropriate to the hour. But that would entail starting from the recognition that Christian tradition has more formidable resources at its disposal than mere emotional succor.

16

The Anti-Theology of the Body

To ask what the legacy of John Paul II's *The Theology of the Body* might be for future debates in bioethics is implicitly to ask what relevance it has for current debates in bioethics; and this creates something of a problem because there is a real sense in which it has none at all — at least, if by "relevance" one means discrete logical propositions or policy recommendations that might be extracted from the larger context of John Paul's teachings so as to "advance the conversation" or "suggest a middle course" or "clarify ethical ambiguities." Simply said, the book does not offer arguments, or propositions, or (thank God) "suggestions." Rather, it enunciates with extraordinary fullness a complete vision of the spiritual and corporeal life of the human being; and that vision is a self-sufficient totality, which one is free to embrace or reject as a whole, but which happily leaves little room for debate. To anyone who holds to John Paul's Christian understanding of the body, and so believes that each human being, from the very first moment of existence, emerges from and is called towards eternity, there are no negotiable or even very perplexing issues regarding our moral obligations before the mystery of life. Not only is *every* abortion performed an act of murder, but so is the destruction of every "superfluous" embryo created in fertility clinics or of every embryo produced for the purposes of embryonic stem cell research. The fabrication of clones, the invention of "chimeras" through the miscegenation of human and animal DNA, and of course the termination of supernumerary, dispensable, or defective specimens that such experimentation inevitably entails are in every case irredeemably evil. Even if, say,

139

research on embryonic stem cells could — as it probably cannot — produce therapies that would heal the lame and the halt, or reverse senility, or repair a damaged brain, or prolong life, this would in no measure alter the moral calculus of the situation: human life is an infinite good, never an instrumental resource, and so is possessed of an absolute sanctity, and no benefit (real or supposed) can justify its destruction.

In a wider sense, though, I would want to argue that it is precisely this "irrelevance" that makes John Paul's theology truly relevant to contemporary bioethics. What makes *The Theology of the Body* an exhilarating book is that it is a text awash in the clear bright light of uncompromising conviction; and one cannot help but admire its author's sublime indifference to the banal pieties and prejudices of modernity. Nowhere does the book pass through any of those moral penumbras that are so populously haunted by penitentially tentative Christian ethicists, timid apologists, Episcopal clergymen, "reflective" theologians, and liberal Catholic journal columnists. It simply restates the ancient Christian understanding of man, albeit in the somewhat phenomenological idiom for which John Paul had so marked a penchant, and invites the reader to enter into the world it describes. And at the heart of its anthropology is a complete rejection — or, one might almost say, ignorance — of any dualism between flesh and spirit.

It is something of a modern habit of thought (strange to say) to conceive of the soul — whether we believe in the soul or not — as a kind of magical essence or ethereal intelligence indwelling a body like a ghost in a machine. That is to say, we tend to imagine the relation between the soul and the body as an utter discontinuity somehow subsumed within a miraculous unity: a view capable of yielding such absurdities as the Cartesian postulate that the soul resides in the pituitary gland or the utterly superstitious speculation advanced by some religious ethicists that the soul may "enter" the fetus some time in the second trimester. But the "living soul" of whom scripture speaks, as John Paul makes clear in his treatment of the creation account in Genesis, is a single corporeal and spiritual whole, a person whom the breath of God has awakened from nothingness. The soul is life itself, of the flesh and of the mind; it is what Thomas Aquinas called the "form of the body": a vital power that animates, pervades, and shapes each of us from the moment of conception, holding all our native energies in a living unity, gathering all the multiplicity of our experience into a single, continuous, developing identity. It encompasses every dimension of human existence, from animal instinct to abstract reason: sensation and intellect, passion and reflection, imagination and curiosity, sorrow and delight, natural aptitude and supernatural longing, flesh and spirit. John Paul is quite insistent that the body must be regarded not as the vessel or vehicle of the soul, but simply as its material manifestation, expression, and occasion. This means that even if one should trace the life of the body back to its most primordial principles, one would still never arrive at that point where the properly human vanishes and leaves a "mere" physical organism or aggregation of inchoate tissues or ferment of spontaneous chemical reactions behind. All of man's bodily life is also the life of the soul, possessed of a supernatural dignity and a vocation to union with God.

THE FAR ANTIPODES of John Paul's vision of the human, I suppose, are to be found at the lunatic fringe of bioethics, in that fanatically "neo-Darwinist" movement that has crystallized around the name of "transhumanism." A satirist with a genius for the morbid could scarcely have invented a faction more depressingly sickly, one would think, and yet — in certain reaches of the scientific community — it is a movement that enjoys some real degree of respectability. Its principal tenet is that it is now incumbent upon humanity to take control of its own evolution, which on account of the modern world's technological advances and social policies has tragically stalled at the level of the merely anthropine; as we come to master the mysteries of the genome, we must choose what we are to be, so as to progress beyond *homo sapiens,* perhaps one day to become beings — in the words of the Princeton biologist Lee Silver — "as different from humans as humans are from . . . primitive worms" (which are, I suppose, to be distinguished from sophisticated worms). We must seek, that is to say, to become gods. Many of the more deliriously visionary of the transhumanists envisage a day when we will be free to alter and enhance ourselves at will, unconstrained by law or shame or anything resembling good taste: by willfully transgressing the genetic boundaries between species (something that we are already learning how to do), we may be able to design new strains of hybrid life, or even indeed to produce an endlessly proliferating variety of new breeds of the post-human that may no longer even have the capacity to reproduce one with the other. (For those whose curiosity runs to the macabre, Wesley Smith's recent *Consumer's Guide to a Brave New World* provides a good synopsis of the transhumanist creed.)

Obviously one is dealing here with a sensibility formed more by comic books than by serious thought. Ludicrous as it seems, though, transhumanism is merely one logical consequence (if a particularly childish one) of the surprising reviviscence of eugenic ideology in the academic, scientific, and medical worlds. Most of the new eugenists, admittedly, see their solicitude for the greater well-being of the species as suffering from none of the distasteful authoritarianism of the old racialist eugenics, since all they advocate (they say) is a kind of elective genetic engineering — a bit of planned parenthood here, the odd reluctant act of infanticide there, a *soupçon* of judicious genetic tinkering everywhere, and a great deal of prudent reflection upon the suitability of certain kinds of embryo — but clearly they are deluding themselves or simply lying. Far more intellectually honest are those who — like the late, almost comically vile Joseph Fletcher of Harvard — openly acknowledge that any earnest attempt to improve the human stock must necessarily involve some measures of legal coercion. Fletcher, of course, was infamously unabashed in castigating modern medicine for "polluting" our gene pool with inferior specimens and in rhapsodizing upon the benefits the race would reap from instituting a regime of genetic invigilation that would allow society to eliminate "idiots" and "cripples" and other genetic defectives before they could burden us with their worthless lives. It was he who famously declared that reproduction is a privilege, not a right, and suggested that perhaps mothers should be forced by the state to abort "diseased" babies if they refused to do so of their own free will. Needless to say, state-imposed sterilization struck him as a reasonable policy; and he agreed with Linus Pauling that it might be wise to consider segregating genetic inferiors into a recognizable caste, marked out by indelible brands impressed upon their brows. And, striking a few minor transhumanist chords of his own, he even advocated — in a deranged and hideous passage from his *The Ethics of Genetic Control* that has been quoted with horror or delight by countless of his critics and disciples — the creation of "chimeras or parahumans . . . to do dangerous or demeaning jobs" of the sort that are now "shoved off on moronic or retarded individuals" — which, apparently, was how he viewed janitors, construction workers, firefighters, miners, and persons of that ilk.

Of course, there was always a certain oafish audacity in Fletcher's degenerate driveling about "morons" and "defectives," given that there is good cause to suspect, from a purely utilitarian vantage, that academic ethicists — especially those among them who, like Fletcher, are notoriously mediocre thinkers, possessed of small culture, no discernible speculative gifts, no records of substantive philosophical contributions, and execrable prose styles — constitute perhaps the single most useless element in society, and that any program for the improvement of the species must necessarily entail their annihilation. What, after all (if I may momentarily borrow Fletcher's own style of reflection), is a man with Fletcher's meager intellectual gifts, grotesquely hypertrophied ego, and pestilentially sociopathic tendencies if not a kind of genetic scurf that ought to be scoured from the skin of the race? If reproduction is not a right, should any woman be allowed to bring this inert excrescence of the social body into the world, or should such a creature be allowed to sire offspring? I ask this question in all earnest, because I think it helps to identify the one indubitable truth about all social movements towards eugenics: to wit, that the values that will determine which lives are worth living, and which not, will always be the province of persons of vicious temperament. I mean to say, if I were asked to decide what qualities to suppress or encourage in the human species, I might first attempt to discover if there is such a thing as a genetic predisposition to moral idiocy and then, if there is, to eliminate it; then there would be no more Joseph Fletchers (or Peter Singers, or Linus Paulings, or James Rachels), and I might think all is well. But, of course, the very idea is a contradiction in terms. Decisions regarding who should or should not live can, by definition, be made only by those who believe such decisions *should* be made; and therein lies the horror that nothing can ever exorcise from the ideology behind human bioengineering.

Transhumanism, as a moral philosophy, is so risibly fabulous in its prognostications, and so unrelated to anything that genomic research yet promises, that it can scarcely be regarded as anything more than a pathetic dream; but the *metaphysical* principles it presumes regarding the nature of the human are anything but eccentric. Joseph Fletcher (not to mince words) was manifestly no more than an undistinguished and petulant little proto-Nazi with a scrofulous and incorrigibly adolescent mind, who was desperately anxious to deceive himself that he was superior to the common run of men, and who all too obviously received some sort of crypto-erotic thrill from his sadistic fantasies of creating a slave race, and of literally branding others as his genetic inferiors, and of exercising power over the minds and bodies of the low-born; and yet his thought continues to win adherents in the academy and beyond it, and his basic presuppositions about the value and meaning of life are the common grammar of a shockingly large portion of bioethicists. If ever the day comes when we are willing to consider a program, however modest, of improving the species through genetic planning and manipulation, it will be exclusively those who hold such principles and embrace such presuppositions who will determine what the future of humanity will be. And men who are impatient of frailty and contemptuous of weakness are, at the end of the day, inevitably evil.

Why dwell on these things, though? After all, most of the more prominent debates in bioethics at the moment do not actually concern systematic eugenics or, certainly, "post-humanity," but center upon issues of medical research and such matters as the disposition of embryos who will never mature into children. It is true that we have already begun to transgress the demarcations between species — often in pursuit of a medical or technological benefit — and cloning is no longer merely a matter of speculation. But even here issues of health and of new therapeutic techniques predominate, and surely these require some degree of moral subtlety from all of us. Am I not, then, one might wonder, simply skirting difficult questions of practical ethics so as to avoid allowing any ambiguity to invade my moral absolutism? Honestly, though, I think that the metaphysics, dogma, and mysticism of "transhumanism" or Fletcherite eugenics hide behind, and await us as the inevitable terminus of, every movement that subordinates or sacrifices the living soul — the life that is here before us, in the moment, in all its particularity and fragility — to the progress of science, of medicine, or of the species. That is to say, I dwell upon extremes because I believe it is in extremes that truth is most likely to be found. And this brings me back to John Paul II's theology of the body.

THE DIFFERENCE between John Paul's theological anthropology and the pitilessly consistent materialism of the transhumanists and their kith — and this is extremely important to grasp — is a difference not simply between two radically antagonistic visions of what it is to be a human being, but between two radically antagonistic visions of what it is to be a god. There is, as it happens, nothing inherently wicked in the desire to become a god, at least not from the perspective of Christian tradition; and I would even say that if there is one element of the transhumanist creed that is not wholly contemptible — one isolated moment of innocence, however fleeting and imperfect — it is the earnestness with which it gives expression to this perfectly natural longing. Theologically speaking, the proper destiny of human beings is to be "glorified" — or "divinized" — in Christ by the power of the Holy Spirit, to become "partakers of the divine nature" (2 Pet. 1:4), to be called "gods" (Ps. 82:6; John 10:34-36). This is the venerable doctrine of *"theosis"* or "deification," the teaching that — to employ a lapidary formula of great antiquity — "God became man that man might become god": that is to say, in assuming human nature in the incarnation, Christ opened the path to union with the divine nature for all persons. From the time of the Church Fathers through the high Middle Ages, this understanding of salvation was a commonplace of theology. Admittedly, until recently it had somewhat disappeared from many Western articulations of the faith, but in the East it has always remained part of the explicit catechesis of the Church; and it stands at the very center of John Paul's theology of the body. As he writes in *Evangelium vitae,*

> Man is called to a fullness of life which far exceeds the dimensions of his earthly existence, because it consists in sharing the very life of God. The loftiness of this supernatural vocation reveals the greatness and the inestimable value of human life even in its temporal phase.

John Paul's anthropology is what a certain sort of Orthodox theologian might call a "theandric" humanism. "Life in the Spirit," the most impressive of the texts collected in *The Theology of the Body,* is to a large extent an attempt to descry the true form of man by looking to the end towards which he is called, so that the glory of his eschatological horizon, so to speak, might cast its radiance back upon the life he lives *in via* here below. Thus, for John Paul, the earthly body in all its frailty and indigence and limitation is always already on the way to the glorious body of resurrection of which Paul speaks; the mortal body is already the seed of the divinized and immortal body of the Kingdom; the weakness of the flesh is already, potentially, the strength of "the body full of power"; the earthly Adam is already joined to the glory of the last Adam, the risen and living Christ. Which is to say that, for the pope, divine humanity is not something that in a simple sense lies beyond the human; it does not reside in some future, post-human race to which the good of the present must be

145

offered up; it is instead a glory hidden in the depths of every person, even the least of us — even "defectives" and "morons" and "genetic inferiors," if you will — waiting to be revealed, a beauty and dignity and power of such magnificence and splendor that, could we see it now, it would move us either to worship or to terror.

Obviously none of this would interest or impress the doctrinaire materialist. The vision of the human that John Paul articulates and the vision of the "transhuman" to which the still nascent technology of genetic manipulation has given rise are divided not by a difference in practical or ethical philosophy, but by an irreconcilable hostility between two religions, two metaphysics, two worlds — at the last, two gods. And nothing less than the moral nature of society is at stake. If, as I have said, the metaphysics of transhumanism is inevitably implied within such things as embryonic stem cell research and cloning, then to embark upon them is already to invoke and invite the advent of a god who will, I think, be a god of boundless horror, one with a limitless appetite for sacrifice. And it is by their gods that human beings are shaped and known. In some very real sense, "man" is always only the shadow of the god upon whom he calls: for in the manner by which we summon and propitiate that god, and in that ultimate value that he represents for us, who and what we are is determined. The materialist who wishes to see modern humanity's Baconian mastery over cosmic nature expanded to encompass human nature as well — granting us absolute power over the flesh and what is born from it, banishing all fortuity and uncertainty from the future of the race — is someone who seeks to reach the divine by ceasing to be human, by surpassing the human, by destroying the human. It is a desire both fantastic and depraved: a diseased titanism, the dream of an infinite passage through monstrosity, a perpetual and ruthless sacrifice of every present good to the featureless, abysmal, and insatiable god who is to come. For the Christian to whom John Paul speaks, however, one can truly aspire to the divine only through the charitable cultivation of glory in the flesh, the practice of holiness, the love of God and neighbor; and, in so doing, one seeks not to take leave of one's humanity, but to fathom it in its ultimate depth, to be joined to the Godman who would remake us in himself, and so to become *simul divinus et creatura*. This is a pure antithesis. For those who, on the one hand, believe that life is merely an accidental economy of matter that should be weighed by a utilitarian calculus of means and ends and those who, on the other, believe that life is a supernatural gift oriented towards eternal glory, every moment of existence has a different significance and holds a different promise. To the one, a Down Syndrome child (for instance) is a genetic scandal, one who should probably be destroyed in the womb as a kind of oblation offered up to the social good and, of course, to some immeasurably remote future; to the other, that same child is potentially (and thus far already) a being so resplendent in his majesty, so mighty, so beautiful that we could scarcely hope to look upon him with the sinful eyes of this life and not be consumed.

It may well be that the human is an epoch, in some sense. The idea of the infinite value of every particular life does not accord with instinct, as far as one can tell, but rather has a history. The ancient triumph of the religion of divine incarnation inaugurated a new vision of man, however fitfully and failingly that vision was obeyed in subsequent centuries. Perhaps this notion of an absolute dignity indwelling every person — this Christian invention or discovery or convention — is now slowly fading from our consciences and will finally be replaced by something more "realistic" (which is to say, something more nihilistic). Whatever the case, John Paul's theology of the body will never, as I have said, be "relevant" to the understanding of the human that lies "beyond" Christian faith. Between these two orders of vision there can be no fruitful commerce, no modification of perspectives, no debate, indeed no "conversation." All that can ever span the divide between them is the occasional miraculous movement of conversion or the occasional tragic movement of apostasy. Thus the legacy of that theology will be to remain, for Christians, a monument to the grandeur and fullness of their faith's "total humanism," so to speak, to remind them how vast the Christian understanding of humanity's nature and destiny is, and to inspire them — whenever they are confronted by any philosophy, ethics, or science that would reduce any human life to an instrumental moment within some larger design — to a perfect and unremitting enmity.

17

Ecumenical War Councils:
On Webster and Cole's The Virtue of War

Alexander F. C. Webster and Darrell Cole, *The Virtue of War: Reclaiming the Classic Christian Traditions East and West* (Regina Orthodox Press)

An Antiochene Orthodox priest of my acquaintance — not long liberated from bondage in the ECUSA — recently told me, with every appearance of sincerity, that he had converted to the Eastern Church because he was a pacifist. For a moment, I was uncertain as to whether he was attempting to baffle me with some cunningly constructed paradox. I would have found it a no more impenetrable *non sequitur* had he announced that he had joined the local Elks' lodge because of his passion for beautiful young women, or that he enjoyed reading Calvin for the witticisms. But it soon became clear that he had meant his remark not only in earnest, but without any sense at all of its absurdity; indeed, he was somewhat disconcerted to discover that my understanding of Orthodoxy differed radically from his on this point.

It strikes me as a singular sort of delusion to imagine that the Eastern Orthodox tradition is any more hospitable to pacifism than the Western Catholic tradition, given the utter absence of pacifist tenets from Orthodoxy's teachings, liturgy, or history. And yet, apparently, it is a delusion shared by a not inconsiderable number of (Western) Eastern Christians at present. Of course, it is something of a cottage industry in the Orthodox Church — especially among converts — to discover and market ever newer ancient differences between Eastern and Western Christian theology, morality, devotion, spirituality, politics, cuisine, or whatever else one can think of. And, since an explicit and elaborate theory of "just war" is the special achievement of Western tradition, it has become received wisdom in some quarters of the Eastern Church that Orthodox tradition *obviously* regards all war as intrinsically "unjust" (which, for obscure reasons, is taken as proof of a certain spiritual superiority on the Eastern side). Thus has been born another fatuous myth regarding the division between the ancient Catholic Churches, one that — like all its predecessors — combines a refusal to learn the meaning of unfamiliar terms with a magnificent indifference to historical fact.

This is not, I hasten to say, to dismiss Christian pacifism out of hand. There may be no good theological reason to prefer an unjust peace to a just war, or to pretend that the undoubted possibility of the former does not — by dialectical necessity — imply the possibility of the latter; but few of us should be confident in our ability adequately to recognize either, and — given the enormities of war — it is always wise to err here on the side of caution. Whether, though, one views pacifists as sinewy heroes of the spirit living out a prophetic life of obedience to the true gospel message, or as pusillanimous moral dilettantes too craven to undertake the discipline of prudential reasoning in the realm of concrete morality, or merely as admirable but excitable irrationalists, it simply is not the case that the Eastern and Western Churches differ significantly in their traditional understandings of war or warfare. And it is as well to acknowledge as much, both for the sake of Christian unity and for the sake of rational theological argument in times of international turmoil.

This, at any rate, is one of the principal arguments of Alexander Webster and Darrell Cole's *The Virtue of War,* a thorough (if not entirely consistent) defense of just war thinking as part of the common inheritance of both the Eastern and the Western Churches. Far more, however, than an exercise in ecumenism, this is a book written with a certain palpable urgency about it: It is intended, quite unambiguously, as an exhortation to Christians to devote themselves wholeheartedly to the current "war on terror," most especially America's invasions of Afghanistan and Iraq. And while, in this latter cause, the book is certainly a failure, this is not necessarily on account of any deficiency in the case it makes for "just" or (in Webster's preferred phrase) "justifiable" war.

The greatest virtue of this book is that it does not advance its case only over against Christian pacifism of the sort one associates with, say, John Howard Yoder, but also over against the "Christian realism" of Reinhold Niebuhr and his disciples. It has long been one of the oddities of American Christian ethics that — in matters pertaining to war — the pacifist and realist positions have been treated as the only available options for Christian moralists. But pacifism and realism are mere inversions of one another, inasmuch as they share more or less the same view of what warfare is. Both accept the premise that war is by its nature evil, while only peace is an unqualified good; the pacifist may believe that peace (understood simply as the absence of strife) is best achieved by refusing to participate in war, and the realist that peace (understood as a secure and just social order) is best achieved by answering violence with violence, but both then accept that the Christian never has any choice in times of war but to collaborate with evil: he must either allow the violence of an aggressor to prevail or employ inherently wicked methods to assure that it does not.

Webster and Cole will have none of this. The bracingly unsentimental argument that they want to make is that war in fact is not intrinsically evil, however tragic it may be, but is a neutral instrument that may be used towards ends either moral or immoral; and, when it is waged on behalf of justice and by just means, it is a positive good, a work of virtue, and an act of charity. Simply said, for Christians, to go to war should never be a tragic choice of the lesser of two evils, for they are forbidden to do evil at all. Rather, if they go to war, it is out of a militant commitment to the peace of God's Kingdom, and when they fight they do so as agents of divine justice in the earth. And that may frequently be cause for sorrow, but should never be cause for contrition.

The Virtue of War is not really a single book; the two authors have not so much collaborated as concurred, each writing one half of the text and each dealing exclusively with his own tradition. Of the two, it is Webster who has the easier task; for while Orthodoxy has never developed an explicit theory of war, the evidence against the pacifist or semi-pacifist account of Eastern tradition is nevertheless so plenteous that Webster's half of the book has for the most part the character of a simple recitation. He gathers his proofs from scripture, the fathers, canon law, hagiography, devotional literature, liturgy, and modern Orthodox theologians and writers; and, by the end, only the most obdurately pacific reader would deny that he has proved his case. In the course of his argument, his epitomes and pericopes do actually concresce into a sort of Eastern theory of justifiable war, but one that consists in nothing more than three general principles: war must be waged only on behalf of a state possessed of a proper political ethos (a state, that is, whose laws are Christian, or at least in accord with natural law); it must be waged in defense of the people of God; and it must be waged with the proper spiritual intent (that is to say, the intention of justice: both as regards the conduct of hostilities and the end towards which they are oriented).

Apart from that, Webster's case is almost entirely historical. He is especially adept at demonstrating that many of the Eastern fathers seem to recognize the legitimacy and merit of the military life (as do the prayers and liturgies of the Church), that the defense of piety and order (even by force of arms) has always been regarded in the Orthodox world as a virtuous undertaking, that priests alone are forbidden to participate directly in war (because of the special purity attaching to the Eucharistic ministry), and that the penitential withholding of the sacraments from warriors lately returned from battle has traditionally been observed not — for the most part — on account of anything essentially evil in a soldier's duties, but on account of sins that might have been committed incidentally or inadvertently in the course of a military campaign.

Where Cole assumes authorial duties, however, the book's argument becomes at once more substantial (at least, in theoretical terms) and more problematic. He somewhat weakens his case at the outset by advocating what he calls a "Christendom-informed political theology," by which he means one that witnesses to God's transcendent goodness, but that does not "call for the aboli[tion] of the liberal state" or for a "theocratic" "collapse of church and state." "The liberal tradition is not to be overturned (even if such a thing were possible), but the church must see that the state recognizes the victory of Christ in the Advent." This — to put it bluntly — is nonsense. Quite aside from the impossibility of Christians in any significant way impeding that process whereby the liberal order has detached itself — and continues to detach itself ever more savagely — from the moral and metaphysical absolutes of Christianity, the notion that the Church can ever wring more concessions from the liberal state than it must make to the state in return is worse than naive.

More importantly, by beginning his account of just war theory by bothering to recognize the legitimacy of a state not explicitly bound to divine law — however much he may urge that Christians must attempt to make the state conscious of that law — Cole puts himself in the odd position of having to argue that Christians must both obey the principles of just war and also resign themselves to fighting at the behest of a political order that has not necessarily placed itself under the sway of those principles. It is, after all, the liberal state that gave us total war in the modern age and that has often, precisely on account of its liberal utopian abhorrence of all war (as Cole himself quite acutely observes), forsaken even the pretense of justice in making war; it is a curious thing indeed, then, for Cole to begin his defense of the just war tradition by arguing on behalf of a political system that is in its essence intractably post-Christian. If the most for which Christians can hope is that they have a "voice" in the political determinations of a government that does not otherwise acknowledge the spiritual and moral supremacy of the Church in worldly affairs, what remains of just war theory but a collection of axioms by which individual Christians must try to ascertain for themselves whether they may or may not consent to a particular war being waged by their government? But surely just war theory is not supposed to function as a private calculus, but as a social and political rationality. In the age of the liberal state, what authority may Christians trust in times of war, if the state cannot — by its own constitutional logic — speak under the clear guidance of the Church? To be fair, Cole does attempt to answer just these questions; his answers are simply completely unconvincing.

Where Cole excels, however, is in providing a concise but comprehensive account of what just war principles are and how they might be brought to bear — if a given government is willing — upon modern conflicts. I know of no better summary in English of the rationality of Western just war principles, as regards both the cause *(ius ad bellum)* and the conduct *(ius in bello)* of hostilities. Concerning the former, Cole enumerates five criteria: war may be entered upon only if it is initiated and governed by proper political authority, only if it is waged in a just cause, only if it is prosecuted with the right intention, only if no other reasonable means for resolving a crisis remains, and only if there is some real hope for success. Concerning the latter, the criteria are only two: war must never be waged with the intent of harming noncombatants, and it must follow strategies whose intended good manifestly outweighs any unintended evils that may follow from them.

And Cole's argument acquires a considerable degree of theological depth when he turns to Augustine and Thomas for support. Here he finds a cogent account — though one, no doubt, somewhat scandalous to modern ears — of justifiable violence as a work of charity. For Augustine, certainly, love occasionally demands violence, such that the failure to use violence is also a failure of love (which is a sin). For Thomas, it is precisely because all human loves must be ordered within the love of God — who is infinite goodness — and governed by the virtue of charity that war may become inevitable for a Christian people: for an unjust peace is not pleasing to God, and the love of any earthly order must conform itself first to the love of divine justice. Cole also shows himself to be quite critically adroit in arguing for the superiority of such a position, intellectually and morally, over both the pacifism of Yoder (with its myriad inconsistencies and incoherencies) and the sub-Christian ethical consequentialism of Niebuhr (who, lest we forget, was all too willing to defend the Allies' saturation bombing of German and Japanese civilians, which no proponent of just war theory could possibly have done).

The Virtue of War is a flawed book, I think it fair to say, for reasons both accidental and essential. At the most trivial level of grievance, I have to confess to a certain degree of annoyance at a book so carelessly edited. It is rather exasperating to see "T. S. Elliot" (sic) described as an "Englishman" (p. 6), or to encounter the catachrestic substitution of "voluntarism" for "volunteerism" (p. 26), or to find *prima facie* rendered as *prima facia* (p. 41), or to endure as absurd and blasphemous a solecism as the transformation of *libido dominandi* into *libido domini* (p. 200). (Surely, at the very least, one should expect scholars of Christian history to have mastered elementary Latin.)

At a somewhat more substantial level, it is strange to see Cole attempting to reconcile the developed Thomistic language of charity as a virtue with the older, somewhat more implausible belief advanced by Ambrose and Augustine (and accepted by Cole) that Christians are forbidden to defend themselves in all circumstances from unjust violence visited upon their own persons lest, in so doing, they offend against charity. Quite apart from the exegetical difficulties such a view presents the theologian (for what purpose were the disciples to use the swords for which Christ prophesied they would sell their cloaks? was he commissioning them as knights errant?), it is clearly incompatible with the rule that *all* earthly loves must be made subordinate to the love of God. It is one thing to turn the other cheek against insult and casual abuse, without seeking vengeance, or even to accept martyrdom, but another thing altogether to permit oneself simply to be murdered to no good end. To love charitably — selflessly — requires that love of self be ordered towards the love of God; to do this, one must learn to love oneself under the rule of justice, and to fail to do so is perhaps no less a sin than refusing to defend one's neighbor. Indeed, defending oneself against unjust violence is one of the few times that one can most assuredly subsume self-love under the law of charity, without egoism or spite intruding at all.

But the greatest problem with this book is that it never succeeds in providing truly compelling arguments regarding how just war principles can be applied by Christians in the age of the secular state. Christians ought not to support or participate in any unjust war, says Cole; but then, also, Christians must not make war except under the authority of a state's duly constituted military. But, surely, if there is no established Church, there is no way of knowing whether any given government will make even a show of limiting its belligerences to causes or practices condoned by Christian moral law. How can we embrace the military profession then? And are we not inevitably reduced (as I have said) to the private prudential calculations of individual believers? When Cole attempts to lend greater moral authority to modern "just wars" by invoking such institutions as international courts while also insisting that Christians must hearken to the verdict of the Church, one wonders why he does not see the incongruity here. And, in any event, if most Christians had listened to the Church in the months leading up to the war in Iraq, would Cole have been pleased with the result?

I do not much blame Webster and Cole for failing to bring their excellent historical and theoretical survey of just war thinking into credible contact with contemporary reality. It seems to me to be a difficulty that is inescapable whenever one attempts to use a moral grammar suited to an age of Christian princes and Christian cultures as a guide to the Church's relations with the post-Christian political order. Webster is almost strident in his assertion that we can credit ourselves with virtuous war-making in both Afghanistan and Iraq, and it would be delightful to imagine he is right. But I cannot imagine anyone not disposed to approve of the invasion of Iraq (in particular) being convinced by any argument this book advances. What exactly, he might ask, are we fighting for? Democracy, freedom of religion? But these are not demonstrably biblical values. Did Iraq constitute a threat to us? Perhaps, but not a threat that can ever definitively be shown to have been more than suppositious. And, even if this were not so, is this a war waged to defend the people of God? Is ours really a Christian culture — our culture of abortion, pornography, and polymorphous perversity — worthy of defending? And has any community suffered more as a result of the war in Iraq than that country's Christians?

I am not urging any particular view of the matter, as it happens; I am only calling attention to how complicated the issue becomes when the Christian just war theorist can no longer claim that we are fighting to defend or restore a Christian order. It may well be that the only argument a Christian could make for our incompetent and disastrous war in Iraq that will not inevitably become at best equivocal when subjected to a sufficiently unyielding moral skepticism is that the suffering of the Iraqis under Saddam's regime was sufficiently monstrous that no Christian conscience could possibly be content to leave that regime in place. But, if this is so, one must then draw a firm demarcation between the aims of Christians in this conflict and the aims of the secular state. Perhaps we should cease to imagine that we can simply translate the principles of just war from the age of Christendom to the age of "the rights of man." If Christians feel moved to make war, and wish to do it justly, they can fight only "alongside" the state, but surely not under its moral or spiritual authority. Their alliance with the state is more or less accidental, and even somewhat opportunistic, and the prudential decisions they make for or against war must be something separate and distinct from the decisions made by their governments. If they go forth to fight for God's justice, they do so as citizens of a Kingdom not of this world, one that can make use of the post-Christian state, but that cannot share its purposes. To the world, this may appear to mean that they go forth only as individuals, driven each merely by the passion of his faith. Perhaps so. And perhaps it is then also the case that, really, they must learn again how to speak not only of just war, but of chivalry.

18

The Angel at the Ford of Jabbok:
On the Theology of Robert Jenson

Not long ago, I was interviewed by a small journal concerning a book of mine that had appeared a few months earlier. Near the end of the conversation, my interlocutor (a young and obviously intelligent divinity student) asked me if there was any modern American theologian whose thinking I find especially provocative, and I answered, without a moment's hesitation, Robert Jenson. My interviewer smiled abashedly and admitted that he had never read any of Jenson's work — whereupon I feigned surprise and began to upbraid the poor fellow (in an affably supercilious way), telling him how very extraordinary this was, and what dereliction it suggested on the part of his teachers, and what a very great pity it all seemed that he had been denied the exhilaration of engaging with Jenson's work . . . (and so on, with a few rueful shakes of the head).

As chance would have it, however, I had scarcely arrived home before I opened an e-mail message — from a fairly authoritative interpreter of Jenson's work — complaining that my critique of Jenson's theology, in the very book upon which I had just been interviewed, had been written in such a way as to appear merely as an exemplary episode within my own narrative of modern philosophy, and thus had all but entirely failed to provide a balanced account of Jenson's theological intentions, or of the greater scope of his thought, or of the biblical concerns animating it. I was slightly indignant, needless to say; this fellow, I surmised, had been drinking, or at any rate trying to read my book while simultaneously watching television and talking to his wife. I repaired to the text itself, murmuring a few angry imprecations, to seek the sentences that would

vindicate me. I have to confess though that, as I read, my indignation began gradually to subside, and then slowly — with the soft relentless in-
exorability of snow gathering upon a bough — to yield to doubt, and then
to dismay, and then at last to morose acquiescence; the complaint, I was
forced to conclude, was probably just.

Well, theology is a particularly savage business (at least when it is
done right), and one that it is never too early to discourage one's children
from entering. I relate the little ironies of that day, however, not as preface to an attempt to remedy any mischief I may have done in the past
(which would be both contrary to my nature and very boring for the
reader). What this incident forced me to reflect upon, though, is the curious neglect Jenson's work has suffered not only among reasonably theologically literate American Christians, but in the academic world. I do
not mean to suggest that Jenson is what one would call an obscure figure: among those who do genuinely care about systematic theology in
this country, his work is known and esteemed (indeed, by many, revered), and the appearance a few years ago of his *Systematic Theology*
confirmed his stature not only as an exciting thinker — more theoreti-
cally audacious than almost all of his compatriots — but one of considerable achievement. But still, relatively speaking, as of yet (and he is over
seventy years of age) his thought is little taught and little studied; few dis-
sertations engage his ideas; scant attention is paid to his contributions
to modern dogmatics; and small note is taken of the dignity his work
lends to American theology. Why, I wonder, should this be so?

One reason, I suspect, is precisely *that* Jenson is an American (to be
exact, a Minnesota Lutheran of Norwegian extraction, and of the "high
church" variety). It is a prejudice widely held — but by no people more fervently than by Americans themselves — that it is not our calling as a nation to indulge in "primary discourse." It is all well and good for an American theologian to write at length about (for instance) what German
theologians might have to say about the Trinity, but it is something altogether different for him to write too boldly about the Trinity as such. We
would not usually — as a rule — presume. Another reason, perhaps, is
Jenson's inveterate and perverse refusal to be long-winded. His books are
not buttressed (as we know such things should be) by long, ponderous
prolegomena on method or on critical history or on the *status quaestionis;*
his scholarly apparatus rarely exceed what is necessary to support his assertions, and are almost ascetically devoid of needless displays of erudi-

tion or Teutonic pedantry; his method and peculiar concerns are typically disclosed in the act of theology itself, on the wing, and he tends to say what he wishes to say once only, and as concisely as he can.

Of course, this last characteristic can occasionally prove daunting. At its most idiosyncratic, Jenson's prose has about it at once a spare tautness and a condensed energy that are almost palpable; one sometimes has the premonition that if certain of his sentences are handled too casually they might detonate. Whether his style is the result of a conscious method, or merely of the legendarily laconic reserve of the Scandinavian upper Midwest translated through a rigorous speculative intelligence, it occasionally produces formulations of a positively oracular terseness. At times, one is conscious of the aphoristic precision of one of his assertions, but not of its meaning. And sometimes he is clearly more concerned for the force of a phrase than for its felicity — "God is a great *fugue*," for instance (the poetry lies here in the idea, I think it safe to say, rather than in the words). Still, for the most part Jenson is always a compelling writer (even to those of us with a taste for the sesquipedalian and pointlessly elaborate), altogether more lucid and precise than one has a right to expect in regard to matters as intricate as he chooses to address, with something of the dramatist's flair for keeping the action moving. And, as a result, it is difficult to resist the power of the story he tells.

PERHAPS THE SIMPLEST THING one might say about Jenson's theology is that it is an attempt to talk about the *living* God. To put the matter thus, however, scarcely conveys any inkling of the vibrancy of Jenson's sense of God's liveliness, or of the force with which that sense has impressed itself upon — and occupies every page of — Jenson's theology: there is nothing in the triune God, one might better say, that is not one infinite act of life — and that life an act of boundless love. God *is* the movement of the Father's love for the Son, and the Son's love for the Father, and their inexhaustible life together in the endless love of the Spirit; and within that movement is contained all beauty, glory, splendor, joy, and future. As Jenson insists upon saying, God is an event — the event, to be precise, of Christ in its eternal fullness — and this event has a real and concrete history. To understand what this means, however, one must understand how Jenson's thought stands in relation to the Christian dogmatic tradition as a whole.

Most Christians, no matter how orthodox or devout they may be, have (through no fault of their own) little notion of how the doctrine of the Trinity took shape, or why it assumed the form it did. Few, certainly, take an interest in the doctrinal disputes of the Church's early centuries, and many harbor at best some vague understanding of the Christian doctrine of God that, if more closely examined, turns out to be either some version of one or another of the heresies rejected by the councils of the ancient Church — "tritheism," "adoptionism," "modalism," even "Arianism" — or a bland ethical Unitarianism bound to the historical career of Jesus of Nazareth by bonds of almost gossamer tenuousness. Many, I suspect, think of the doctrine of the Trinity (when they have occasion to think of it at all) either as a mere revealed "fact" susceptible of no rational investigation or as something rather arbitrary and historically fortuitous, to be embraced *ex convenientia,* but accorded little serious reflection. In fact, however, the orthodox articulation of Trinitarian theology came at the end not only of many decades of extremely complicated theological dispute, but at the end of centuries of meditation upon the meaning of the scriptural account of Christ's life, death, resurrection, and continued presence to the Church in the Holy Spirit.

At the beginning of the fourth century, there were many models by which Christian theologians attempted to grasp the nature of the interrelations of Father, Son, and Spirit, and to determine to which of the three Persons — and in what manner — it was correct to apply the name "God." Scripture made it impossible, of course, to deny Christ at least some ascription of divinity, and equally difficult entirely to reject the divinity of the Spirit; but it was by no means clear to all that the three divine Persons should be understood as co-equally, co-eternally, or "co-essentially" one and the same God. Hence, the most appealing, intellectually sophisticated, and plausible fourth century alternative to what would become Nicene orthodoxy was some variant of "subordinationism": that is, the school of thought (especially well established in the great city of Alexandria) that saw the Son and Spirit as derivative and lesser emanations of the Godhead of the Father, "economically" reduced versions of God mediating between the transcendence of the Father, dwelling in light inaccessible, and the darkness of this material world.

This was a version of what is sometimes called the "pleonastic fallacy," which pervaded almost every school of Alexandrian thought: the fallacy that — if there is an infinite qualitative distance between the ultimate principle of all reality and the world of "unlikeness" here below — then it is necessary to posit a certain number of intermediate principles or "hypostases" in the interval between the two in order to bridge that distance. The most speculatively accomplished forms of this fallacy were to be found among the Neoplatonists, and the most barbarous, fabulous, and risible among the various "Gnostics." But, among Christian thinkers, the most consistent and austere form of this subordinationism was to be found among the "Arians," who were so intent upon preserving a proper sense of the Father's transcendence that they were moved to assert that the Son was a creature — the highest and most godlike of creatures, of course, worthy even of being called "God" honorifically, the Great High Priest of heaven who leads all intellectual creation in its worship of the unknowable Father, but a creature for all that.

There would be no purpose in rehearsing here the long history of the Arian controversy and its sequelae. What is important in this context is that the dogmatic discords of the fourth century forced theologians to examine perhaps more deeply than ever before (or, at least, more explicitly) the governing logic of the Church's immemorial Trinitarian diction. The greatest achievements of this period in defense of Nicene orthodoxy were those of the so-called Cappadocian fathers: Basil of Caesarea, Basil's younger brother Gregory of Nyssa, and Basil's friend Gregory of Nazianzus. These three, in the course of their disputes with the "Eunomians" — the intellectual heirs of the Arians — grasped with a special urgency that a proper attention to biblical language regarding Father, Son, and Spirit — and, most particularly, regarding the story of our salvation in Christ — makes a subordinationist construal of that language impossible. I am afraid I simplify their arguments rather brutally in phrasing the matter thus, but the essence of their position — quite incontrovertible to my mind — was that, if the Son and Spirit are not God in the same sense as the Father, we cannot be saved.

It must be appreciated, I hasten to add, that "salvation" was not understood by the Cappadocian fathers in that rather feeble and formal way many Christians have habitually thought of it at various periods in the Church's history: as some sort of forensic exculpation or official exoneration accompanied by a ticket of entry into an Elysian aftermath of sun-soaked meadows and old friends and consummate natural beatitude. Rather, salvation meant nothing less than being joined to the living God by the mediation of the God-man himself, brought into living contact with the transfiguring glory of the divine nature, made indeed partakers of the divine nature itself (2 Pet. 1:4) and co-heirs of the Kingdom of God; in short, to be saved was — is — to be "divinized" in Christ by the Spirit. In the great formula of St Athanasius (and others), "God became man that man might become god."

It is precisely here, therefore, in the economy of salvation, that the true nature of the eternal Trinity must declare itself: for, simply said, no creature could ever join us to God. The calculus of the infinite is absolute: the finite can never reach the infinite, the created can never aspire to its transcendent source, and nothing — no economically reduced manifestation of the Godhead, no "ontological pleonasm" of mediating principles, no conceptual Tower of Babel erected upon the foundations of the human spirit — can unite us with God save that God in his mercy condescend to unite us to himself, by becoming one of us. If the Son saves us by joining us to the Father, then the Son must necessarily be, in every sense, God of God, essentially and infinitely. But, then again, how are we joined to the Son? By the Holy Spirit — in the sacraments and corporate life of the Church and in his sanctifying work within the soul — and so the Spirit too, it follows, must be God of God, no less than the Son. Only God can join us to God, and so we must affirm that in the incarnation of the Son and actions of the Spirit God himself is in our midst; or rather, more wonderfully, we are in the midst of God, and the movement of relation among the three divine Persons, as it is unfolded through salvation history, is nothing less than the triune God drawing us into the infinite splendor of his life.

Again, I oversimplify in many ways; but what I want to emphasize here is that Trinitarian doctrine is not merely an abstract metaphysics forcibly imposed from above upon the more spontaneous and vital experiences of the Church (though it most certainly requires and gives shape to a number of profound metaphysical conclusions); it is first and foremost a "phenomenology of salvation," a theoretical articulation of the Church's experience of being made one in Christ with God himself. It would not be too much to say, in fact, that this is the central and guiding maxim of all Christian dogmatics, which was enunciated in the twentieth century, with admirable clarity, by Karl Rahner: the "economic" Trinity (that is, God in the history of salvation) is the "immanent" Trinity (that is, God in himself) and the "immanent" Trinity is the "economic" Trinity. In witnessing the drama of redemption, we are seeing nothing less than the triune God's revelation of his eternal life within time; and so, in that drama, we may discern (within the limits of our created intellects) who God is.

This, at last, brings me back to Jenson, for it is Jenson's special distinction to have pursued the logic of this equation — at least, along a very particular path — more relentlessly than almost any other American theologian, in a way at once faithful to and (frankly) defiant of classical Christian language. Traditionally, even in implicitly acknowledging the necessary identity of the economic Trinity and immanent Trinity, Christian theology has striven to preserve a strict and inviolable "analogical interval" between the two: that is to say, it has always asserted that what happens in the story of salvation is a perfect *expression* (or dramatic *revelation*) of how it is with God in his timeless eternity, and how it would be even were there no creatures at all, but between that temporal expression and its eternal source there is a relation of grace. God is not affected by time, his eternal identity knows neither before nor after, and the incarnation of the Logos is in no sense necessary to or determinative of that identity. Jenson, however, falls within a school of modern, predominantly Protestant thought that chooses to collapse this analogical interval, and to assert that the event of our salvation in Christ and the event of God's life as Trinity are simply one and the same; what occurs in Jesus of Nazareth is in some sense the story of God becoming the God he is, within which story we are also included — for love's sake.

THE FIRST and most enormous consequence of the course of reflection Jenson takes — a consequence he exuberantly embraces — is that he must reject many of the classical perfections ascribed to God, at least as they have traditionally been understood. For instance, the venerable teaching that God is, in his nature, impassible — that is, immune to suffering and change — Jenson all but absolutely abjures. More to the point, the very definition of God's eternity as "timeless" Jenson regards as unbiblical and incompatible with the story of creation and redemption. God's eternity, he claims, is intrinsically temporal, however much that temporality may transcend the fragmentary successiveness by which the days of creatures are measured; God possesses a past, present, and future, though in his infinity he possesses all of these in perfect fullness. The Father, for Jenson, is the whence of the divine life, the Spirit the whither, and the Son the present in which the divine past and divine future hold together in one life and identity.

Moreover, God's "present" is not something that can be abstracted from the particular historical identity of Jesus of Nazareth. Here is where Jenson's thought is perhaps most radical, and most in accord with one very pronounced extreme within modern Protestant dogmatics; for, in his theology, it is as the man Jesus — and in no other fashion — that Christ is the eternal Son and Word of the Father. There is no *"Logos asarkos"* for Jenson — that is, no timeless and "fleshless" Word of God; rather, God the Father has decided from all eternity to determine himself in this man as his Son, to make Jesus the object of his perfect attention and complete preoccupation, and thereby to determine himself as the Father of this Son. As the unique object of the Father's absolute concern (to phrase the matter differently), the man Jesus "stays" the consciousness of the Father and gives it the shape that it has. The eternity of the Son, therefore, begins in the eternal presupposition of Jesus in the infinity of God's choice, and the pre-existence of the Son in a pattern of movement within salvation history towards the arrival of this "incarnation."

Who God is, therefore, subsists in the Father's loving concern for the Son and the Son's loving obedience to the Father, and in the freedom of the Spirit who — as unending divine futurity — makes this relation eternal. In Jenson's rather daring formulation, the Spirit "frees" the Father and the Son for the adventure of this love, and for the infinite possibility that is this love's perfection. As for us, our place in this drama is that of the companions of the Son; we are included in the story of God's freedom because Christ is the man who is for all men, and so for the Father to have Christ as his Son he must have us as well; for there is no Son apart from him who said "Father, forgive them." And thus we are taken up into the one story of God's infinite love, in which all our particular and shared stories — insofar as they are true stories — live, and move, and have their being.

Another implication of this line of thought, from which Jenson does not shrink, is that not only does God overcome death for us in the death and resurrection of Christ, by virtue of his transcendence; he in fact overcomes death *for himself*, indeed constitutes himself *as* transcendent of death by way of his confrontation with death upon the cross and his triumph over death at Easter. Which is also to say that — inasmuch as God has eternally decided to determine his identity in this man — God has eternally elected the world of sin, death, and the devil "alongside" his election of the Son, as the context in which the drama of triune love must be played out. That is to say, even the fallenness of our world falls within the story of God's life as Trinity, but only insofar as that fallenness is overcome by God in Christ. There is sin only that we might be saved, for it is as the God who saves that the Father determines himself in his Son, and raises the Son by the Spirit, and draws us into that mystery. The triune "event" that God is, then, involves the cross of Christ not as something incidental or subsidiary, but as (so to speak) its axis: the moment in which the Father's love for the Son and the Son's obedience to the Father arrive at their crisis, and in which the Spirit lifts up that love and obedience into an eternal living future.

How, though, one might justly wonder, does such thinking accord with traditional understandings not only of God's transcendence, but of the Person and nature of Christ? After all, if indeed Athanasius's formula is correct (and it most certainly is), how can the man Jesus — as a man — be the unique instance of a perfect union between divine and human natures in a single Person, through whom we are admitted to a share in divinity? And how can the consent of Jesus' human will to the obedience of the divine will within him serve to reconcile humanity with God? How can the divine and human wills be said to subsist together in his one Person if it is only as the man Jesus that he is the Son of the Father? But, again, Jenson's central claim is that God *is* the event of what happens between the Father and Jesus, as enabled by and lifted up in the Spirit; and so it is the human Jesus who is the second Person of the Trinity, and the human will within Jesus that *is* the divine will of the Son. Hence, the perfect human love of Christ for the Father, and his perfect assent to the Father's will, is also the salvific divine decision that sets all of us free, and the one great High Priestly act whereby the Son hands all of us over — in our corporate nature — to the Father's love.

SUMMARY IS USUALLY invidious. I cannot really provide any glimpse of the subtleties of Jenson's arguments here, nor can I sketch in many of the more beguiling details of his exposition, nor certainly can I convey any sense of the biblical sweep of his narrative. For all I know, I have merely compounded my earlier malfeasances by attempting to force Jenson's thought into so narrow a frame, and readers of a particularly traditionalist temperament might wonder what makes his work of interest to me.

Let me state flatly that I write neither as a disciple of Jenson's, nor as a "Jensonian," nor even as his theological ally. To be perfectly candid, there is scarcely any aspect of the theological story I have just told with which I am not in profound disagreement — for reasons I believe to be at once biblical, doctrinal, philosophical, and historical. I find it impossible to do without the "analogical interval" between God's immanent life and economic revelation, I deny the identity of divine and human will in Christ, and I insist upon the necessity of affirming the *Logos asarkos;* Jenson's interpretations of many of the Church fathers — the Cappadocians, Augustine, Cyril of Alexandria, Maximus the Confessor — differ from my own radically; I regard it as logically impossible to attribute actual temporality of any kind to God's eternity, and indeed would argue that it was Christian philosophy (not pagan Greek thought) that first enucleated a perfectly coherent account of God's transcendence of temporal succession; and I believe that the classical perfections traditionally ascribed to God — simplicity, timelessness, and above all impassibility — are vital not only to a rationally coherent description of the Christian faith, but to a consistent interpretation of scripture, and indeed to the very essence of the gospel.

None of this I can argue here; but, in acknowledging the range of my differences with Jenson, I think I give myself license to declare something like perfect disinterest in the claims I wish to make on his behalf. My profession of interest in his work is not some devious and elliptical path back towards praise of my own, nor in celebrating him am I merely using him as a mirror in which to admire myself. I praise him simply as the most provocative, original, and challenging proponent in America of an approach to Trinitarian theology to which I am implacably averse. More to the point, I praise him for enunciating a Trinitarian theology with whose biblical *shape* — I mean specifically his reading of scripture as Trinitarian throughout — it is difficult to take issue. Indeed, in contemplating that shape in all its various contours, I am conscious that, were it not for the absence of that aforementioned "analogical interval," Jenson's theology might appear to me impeccably sound. And yet that interval remains absent: it is a small difference; it is an immense difference; and it is a difference that cannot be negotiated away, mediated in some third term, or reconciled.

I cannot deny, however, that there is something of an historical fatedness in this irreconcilability; and this is a chastening thought.

Jenson most definitely comes from that Protestant tradition that has long deplored the (no doubt historically necessary) alliance struck between the theology of the early Church and "Hellenism" or (to be more precise) "Platonism." I, on the other hand, as a proud scion of this alliance, am predisposed to view that aspect of Protestant tradition as misguided and destructive: I regard what many call "Hellenism" as already an intrinsic dimension of the New Testament, some form of "Platonism" as inseparable from the Christian faith, the development of Christian metaphysics over the millennium and a half leading to the Reformation as perfectly in keeping with the testimony of scripture, and "Hellenized" Christianity as the special work of the Holy Spirit — with which no baptized Christian may safely break. Hence my great regret is the alliance struck in much modern dogmatics between theology and what I can only call "Teutonism" or (to be more precise) German idealism.

Here, however, I must tread cautiously. There was among theologians a great revival of interest in Trinitarian theology during the latter half of the twentieth century, but it tended to fall into two distinct camps: those who sought to rearticulate the doctrine of the Trinity by way of a full return to the patristic and mediaeval sources of the tradition, and those who did so directly in response to — and so largely in the terms of — the "Trinitarian" metaphysics of Hegel and others. It is with this latter camp that one tends to associate that collapse of the analogical interval that I have so roundly lamented to this point; and it had been my habit for some time to read Jenson merely as a representative of the German idealist tendency in modern dogmatics — and as a disciple specifically of the greatest of the German idealists, Friedrich Wilhelm Joseph von Schelling (1775-1854), in his early phase — until someone of considerable authority on the matter (Jenson himself, to be exact) informed me that Schelling's thought had had no appreciable influence on Jenson's at all.

Nevertheless, I find it hard not to place Jenson in that company, if for no other reason than that he is willing to speak of God becoming the God he is, determining himself in time, *choosing* to be *this* God — the Father of Jesus of Nazareth — and doing so in an irreducibly temporal fashion. If nothing else, in reading Jenson I often find myself suffering from the same apprehensions inspired in me by other, more indisputably "Teutonized" theologians, and find myself also compelled to raise certain very classical objections to what I am reading: Does it make sense, ultimately, to speak of God both as the source of all being and yet as *becoming* the God he is? Can temporality be intelligibly ascribed to God without one's theology lapsing into contradiction? What of the moral nature of God, if he must elect sin, death, and evil as the context of his self-determination in time? If it is true that, in order for God to transcend death, he must triumph over it in time, is death then an independent reality over against God?

Perhaps most crucially, what could it mean to speak of God determining himself, of choosing to be the God he is? Could he choose otherwise? Is there — as classical Christian thought has always denied there is — "possibility" in God, potential that must be realized? How then could he be the infinite source of all actuality, from which everything draws its being? I know that I am flinging these questions out with such haste, and in so abridged a form, that their substance is all but invisible. But I must insist that there are many very sound reasons why the Church has long maintained that this sort of deliberative choice — this sort of arbitrary power of decision — would be an imperfection in the divine nature, a mark of finitude, in fact a limitation upon the divine freedom. God *is* God, and the infinite eternal actuality of this "is" — unbounded by any outward necessity, never needing to become what it is, undimmed by possibility, undivided by succession — is absolute freedom. And so it must surely be degrading to the divine majesty, many would say, to speak of God *choosing* to be the God he is.

And yet precisely here, I find, the biblical shape of Jenson's theology makes me poignantly conscious of the metaphoric limitations that encumber all the words we attempt to use of God, and of how quickly our terms can disintegrate into incoherence when we attempt to press them past a very rudimentary level of signification. When Jenson speaks of divine temporality, he manifestly does not mean to suggest that God experiences time as we do: as loss, as the possibility of things that may never come, as always fragmentary and haunted by disappointments and vain longings, as a future never yet possessed and only dimly imagined, as a present forever slipping away into oblivion, as a past mourned or regretted. Nor certainly, I am sure, does he speak of God's decision to be *this* God intending us to understand that decision in a human way. For us, after all, decision is always preceded by some kind of indecision, and no decision can be reached that is not in some sense the arbitrary selection of possibilities confronting us from outside ourselves. I may find the language of "choice" unsatisfactory, but when I read Jenson I cannot help but acknowledge that the mere denial of "choice" within God is no less inadequate to the truth I want to describe. For in saying that God's nature suffers no constraints, I want also to urge that God is not passively or indifferently the God he is, and that his will abides in perfect freedom. And to speak of this mystery, no language really suffices.

MY PRINCIPAL REASON, however, for thinking Jenson's work important for serious theologians, or even just for reflective Christians who have had the good sense not to become theologians, has to do with the single great Christian mystery from which all theology arises: the mystery of the Person of Christ. For numerous reasons (which I regret I cannot enumerate here), it is absolutely essential to theology that there is nothing arbitrary or accidental in the relation of the identity of Jesus of Nazareth to that of the eternal Logos. Jesus is not an avatar of the Logos, a mask the Son assumes in a transient or extrinsic fashion, or a part he plays in some grand cosmic charade. When God becomes man, this is the man he becomes — and there can be no other. That is why it is silly to ask the questions that bad theologians, or casual catechists, or well-meaning Sunday School teachers have sometimes felt moved to ask: whether the Son might have been incarnate as someone else — as a Viking, or a Nigerian, or a woman, or simply another first-century Jew. The Logos, when he divests himself of his divine glory, is this man; between this finite historical individual and the eternal and infinite Son of God, there is no caesura. Jesus is not a manifestation of the Son, but the Son in his only true human form.

It is an understanding of just this truth, I make bold to assert, that lies at the very heart of Jenson's theology, and that constitutes its secret motive power. Jenson's thought represents, to my mind, the most ambitious and unflagging attempt any American theologian has yet made fully to grasp the uniqueness of Christ — the one incommutable human identity of the incarnate God — which is no simple thing. When any theologian is daring enough to risk reflection upon this mystery, he is immediately immersed in all the other mysteries that must attend it: time and eternity, necessity and freedom, divine sovereignty and divine abasement — above all the mystery of where Christ's cry of dereliction on the cross ("My God, my God, why hast Thou forsaken me?") falls within the life of the Trinity. Jenson has never failed to struggle with any of these questions. True, all my convictions in this matter run counter to his: I think that only by affirming God's timelessness and the reality of the *Logos asarkos* can we truly say that the identity of Jesus of Nazareth is in no sense arbitrary, that God has not somehow chosen this one man out of an infinity of other possibilities. But I am also aware that the arguments Jenson would make to the contrary cannot simply be dismissed; they must be engaged directly.

In the end, as I have already more or less said, it is the entire shape of Jenson's narrative that remains compelling, as that narrative unfolds around the Person of Christ, whether one is ultimately persuaded by it or not. Here I can only direct the reader to Jenson's work: there (especially in his *Systematic Theology*) one will find an account of the triune God drawing nigh to us — and of us drawing nigh to him — an account of extraordinary imaginative richness, one that is (depending on one's temperament or intellectual affiliations) either seductive or scandalous, but one that is also impossible to forget. For myself, I can say only that I have returned often to his work, and found it an inexhaustible challenge to refine and clarify my own thought. And whenever I make that return, I cannot help but feel that, in a small way, the experience is rather like that of Jacob wrestling with God in his angel at the ford of Jabbok. No one of my theological persuasion, I think, who engages Jenson's thought in earnest can doubt that it is indeed the living God with whom he has come to grips therein: not some fabulous metaphysical phantom conjured out of Jenson's fixations or fantasies, but a genuine attempt to describe the God of scripture in the fullness of his historical presence and eternal identity; nor can he hope to retreat from that contest without a wound — or, for that matter, without a blessing.

19

Infinite Lit:
On William Lynch's Christ and Apollo

William Lynch, *Christ and Apollo: The Dimensions of the Literary Imagination* (ISI Books)

F ew American literary scholars could have known in 1960 — the year in which Fr. William Lynch's *Christ and Apollo* first appeared — that the reigning school of the "New Criticism" was entering into its twilight. The Eliotic rebellion against Romanticism and the consequent elevation of the Metaphysical Poets to canonical supremacy had become, by this point, simply an established orthodoxy, as yet untroubled by any serious agitations of counterrevolution. A high formalism — hostile to subjective affectivity, false transcendence, or empty enthusiasm — enjoyed all but unquestioned authority. Allen Tate was still in his caustic and devastating prime. Yet only eight years later, Jacques Derrida's notoriously oracular encomium on structuralism at Johns Hopkins would leave many of the younger denizens of American English departments hopelessly infatuated with movements in French postmodernism that they would possess neither the philosophical erudition to understand nor the good taste to despise. Soon American literary academe's quest for its holy grail — the "well-wrought urn" — would be abandoned in favor of more exciting (because somewhat more degenerate) critical pursuits.

This perhaps explains, at least in part, how it is that a book of such impressive originality as Lynch's should have fallen into obscurity so soon after its publication, and should have languished in near oblivion for at least three decades. Admired as it once was, it was too much a part of a fading moment in intellectual history. Not to say that Lynch was a slave of his time. True, he (like the New Critics) harbored a wholesomely robust distaste for tendentious schools of literary criticism devoted to questions of ideological or social "relevancy," but he was also impatient with the desire of many of his contemporaries to seal off the literary artifact so jealously against the contamination of any concern beyond itself as to reduce the literary act itself to a kind of exquisite and intricate autism. Still, where Lynch diverged from the critical dogmas of his day, he was not, it seems, "precocious": his book contained no hint of an interest in "transgression," expressed no loathing for "patriarchy" or "phallogocentrism," evinced no concern for "post-colonial" consciousness, betrayed no anxiety regarding "the absence of the signified"; "queer theory," "eco-feminism," "post-globalist Marxism" — none of this was even so much as foreshadowed in its pages. His was, in short, a reactionary text.

Therein, of course, lies its charm: *Christ and Apollo* is a remarkably coherent — if eccentric — attempt to address the critical concerns of its day by way of a retreat to perhaps the most conceptually sophisticated "formalism" of all: the classical Christian metaphysics of the transcendental perfections of truth, goodness, beauty, and (above all) being. Lynch was, after all, not only a literary scholar, but a philosopher and theologian of some considerable erudition; and, as such, his inclination was to approach literature not simply as an object of aesthetic concern, nor even more broadly as a matter of general culture, but as a particular path to a truer vision of humanity, creation, and God.

LIKE ALLEN TATE, Lynch felt a special aversion to any art that too obviously presumes the vantage of the "angelic intellect" — that is, an intellect capable of an immediate intuition of the essences of things, without any passage through empirical experience or any conversion of that experience into knowledge by way of the imagination. Meaning is won through the concrete — at least for us mortals — or it is a meaning either false or vapid. This is in a sense the single "large claim" animating Lynch's project, and it is for this reason that the first half of *Christ and Apollo* is taken up with an indictment of various tendencies within modern literature towards a kind of irrepressible abstraction (albeit an abstraction often veiled behind a counterfeit realism). Lynch's model of the creative act is entirely theological, and is in fact specifically conformed to the doctrine of Christ's incarnation. It is in this doctrine, Lynch believes, that Western consciousness' unique attention to particularity — the particularity of time, of flesh, of personality — finds its highest rationale, and that the way to true beauty and wisdom (*through* limitation and finitude) is laid open. It was in the broken particularity of Christ's humanity — a humanity plumbed to its uttermost depths — that the nature of his divinity was revealed. And, in light of this belief, Lynch concludes that the highest literary accomplishments are the result of an imagination that, by suffering the probation of the particular, arrives at a "universality" richer than any that mere abstraction could provide.

This is the meaning, as it happens, of the title of Lynch's book. His Apollo is not the god of myth so much as Nietzsche's Apollo in *The Birth of Tragedy:* the god of the dream image, of lovely and mesmerizing spectacle, of timeless and serene proportion, whose chief function is to master the creative and destructive energy of Dionysus — of life and death, that is — and convert it into enchanting artifice. "I take even the symbol of Apollo," writes Lynch, "as a kind of infinite dream over against Christ, who was full of definiteness and actuality. . . . [L]et Apollo stand for . . . that kind of fantasy beauty which is a sort of infinite, which is easily gotten everywhere, but which will not abide the straitened gates of limitation that leads to stronger beauty." The world of the finite, argues Lynch, should never be treated simply as a land of magical symbols, where the author briefly sojourns before springing up into the "infinite" or retreating into a private realm of personal sensibility (Proust is singled out for special censure on this point). Nor should it be treated — in dialectical fashion — merely as a universe of horror, nausea, absurdity, or ennui, and so as the occasion either of flight to the "real world" of heaven (as in the theology of Karl Barth) or of hopeless but heroic existential authenticity (as in the work of Camus). Most importantly, says Lynch, the writer must never seek to escape from the constraints of time into a world of pure ideas, affect, or vision. It is by the hard way of time only ("Christic temporality," as Lynch calls it) that the fruit of finitude (the "fullness of time") is to be reaped. It is for this reason that much of modern tragedy — with its cheap triumphalism, false sublimities, and obstreperous humanist optimism — earns Lynch's special contempt.

IN THE SECOND HALF of *Christ and Apollo,* Lynch attempts to set his critical philosophy upon a metaphysical foundation, and this he does by resorting to the theological language of the *analogia entis* or "analogy of being." One must say, however, that he rather too quickly presumes (and this, surely, is another cause of the book's meager posterity) that his terms will be recognizable to his readers (which is a very great deal to presume indeed). So here — to risk a trying descent into the abstruse — some elucidation is probably necessary.

To begin with, as a purely philosophical question, the issue of "analogy" concerns the power of a single predicate to refer to two different realities without being reduced to a single meaning (which would make its usage "univocal") or divided into two utterly different meanings (which would make its usage "equivocal"). For instance, one might describe a river's tributary or a journalist's informant as a "source," not because the word has exactly the same acceptation in either case, but because there is a certain discernible "proportion" (which is what "analogy" properly means) between the two cases that holds the predicate together. The "analogy of being," then, concerns first the application of the word "being" to both God and creatures: how can *this* word be used both of finite temporal reality and infinite eternal reality without its meaning disintegrating into complete equivocity? One traditional way of framing an answer is to say that in God "essence" (*what* he is) and "existence" (*that* he is) are the same — one infinite and simple "subsistent act of being." For us, however, what we are in no way naturally implies that we must be, for existence is graciously superadded to our essence by our creator, and even our essence is not our own: it is given to us by God, and we possess it always only in part, as we pass through time, becoming what we are always by losing what we have been. This yields one very delightful consequence. If it is the wholly fortuitous synthesis of essence and existence within us, in becoming, that constitutes our analogy to the perfect identity of essence and existence in God, in its eternal changelessness, then the more we become the particular beings that we are, the more we show forth (precisely through our "infinite difference" from God) the being of God. It is our very particularity — in all the richness and poverty of its limited existence — that is also our universality.

Why, though, does Lynch need to resort to this particular metaphysical grammar? Because, in his view, the great failure of much of modern literature often lies in its implicit rejection of the principle of analogy, and its consequent subjugation to either the univocal or the equivocal imagination. The former is that of the passionate idealist or apostle of pity or merciless social engineer, who sees truth as lying only in some single grand abstraction, in service of which all the uniqueness and difference of the particular is reduced to allegory or instrumental detail. The latter is that of the tedious and solipsistic absurdist, for whom nothing means anything beyond itself, and for whom then only an art of pure suddenness, arbitrariness, and spontaneity can correspond to the private hell from which it issues. Only the truly analogical imagination, Lynch believes, can hold the same and the different together in a single creative act able to reach the universal by way of the particular and to illuminate the particular through the universal.

COMING TO *Christ and Apollo* forty-five years after its debut, one cannot help but be impressed by Lynch's prescience. In many ways, of course, the book is an artifact of its age and deals with artists from whose influence, in many cases, time has mercifully delivered us. (Did anyone ever really take Archibald MacLeish seriously? Why, for God's sake?) But more striking is how prophetically this book adumbrates and inveighs against the very critical movements that would soon emerge in academia. For, indeed, the new orthodoxy consists quite explicitly in an intellectually inept but still triumphalist rejection of analogy. One need only note how enthusiastically the formula of the philosopher Gilles Deleuze — "the univocity of being, the equivocity of beings" (i.e., the meaningless sameness of existence, the meaningless difference of things) — has been embraced by literary scholars to grasp this.

That said, it is a flawed book. At times, its insistence upon "limitation" becomes doctrinaire and somewhat silly. While reading it, I could not help but sense (especially in the supplemental chapters) that I was being told that I had no choice but to prefer not only the character, but the art, of Mauriac to that of Proust; and this, alas, I am unable to do. In fact, I would feel very suspicious of anyone who could, though I will gladly grant that Mauriac was certainly the more adept purveyor of "limitation" (in every sense). Too often Lynch fails to grasp that, as much as knowledge of the universal is to be gained through the particular, the reverse is always also true. Moreover, how an artist goes about negotiating this circle of knowledge is not something one should be too eager to prescribe. It would be perfectly possible for a dissenting critic to argue that when Proust (or, say, Nabokov) attempts to gather up the moments of experience into a coherent pattern of sensibility or symbolism, this is not merely an aesthete's recreation from the real or a flight to the timeless, but is also an attempt to glimpse time *sub specie aeternitatis,* indeed to recognize eternity *within* becoming without abandoning the particular. The theologian may, of course, take exception to the understanding of eternity thus produced; but the critic has no grounds by which to indict the novelist of inattention to the real. And no artist should care a whit whether his practice accords with the expectations of either theologians or critics (two of the more insignificant classes of men).

Nonetheless, all that said, Lynch's book remains a fascinating work, original and audacious in argument, penetrating in critique, and rigorous in its speculative architecture. ISI is to be commended for rescuing it from its archival exile. And who knows? Now that the epoch of postmodern literary criticism is *(Deo gratias)* entering into its own twilight, the time for the reappropriation of Lynch's *magnum opus* has finally arrived.

20

Theology as Knowledge

On a great number of points, James Stoner's argument is obviously right. Certainly the long, inglorious, forced retreat of religious reasoning from the commanding heights of civic and legal culture has been, at the very least, *hastened* by the displacement of theology from the center of the modern university's curriculum. Once, in an age now rapidly receding into legend, theology enjoyed the status not merely of a science, but of the "queen of sciences," whose special preoccupation with the highest things — God, being, the soul, the virtues, the transcendentals, metaphysics — invested her with the privilege of legitimating, inspiring, and unifying all those lesser disciplines over which she exercised her benevolent rule. Now, though, her estate is very much diminished. In most private institutions of higher learning, she may be tolerated, but is rarely invited to dine at the high table, and on more resplendent occasions is not encouraged to show herself. She has become something of a shabby and demented elderly relative, relegated to an attic apartment: the family may still grant her shelter, but only with considerable embarrassment.

As for Stoner's larger question, however — whether theology might once again be recognized as a genuine kind of knowledge, and readmitted into full society with the humane sciences on those terms — it shows how astutely he has identified the present condition of academic theology, and it is undoubtedly, in some sense, the *correct* question to ask; but, to be frank, it is also a question rather along the same lines as asking whether Arthur might soon return from Avalon to rescue Britain from the European Union. No — the answer seems fairly certain — in all likelihood not. The majority of the faculty of most modern universities, one can safely say, would regard the claim that theology constitutes some kind of "science" as absurd and rather presumptuous. Religion, after all (and as *everyone* knows), is a realm of purely *personal* conviction (isn't it?) sustained by faith, which is (as everyone also knows) an entirely irrational movement of the will, an indistinct impulse of saccharine sentiment, pathetic longing, childish credulity, and vague intuition. And theology, being the special language of religion, is by definition a collection of vacuous assertions, zealous exhortations, and beguiling fables; it is the curious *patois* peculiar to a certain private fixation or tribal allegiance, of interest perhaps to the psychopathologist or anthropologist, but of no greater scientific value than that; surely it has no proper field of study of its own, no real object to investigate, and whatever rules it obeys must be essentially arbitrary.

From a purely scholarly point of view, of course, such prejudices are simply tiresome and silly. After all, theology is — if scrupulously pursued — a complex and pitilessly demanding discipline concerning an immense, profoundly sophisticated legacy of hermeneutics, dialectics, and logic; it deals in minute detail with a vast variety of concrete historical data; over the centuries, it has incubated speculative systems of extraordinary rigor and intricacy, many of whose questions and methods continue to inform contemporary philosophy; and it does, when all is said and done, constitute the single intellectual, moral, spiritual, and cultural tradition uniting the classical, mediaeval, and early modern worlds. Even if one entirely avoids considering what metaphysical content one should attach to the word "God," one can still plausibly argue that theology is no more lacking in a substantial field of inquiry than are history, philosophy, the study of literature, or any of the other genuinely respectable human sciences; and that neither is its object of study anywhere near so chimerical, nor are its rules anywhere near so impressionistic, as are those proper to certain of the fields more recently admitted to the humanities.

It is perhaps worth considering, moreover, that theology requires a far greater scholarly range than does any other humane science. The properly trained Christian theologian, perfectly in command of his materials, should be a proficient linguist, with a mastery of several ancient and modern tongues, should have a complete formation in the subtleties of the whole Christian dogmatic tradition, should possess a considerable knowledge of the texts and arguments produced in every period of the Church, should be a good historian, should be thoroughly trained in philosophy, ancient, mediaeval, and modern, should have a fairly broad grasp of liturgical practice in every culture and age of the Christian world, should (ideally) possess considerable knowledge of literature, music, and the plastic arts, should have an intelligent interest in the effects of theological discourse in areas such as law or economics, and so on and so forth. This is not to say that one cannot practice theology without all these attainments; but such an education remains the scholarly ideal of the guild.

And, of course, as Stoner rightly notes, the absence or near-absence of theology from the general curriculum of students in other disciplines has done incalculable harm to their ability to understand their own fields. This is perhaps especially — or at least most obviously — true in the case of literary studies; but, in fact, it would be hard to name any genuine academic discipline outside the hard sciences or mathematics that can be mastered adequately without some degree of theological literacy. Certainly students of the arts, history, law, political theory, philosophy, and classics can possess only a partial command of their fields without any knowledge of Christian doctrine and practice. And any scholar in the least concerned for the history of ideas — or, more broadly, in the genealogy of culture — can scarcely begin fully to understand certain aspects of our modern concepts of freedom, right, morality, truth, justice, and so on, without knowing something of, say, their provenance in a number of movements of late mediaeval scholasticism (and it is difficult to exaggerate the value of a proper appreciation of the historical contingency of accepted notions). All of this is susceptible of little or no doubt, I think; and, on these matters, Stoner's case is incontrovertible.

That said, I should like to venture two assertions that, if not contrary to Stoner's argument, at least cut across its grain. The first, simply enough, is that theology will never be restored in the modern university to anything like the status it once enjoyed, or even to the status of a particularly reputable form of knowledge. And the second is that it is not at all certain that theologians should wish it to be.

ONE OF THE guiding premises of Stoner's article is that the secularization of "the public square" is something of a historical accident, and that the progressive exclusion of religious reasoning from civil law was never historically necessary. At one level, this is true. In purely constitutional terms, the wall of separation between public institutions and faith has no legitimate basis, and the ever more invasive and dictatorial peremptoriness with which generations of dishonest or incompetent jurists have forced a boring institutional laicism upon every stratum of civil society, no matter how local, is a betrayal of the federal principle and an unconscionable violation of genuine republican liberties.

Nevertheless, modernity *is* secularization; it is, in its inmost essence, a project of detaching moral, legal, and governmental reasoning from any authority transcendent of the state or of the individual. It is the project of an ethics conformed not to divine justice, but to human "reason" and popular consensus; of a politics authorized not by divine ordinance, but by the absolute sovereignty of the nation state; and of a model of freedom based not on the perfection of human nature, but on the unconstrained liberty of individual will. And America is a *modern* nation — the first, indeed, explicitly to constitute itself without reference to any sacral institution of its authority (vague, ceremonial invocations of divine providence notwithstanding). The putative intentions of the founders aside, in a nation so formed nothing was more inevitable than a subtle, chronic antagonism between religious and state authority; and, to secure itself against any rival source of moral legitimacy, such a state could do no other than drive religious adherence ever farther away from the public realm into the private realm of "values" (where, of course, it is free to do what it likes). It scarcely constitutes a kind of fatalism, it seems to me, to acknowledge that, for all the enormous virtues of its constitution, and despite the piety of many of its citizens, America enjoys no miraculous immunity from the logic of modernity.

The "secular" order was born only a few centuries ago, making its first systematic appearance under the guise of a novel doctrine of "absolute monarchy" and of the total sovereignty of the state over its subjects or citizens. And it was an order born in blood: to free themselves from the lingering constraints of an old, moribund, now largely nominal system of political subsidiarity — with its plurality of powers, estates, spheres of competence, and obligations — the modern states of Europe were forced not only to subdue the Church within their territories (whether through concordats like those of Gallican France or state establishments like that of Tudor England), but to shatter the power of both the Church and the Habsburg Holy Roman Empire by waging what, to that point, were the most sanguinary wars ever fought upon European soil (wars that we are still — as a testament to the power of propaganda — in the habit of remembering simply as "wars of religion"). In the wake of the final triumph of the modern centralized state, and of the breaking of the Church, followed a protracted period of wars, revolutions, tyrannies, and attempted genocides that spilled oceans of blood and that, for rather obscure reasons, we are supposed to think morally superior to the age of "religious intolerance." And so we are all now the beneficiaries of "enlightened" secular governance and its special achievements: the absolute state and total war (and, of course, a universal right to legal abortion).

Which brings me to my second claim. When I say that it is not obvious to me that theologians should desire the restoration of their discipline within the modern university, it is not because I believe in a wall of separation, or because I am some sort of Christian separatist who believes the Church should never have had any relations with kings and princes (though perhaps it should not have done). Rather, it is because I find it impossible to grant that the modern secular state is anything other than a wicked and murderous perversion of social order. This is not to say that the time has come for theologians simply to sound their mournful recessional, furl up their pennons and gonfalons, and withdraw from the stage of history; it is worth noting, though, that inasmuch as it was on the terms decided by the secularized university that theology was driven out from the inner chambers of the curriculum, only on those same terms would it be admitted back. This is obvious even from the somewhat disappointingly bland conclusion of Stoner's argument, with its theologically suspect invocation of providence and its exhortation to a Christian appreciation of the pluralism of the modern university. Christians should embrace and celebrate truth wherever they find it, undoubtedly; but it is not natural to theology that it should function as one discipline among others, attempting to make its "contribution" to some larger conversation; as soon as it consents to become a "perspective" among the human sciences, rather than the final cause and consummation of all paths of knowledge, it has ceased to be theology and has become precisely what its detractors have long suspected it of being: willful opinion, emotion, and cant.

I confess, I am being intentionally extreme; and what practical implications follow from my remarks I really do not know. What I fear, however, is that theology would — as a more generally accepted form of academic knowledge — be required to give its parole, and that the price of its recognition by the post-Christian university would be its reciprocal recognition of the secular order. Given those terms, ignominious exile might be preferable to repatriation on sufferance. The academic margins might be a more hospitable and healthy climate just at the moment; the desert, after all, has often proved the most fertile garden of the spirit; and it may be that a vocation to theology and the ethos of the academy are — for the time being, at least — essentially inimical.

21

*On the Trail of the Snark
with Daniel Dennett*

Lewis Carroll, surely, was the supreme poet of the Voice of Authority — or of, rather, the authoritative *tone* of voice, which is, as often as not, entirely unrelated to any actual *authority* on the speaker's part. No other writer ever captured its special cadences and inflections with such delicate care, or reproduced them with such loving fidelity. It runs like a variable theme through all his books, migrating from character to character, and passing through all conceivable modulations — pomposity, severity, pedantry, didacticism, imperiousness, sophistry, abstraction — as it goes. It is probably most persistently audible in the Alice books: one hears it in the White Rabbit, the Mouse, the Caterpillar, the Duchess, the Queen of Hearts, the King of Hearts (in his capacity as judge), the Mad Hatter, the Mock Turtle, the Red Queen, Humpty Dumpty, and others. And, in the Sylvie and Bruno novels, there are the Lord Chancellor, the Professor, the Other Professor, Mein Herr, the metaphysical young lady in spectacles, and so on.

Nowhere, though, does Carroll render the authoritative tone at a purer pitch than in England's great national epic, *The Hunting of the Snark*. It rings out with particular plangency, for instance, in the poem's second "fit," where the Bellman lectures his crew on the creature they have just crossed an ocean to find. There are, he tells his men, "five unmistakable marks" by which genuine Snarks may be known. First is the taste, "meagre and hollow, but crisp:/ Like a coat that is rather too tight in the waist,/ With a flavour of Will-o'-the wisp." Second is its "habit of getting up late," which is so pronounced that it frequently breakfasts at tea time and "dines on the following day." Third is "its slowness in taking a jest," evident in its sighs of distress when a joke is ventured and in the grave expression it assumes on hearing a pun. Fourth is its "fondness for bathing-machines," which it thinks improve the scenery. Fifth is ambition. Then, having enumerated the beast's most significant general traits, the Bellman proceeds to dilate upon its special variants:

> . . . It next will be right
> To describe each particular batch:
> Distinguishing those that have feathers, and bite,
> From those that have whiskers, and scratch.

He never completes his taxonomy, however. He begins to explain that, while most Snarks are quite harmless, some unfortunately are *Boojums,* but he is almost immediately forced to stop because, at the sound of that word, the Baker has fainted away in terror. One senses, though, that the Bellman could have continued indefinitely.

The delightful thing about these verses, obviously, is the way in which they mimic a certain style of exhaustive empirical exactitude while producing a conceptual result of utter vacuity; and, for this reason, they strike me as exquisitely germane to Daniel Dennett's most recent book, *Breaking the Spell: Religion as a Natural Phenomenon,* which was published earlier this year (and which, in fact, is my actual topic here). This, I hasten to add, is neither a frivolous nor a malicious remark. The Bellman — like almost all of Carroll's characters — is a rigorously, even remorselessly rational person, and is moreover a figure cast in a decidedly heroic mold. But, if one sets out in pursuit of beasts as fantastic, elusive, and protean as either Snarks or religion, one can proceed from only the vaguest idea of what one is looking for. So it is no great wonder that, in the special precision with which they define their respective quarries, in the quantity of farraginous detail they amass, in their insensibility to the incoherence of the portraits they have produced — in fact, in all things but felicity of expression — the Bellman and Dennett sound much alike.

For those who do not know, Dennett is a widely respected professor of philosophy at Tufts University, a co-director of the Center for Cognitive Studies (also at Tufts), and a self-avowed "Darwinian fundamentalist." That is to say, he is not merely a Darwinian; rather, he is a dogmatic materialist who believes that Darwin's and Wallace's discovery of natural selection provided us with a complete narrative of the origin and "essence" of all of reality, physical, biological, psychological, and cultural. And in *Breaking the Spell* he sets out to offer an evolutionary account — admittedly provisional in form — of human religion, to propose further "scientific" investigations of religion to be undertaken by competent researchers, and to suggest what forms of public policy we might wish, as a society, to adopt in regard to religion, once we have begun to acquire a proper understanding of its nature. It is, in short, Hume's project of a natural history of religion, embellished with haphazard lashings of modern evolutionary theory and embittered with draughts of dreary authoritarianism. When the book appeared, it provoked many indignant groans from the faithful and much exultant bellowing from the godless; but, honestly, both tribes might have been wiser to treat it with quiet indifference.

I confess that I have never been an admirer of Dennett's work. I have thought all of his large books — especially one entitled *Consciousness Explained* — poorly reasoned and almost comically inadequate in their approaches to the questions they address. Too often, it seems to me, he shows a preference for the cumulative argument over the cogent, and for repetition over demonstration. The Bellman's maxim, "What I tell you three times is true," is not alien to Dennett's method. He seems to work on the supposition that an assertion made with sufficient force and frequency is soon transformed, by some subtle alchemy, into a settled principle. And there are rather too many instances when Dennett seems either clumsily to miss or willfully to ignore pertinent objections to his views, and so races past them with a perfunctory wave in what he takes to be their general direction — though usually in another direction altogether. Consider, for example, this dialectical gem, plucked from his book *Darwin's Dangerous Idea:* "Perhaps the most misguided criticism of gene centrism is the frequently heard claim that genes simply cannot have interests. This . . . is flatly mistaken. . . . If a body politic, or General Motors, can have interests, so can genes." At moments like this, needless to say, one cannot help but feel that something vital has been overlooked.

Dennett's general method is often, I think it fair to say, rather reminiscent of the forensic technique employed by the Snark, in the Barrister's dream, to defend a pig charged with abandoning its sty: the Snark admits the desertion, but then immediately offers this as proof of the pig's alibi (for the creature was obviously absent from the scene of the crime at the time of its commission). Even among Dennett's detractors, however, my low opinion of his gifts places me in a distinct minority. So let me simply say that I came to *Breaking the Spell* with a fixed prejudice against its author. Even so, I was entirely unprepared for how exorbitantly bad an argument the book advances — so bad, in fact, that the truly fascinating question that it raised for me was how so many otherwise intelligent persons could have mistaken it for a coherent or serious philosophical proposition.

THE CATALOGUE of complaints that might be brought against *Breaking the Spell* is large, though no doubt many of these are trivial. The most irksome of the book's defects are Dennett's gratingly precious rhetorical tactics, such as his inept and transparent attempt, on the book's first page, to make his American readers feel like credulous provincials for not having adopted the European's lofty disdain for religion; or his use of the term "brights" to designate atheists and secularists of his stripe (which reminds one of nothing so much as the sort of names packs of "popular" teenage girls dream up for themselves in high school, but which also — in its favor — is so resplendently asinine a habit of speech that it has the enchanting effect of suggesting precisely the opposite of what Dennett intends). There are also the embarrassing moments of self-delusion, such as when Dennett, the merry "Darwinian fundamentalist," claims that atheists — unlike persons of faith — welcome the ceaseless objective examination of their convictions, or that philosophers are as a rule open to all ideas (which accords with no sane person's experience of either class of individuals). And then there is his silly tendency to feign mental decrepitude when it serves his purposes, as when he pretends that the very concept of God possesses too many variations for him to keep track of, or as when he acts scandalized by the revelation that academic theology sometimes lapses into a technical jargon full of obscure Greek terms like "apophatic" and "ontic." And there are those almost stirring moments when the magnificent and imposing peaks and promontories of his immeasurable historical ignorance swim into view, such as when he asserts that the early Christians regarded apostasy as a capital offense. And the prose is rebarbative. And the book is unpleasantly shapeless: it labors to begin and then tediously meanders to a drab and slightly delirious conclusion. And one can scarcely fail to notice the magnificent *non sequitur* that "unites" the first to the second half of the book — the "science" of the former, that is, to the prescriptions of the latter.

There is, moreover, the utter tone-deafness evident in Dennett's attempts to describe how persons of faith speak or think, or what they have been taught, or how they react to challenges to their convictions. He even invents an antagonist for himself whom he christens "Professor Faith," a sort of ventriloquist's doll that he compels to utter the sort of insipid bromides he imagines typical of the believer's native idiom. In fact, Dennett expends a surprising amount of energy debating, cajoling, insulting, "quoting," and taking umbrage at nonexistent persons. In the book's insufferably prolonged overture, he repeatedly tells his imaginary religious readers — in a tenderly hectoring tone, as if talking to small children or idiots — that they will probably not read his book to the end, that they may well think it immoral even to consider doing so, and that they are not courageous enough to entertain the doubts it will induce in them. Actually, there is nothing in the book that could possibly shake anyone's faith, and the only thing likely to dissuade religious readers from finishing it is its author's interminable proleptic effort to overcome their reluctance. But Dennett is convinced he is dealing with intransigent oafs, and his frustration at their inexplicably unbroken silence occasionally erupts into fury. "I for one am not in awe of your faith," he fulminates at one juncture; "I am appalled by your arrogance, by your unreasonable certainty that you have all the answers." And this demented apostrophe occurs on the fifty-first page of the book, at which point Dennett still has not commenced his argument in earnest.

I could go on, but these are all minor annoyances, really. The far profounder problem with *Breaking the Spell* is that, ultimately, it is a sublimely *pointless* book, for two quite uncomplicated reasons: first, it proposes a "science of religion" that is not a science at all, except in the most generously imprecise sense of the word; and, second, even if Dennett's theory of the phylogeny of religion could be shown to be largely correct, not only would it fail to challenge belief, it would in fact confirm an established tenet of Christian theology, and a view of "religion" already held by most developed traditions of faith.

THE PRINCIPAL WEAKNESS of Dennett's argument stems from his unfortunate reliance on certain metaphors, most particularly that of parasitism. For what Dennett most definitely does not wish to argue — as other, more "functionalist" evolutionary theorists of religion are wont to do — is that the intellectual and social artifacts of human culture have evolved solely on account of the benefits they confer upon us, or of the contribution they make to our survival. Though he believes that those natural faculties that render us *accidentally* susceptible to religious belief have certainly been bred into us on account of the evolutionary advantages they bestow, religion itself, he thinks, in its developed form, is something more on the order of a parasite whose only interest is its own propagation, even if that should involve the destruction of its host. This is the very heart of his case, since he wants at all costs to avoid giving the impression that religion is in any sense — even evolutionarily — good for us. And to achieve his end, he finds it necessary not only to employ, but to treat almost as an established scientific fact, the infinitely elastic and largely worthless concept of "memes."

"Memes," for those unfamiliar with them, were invented thirty years ago by Dennett's fellow Darwinian fundamentalist, the zoologist and fanatical atheist tractarian Richard Dawkins, in his immensely popular *The Selfish Gene.* This is not, I think it fair to say, an altogether logically consistent book, at least as regards human beings, inasmuch as it seems to argue simultaneously for and against a purely deterministic account of human behavior; and it is, to say the least, debatable whether the introduction of the notion of memes alleviates or aggravates this ambiguity. Whatever the case, though, here it is enough to know that memes are culturally transmitted ideas, habits, behaviors, motifs, styles, themes, turns of phrase, structures, tunes, fashions, patterns, and in fact just about any other items or aspects of our shared social world, all of which, like genes, "selfishly" seek to persist and replicate themselves. That is to say, to take the obvious example, if most human beings believe in God, this has nothing to do with any sort of rational interpretation of their experience of reality; nor is it even simply the influence of traditions that illuminate or confine their reasoning; rather, the meme for God has implanted itself in their minds and has replicated itself through adaptation, while successfully eliminating any number of rival "memetic" codes. We may like to think we believe because we have been "convinced" or "awakened" by — or that we have "chosen" or "discovered" — certain ideas or realities; but, in fact, our concepts and convictions are largely the phylogenic residue of a host of pre-conscious, invisible, immaterial agencies that have made our languages, cultures, and thoughts the vehicles by which they disseminate and perpetuate themselves.

This is, needless to say, a theory of absolutely preposterous pliancy, however momentarily beguiling it might be, and few philosophers apart from Dennett have shown any enthusiasm for it. Of course, human beings most definitely are shaped to some degree by received ideas and habits, and copy patterns of behavior, craft, and thought from one another, and alter and refine these patterns in so doing. But, since human beings are also possessed of reflective consciousness and deliberative will, memory and intention, curiosity and desire, talk of "memes" is an empty mystification; and the word's phonetic resemblance to "genes" is not quite enough to render it respectable. Meme language might provide Dennett a convenient excuse for not addressing the actual content of religious beliefs, and for concentrating his attention instead upon the "phenomenon" of religion as a cultural and linguistic "type"; but any ostensible science basing itself upon memetic theory is a science based, again, upon a metaphor — or, really, upon an assonance. Dennett, though, is as indefatigable as the Bellman's crew in his pursuit of that ghostly echo. He is desperate to confine his thinking to a strictly Darwinian model of human behavior, but just as desperate to portray religion as a kind of "cultural symbiont" that is more destructive than beneficial to the poor unsuspecting organisms it has colonized. And so memes, for want of more plausible parasites, are indispensable to his tale.

Dennett's actual narrative of the genesis of religion is the most diverting part of his book, if only because it is so winsomely *quasi una fantasia*. He begins by considering the evolutionary advantages of the "intentional stance" — the ability to recognize or presume agency in one's surroundings — and the very special advantages of language. From these he deduces the origins of primitive animism and the development of the earliest religious memes (such as the personification of natural forces). From there he attempts to imagine how these vague apprehensions of the supernatural mutated — by associating themselves with the tendency of children to exaggerate the powers of their parents — into the idea of omniscient and omnipotent ancestor gods, and also how this idea was subsequently fortified by the invention of divination. He hypothesizes that those early humans who were most susceptible to hypnotic suggestion and the "placebo effect" were better able to survive severe illnesses because the ministrations of shamans would be more likely to take effect with them; and it is perhaps this mesmeric gene that is responsible for that part of our brain that is especially hospitable to the god meme. He ponders also the development of those rituals by which religious memes scaffold themselves in more enduring social structures, and reflects upon the phenomena of mass hypnosis and mass hysteria, which help to explain how the contagion of religion spreads and sustains itself; he considers the transformation of folk religion into organized religion, especially as agriculture and urban society developed, as well as the kleptocratic alliances struck between organized religion and political power; and he contemplates the way in which religions deepen their complexity and mystery, and in which believers begin to take responsibilities for the memes that shape them by producing ever more sophisticated rationales for their beliefs and forming allegiances to those rationales. And he describes the way in which "belief in belief" — a desire to believe, or a sense that belief is good, rather than actual conviction — becomes one of the most effective ways by which religious memes render themselves immune to the antibodies of doubt. And so on and so forth. Near the end of these reflections, Dennett feels confident enough to assert that he has just successfully led his readers on a "nonmiraculous and matter-of-fact stroll" from the blind machinery of nature up to humanity's passionate fidelity to its most exalted ideas. He has not, obviously: his story is a matter not of facts but of conjectures and intuitions, strung together on tenuous strands of memetic theory; but it is as good a story as any.

Unfortunately, all evolutionary approaches to culture suffer from certain inherent problems. Evolutionary biology is a science that investigates chains of physical causation and the development of organic life, and these are *all* it can investigate with any certainty. The moment its principles are extended into areas to which they are not properly applicable, such as human culture, it begins to cross the line between the scientific and the speculative. This is fine, perhaps, so long as one is conscious from the first that one is proceeding in stochastic fashion and by analogy, and that one's conclusions will always be unable to command anyone's assent. When, though, those principles are translated into a universal account of things that are not actually, in any definable way, biological or physically causal, they have been absorbed into a kind of impressionistic mythology, or perhaps into a kind of metaphysics, one whose guiding premises are entirely unverifiable.

In fact, the very presuppositions that all social phenomena must have an evolutionary basis and that it is legitimate to attempt to explain every phenomenon solely in terms of the benefit it may confer (the *"cui bono?"* question, as Dennett likes to say) are of only suppositious validity. Immensely complex cultural realities like art, religion, and morality have no genomic sequences to unfold, exhibit no concatenations of material causes and effects, and offer nothing for the scrupulous researcher to quantify or dissect. An evolutionary sociologist, for instance, might try to isolate certain benefits that religions bring to societies or individuals (which already involves attempting to define social behaviors that could be interpreted in an almost limitless variety of ways), so as then to designate those benefits as the evolutionary rationales behind religion; but there is no warrant for doing so. The social and personal effects of religion, even if they could be proved to be uniform from society to society or person to person, may simply be accidental or epiphenomenal to religion itself. And even if one could actually discover some sort of clear connection between religious adherence and, say, social cohesion or personal happiness, one still would have no reason to assume the causal priority of those benefits; to do so would be to commit one of the most elementary of logical errors: *post hoc ergo propter hoc* — "thereafter, hence therefore" (or really, in this case, an even more embarrassing error: *post hoc ergo causa huius* — "thereafter, hence the cause thereof").

In the end, the most any "scientist of religion" can do is to use biological metaphors to support (or, really, to illustrate) an essentially unfounded philosophical materialism. When one does this, however, one is not investigating or explaining anything; one is merely describing a personal vision. One will never arrive anywhere but where one began — rather like the Butcher at the end of his mathematical demonstration to the Beaver that two added to one equals three (which starts with three as its subject and yields three as its result, but only because it is so constructed as always to yield a result equivalent to its subject). And Dennett's "non-functionalist" story of religion's development is no exception to this. He may wish to argue that the principal beneficiaries of religion are not men but memes; but he still assumes that, to understand the essential nature of a thing, it is enough to know who benefits from it — *cui bono?* — which is, of course, the very thing he should be trying to prove. In fact, in Dennett's case, it becomes especially difficult to distinguish conclusions from premises. After all, he wishes to argue — first —

that the most rudimentary religious impulses sprang from purely natural causes, which originally involved useful evolutionary adaptations, and — second — that most subsequent developments of religion have come about not because they make any useful contributions to the species, but because certain memes have spun off into self-replicating patterns of their own, and metastasized into vast self-sustaining structures without much practical purpose beyond themselves. Sadly, these claims render one another useless as explanatory instruments for evaluating the evidence Dennett would like to see collected; for, wherever his primary premise proves inadequate as a predictive model for explaining the phenomena of religion, he need only shift to his secondary premise — from genes to memes, so to speak — which means he has effectively insulated his results against the risk of falsification. If one proceeds in that fashion, all one can ever really prove is that, with theories that are sufficiently vacuous, one can account for everything (which is to say, for nothing).

There are few alternative approaches open to Dennett, though. The data provided by religion, or by any other comparably enormous cultural reality, are so multifarious and polymorphous that they cannot be made to fit comfortably into any simple causal paradigm without significant remainder. The "scientist of religion" will always turn out to be someone who simply employs a particular preferred evolutionary model as a kind of filter, by which to identify those religious phenomena that seem to conform to his expectations, so as arbitrarily to isolate them as indicators of religion's "essence." As for those religious phenomena that cannot easily be accommodated within a simple biological explanation of religion, these he will have to explain away by one or another purely speculative evolutionary principle, like "group selection" or "hidden benefits" or "memes." This process might be an interesting imaginative exercise, but it could never be a science. One can devise all the evolutionary models of religion one likes, but one will never be able to establish which, if any, is the most accurate; and the most successful models will simply be those that best conceal their own circularity.

This, though, may be the least of Dennett's problems. Questions of method, important as they are, need not be raised at all until the researcher can first determine and circumscribe the object of his studies in a convincing way. And here, I think, it seems worth mentioning — just for precision's sake — that religion does not actually exist. Rather there are a very great number of traditions of belief and practice that, for the sake of convenience, we call "religions," but that could scarcely differ from one another more. Perhaps it might seem sufficient, for the purposes of research, simply to identify general resemblances among these traditions; but even that is notoriously hard to do, since the very effort to ascertain what sort of things one is looking at involves an enormous amount of interpretation, and no clear criteria for evaluating any of it. One cannot establish where the boundaries lie between "religious" systems and magic, or "folk science," or myth, or social ceremony. There is not even any compelling reason to assume a genetic continuity or kinship between, say, shamanistic beliefs and developed rituals of sacrifice, or between tribal cults and traditions like Buddhism, Islam, and Christianity, or to assume that these various developed traditions are varieties of the same thing. One may feel that there is a continuity or kinship, or presuppose on the basis of one's prejudices, inklings, or tastes that the extremely variable and imprecise characteristic of "a belief in the supernatural" constitutes proof of a common ancestry or type; but all of this remains a matter of interpretation, vague morphologies, and personal judgments of value and meaning, and attempting to construct a science around such intuitions can amount to little more than mistaking "all the things I don't believe in" for a scientific genus. One cannot even demonstrate that apparent similarities of behavior between cultures manifest similar rationales, as human consciousness is so promiscuously volatile a catalyst in social evolution. And of course, conversely, neither can one demonstrate that such similarities would not indicate a common experience of supernatural reality — however risible one might find that suggestion.

Moreover, the task of delineating the "phenomenon" of religion in the abstract becomes perfectly hopeless as soon as one begins to examine what particular traditions of faith actually claim, believe, or do. It is already difficult enough to define what sort of thing religion is. But what sort of thing is the Buddhist teaching of the Four Noble Truths? What sort of thing is the Vedantic doctrine that Atman and Brahman are one? What sort of thing is the Christian belief in Easter? What is the core and what are the borders of *this* "phenomenon"? What are its empirical causes? What are its rationales? Grand, empty abstractions about religion are as easy to produce as to ignore. These, by contrast, are questions that touch upon what persons actually believe; and to answer them requires an endless hermeneutical labor — an investigation of history, and intellectual traditions, and contemplative lore, and so on and so forth — which ultimately requires a degree of specialization that few can hope to achieve; and even then the specialist's conclusions will always be subject to revision, dispute, or doubt.

Dennett, incidentally, is conscious of this "hermeneutical objection," but he thinks it enough to dismiss it as nothing more than an expression of territorial anxiety on the part of scholars in the humanities who fear the invasion of their disciplines by little gray men in lab coats. His only actual reply to the objection, in fact, is simply to assert yet more stridently that human culture's "webs of significance" (as Clifford Geertz phrases it) "*can* be analyzed by methods that critically involve experiments and the disciplined methods of the natural sciences." Well, if Dennett is going to resort to *italics* (that most devastatingly persuasive weapon in the dialectician's arsenal), one can do little more than shamelessly lift a page from his rhetorical portfolio and reply: No, they *cannot*. This is not a matter of territoriality, or of resistance to the most recent research, but of simple logic. There can be no science of any hard empirical variety when the very act of identifying one's object of study is already an act of interpretation, contingent upon a collection of purely arbitrary reductions, dubious categorizations, and biased observations. There can be no meaningful application of experimental method. There can be no correlation established between biological and cultural data. It will always be impossible to verify either one's evidence or one's conclusions — indeed, impossible even to determine what the conditions of verification should be.

AT ONE POINT in his argument, Dennett discusses "cargo cults," those fascinating and troubling religions invented by various Pacific islanders in response to their first encounters with visitors from the technologically advanced West. During the Second World War, for example, the construction of an American airbase on the island of Efate and the subsequent arrival there of riches from the heavens understandably aroused the envy of the people of the island of Tana; the latter, therefore, built their own airbase from bamboo, complete with warehouses, landing strips, and aeronautical icons, and devised religious rituals incorporating elements of American military pageantry, in the expectation that the same gods who had blessed their neighbors with such abundant cargo could be persuaded to visit Tana as well. Now, of course, Dennett wants his readers to see these cults as specimens of religion as such, their evolution conveniently accelerated (almost as if in a laboratory), and so not yet obscured by any of the imposing venerability or mysterious antiquity of more established traditions. Obviously, though, these cults are far too anomalous, and local, and bound to a very special set of conditions to tell us much about religion in general; and obviously, also, they are variations within traditions of cultic practice already long established in those islands, and so they pose the same hermeneutical problems as any other set of religious practices. But, while they may not teach us much about religion in the abstract, they may help to explain the kind of thinking animating *Breaking the Spell*.

That is to say, in a sense Dennett is himself a kind of cargo cultist. When, for instance, he proposes statistical analyses of different kinds of religion, to find out which are more evolutionarily perdurable, he exhibits a trust in the power of unprejudiced science to demarcate and define items of thought and culture like species of flora that verges on magical thinking. It is as if he imagines that by imitating the outward forms of scientific method, and by applying an assortment of superficially empirical theories to non-empirical realities, and by tirelessly gathering "information," and by asserting the validity of his methods with an incantatory repetitiveness, and by invoking invisible agencies such as "memes," and by fiercely believing in the efficacy of all that he is doing, despite the elements of fantasy and improvisation involved, he can summon forth actual hard clinical results, as from the treasure houses of the gods. Perhaps, though, this is inevitable. When one does not really know what one is looking for, the proper method to adopt is probably just to look busy. As the Bellman says to his men, "Do all that you know, and try all that you don't."

> They sought it with thimbles, they sought it with care;
>   They pursued it with forks and hope;
> They threatened its life with a railway share;
>   They charmed it with smiles and soap.

At the end of the day, it is the quarry that determines the manner of the hunt.

By the same token, perhaps it is also inevitable that Dennett should defer the corroboration of his arguments to future research, as he constantly does. I confess, though, I find it difficult to judge whether this is simply a rhetorical ploy on his part or is indeed the vaguely messianic delusion it occasionally appears to be. At the end of *Breaking the Spell,* he provides a list of some of the "unanswered empirical questions" raised in its pages, as recommendations for future research. But they are almost all questions that are, quite clearly, unanswerable — or, rather, answerable in innumerable, imprecise, and contradictory ways — and Dennett seems strangely unaware of this. His book abounds in sentences such as these: "We don't have to settle the empirical question *now* of whether divination memes are mutualist memes and actually enhance the fitness of their hosts, or parasite memes that they'd be better off without. Eventually, it would be good to get an evidence-based answer to this question, but for the time being it is the questions I am interested in." And he appears earnestly to believe that there truly is some question here — or some means of resolving it — that is in some intelligible sense "empirical." This is worse than quixotic. A century hence, our knowledge of physics will have no doubt advanced far beyond what we can now conceive, but our knowledge of issues such as these (and of memes especially) will have advanced not a step, except perhaps in the direction of ever more inventive conjectures. As used to be said of Brazil by the spitefully droll, Dennett's science of religion has a great future, and always will have.

In the end, though, I am not altogether certain Dennett believes much of what he is saying; in all likelihood, it seems to me, he harbors no more than a sort of wistful "belief in belief" with regard to it. I doubt it matters much to him whether future research on religious memes is a concrete possibility or not. I doubt even that he is really interested in the questions he raises, except insofar as they might induce salubrious doubts in his readers, through appearing more probative than they are. *Breaking the Spell* is a thoroughly tendentious book, and in a rather vicious way, for Dennett's ultimate aim is to propose certain social policies of a distinctly dictatorial sort. For instance, he sympathetically cites the view of Richard Dawkins and others that religious indoctrination of children should be considered a form of child abuse, and suggests that we might need to consider what measures our society should take to protect children from their parents' superstitions. He also pompously proclaims that we cannot as a society tolerate certain Catholic or Mormon teachings. And so on.

This, I imagine, partially explains his devotion to the concept of memes: it gives him license to indulge a small taste for the totalitarian without any undue stress upon his conscience. If, after all, the only beneficiaries of memes are memes themselves, and if religious memes are an especially toxic strain, then surely it is nothing but prudence and benevolence to seek the extermination of these parasites, ideally by preventive measures. And it hardly matters that the argument by which Dennett reaches his conclusions is patently absurd. He can assume the credulity of a compliant journalistic class and the tacit collaboration of his ideological allies; and he is convinced of the stupidity of his religious readers. His book's digressions and longueurs, its coarse jargon and fraudulent tone of authority, its parodies of logic and science, are all part of an immense and ponderous obfuscation, behind which is concealed a thoroughly authoritarian agenda. And behind that is concealed only ignorance and apprehension.

Dennett, needless to say, has no curiosity regarding any actual faith or its intellectual tradition. His few references to Christian history make it clear that, on that matter, his historical consciousness is little more than a compilation of threadbare eighteenth- and nineteenth-century caricatures. In the six spacious pages he devotes to the question of whether there is any reason to believe in God (or, really, devotes mostly to quoting himself at length on why the question is not worth considering), he does not address any of the reasons for which persons actually do believe, or any of the cases made by the most formidable of religious philosophers, but merely recites a few of the arguments that freshmen are given in introductory courses on the philosophy of religion; and, even then, so enormous is his mental sloth that he raises only those counterarguments that all competent scholars of philosophical history know to be the ones that do not work. The world of faith is all a *terra incognita* to Dennett; the only map he knows of it is, like the map used by the Bellman, "A perfect and absolute blank!" — though, in Dennett's case, bearing a warning that "Here there be dragons." Or, perhaps, "Here there be Boojums":

> . . . beware of the day,
> If your Snark be a Boojum! For then
> You will softly and suddenly vanish away,
> And never be met with again!

All Dennett knows is that something he very much dreads haunts that world, something intolerant and violent and irrational, and he wants to conjure it away. This, of course, raises the now quite hoary-headed question of how, in the wake of the twentieth century, the committed secularist dare wax either sanctimonious towards faith or sanguine towards secular reason; but Dennett is not one to be detained by doubts of that sort. He is certain there is some single immense thing out there called religion, and that by its very nature it endangers all of us, and that it ought as a whole to be abolished. This being so, it is probably less important to him that his argument be good than that, for purely persuasive purposes, it appear to be grounded in irrefutable science — which it can never be.

AGAIN, HOWEVER, all of this probably matters very little, because the most crucial defect of *Breaking the Spell* is, as I have said, its ultimate pointlessness. Let us assume I am wrong about Dennett's motives and intentions. More graciously, let us assume that there is far greater substance to Dennett's argument than I grant. Very well. Dennett need not have made such an effort to argue his point in the first place. *Of course* religion is a natural phenomenon. Who would be so foolish as to deny that? Religion is ubiquitous in human culture, and obviously constitutes an essential element in the evolution of society, and obviously has itself evolved. It is as natural to humanity as language or song or mating rituals. Dennett may imagine that such a suggestion is provocative and novel; and he may believe that there are legions of sincere souls out there desperately committed to the notion that religion itself is some sort of miraculous exception to the rule of nature; but, in either case, he is deceived.

For one thing, it does not logically follow that, simply because religion *as such* is a natural phenomenon, it cannot become the vehicle of divine truth, or that it is not in some sense oriented towards a transcendent reality. To imagine that it does so follow is to fall prey to a version of the "genetic fallacy," the belief that one need only determine the causal sequence by which something comes into being in order to understand its nature, meaning, content, uses, or value. (As far as I can tell, the only reviewer to have attempted to defend Dennett's book on this score is Kim Sterelny, writing in *American Scientist Online;* but, inasmuch as Sterelny's strategy is simply to repeat the original error in a slightly different combination of words, his defense amounts to very little.)

For another thing, no one believes *in* religion. Christians, for instance, believe that Jesus of Nazareth, crucified under Pontius Pilate, rose from the dead and is now, by the power of the Holy Spirit, present to his Church as its Lord. This claim is at once historical and spiritual, and has given rise to an immense diversity of *natural* expressions: moral, artistic, philosophical, social, legal, and (of course) religious. Regarding "religion" as such, though, it is perfectly consonant with Christian tradition to see it as an impulse common to all societies, many of whose manifestations are violent, idiotic, despotic, superstitious, amoral, degrading, and false. The most one can say from a Christian perspective concerning religion in the abstract is that it gives ambiguous expression to what Christian tradition calls the "natural desire for God," and to a human openness to spiritual truth, revelation, or grace. When, therefore, Dennett solemnly asks (as he does) whether religion is worthy of our loyalty, he is posing a nonsensical question. The only pertinent question for Christians is whether Christ is worthy of loyalty; and, by gravely informing us that the "natural desire for God" is in fact a desire for God that is natural, Dennett really has not cast much light upon this question at all. He would not, however, be the first analytic philosopher to have mistaken a minor modification of syntax for a conceptual revolution.

Dennett, moreover, seems curiously unaware of what belief in a transcendent God actually entails; and he wildly exaggerates what relevance a purely naturalistic account of religion should have for such a belief. After all, the marvelous strength and fecundity of modern science is the result of its narrowness, and of the ascetical rigor with which it limits the scope of its inquiries. Herein lie its greatest virtue and its greatest (albeit self-imposed) limitation. In the terms of Aristotle's fourfold scheme of causality, science as we understand it now — Baconian science, if one likes — concerns itself solely with efficient and material causes, while leaving the questions of formal and final causes unaddressed. That is to say, its aim is the scrupulous reconstruction of *how* things and events are generated or unfold, not speculation on *why* things become what they are, or on the purpose of their existence. Much less is it concerned with the ontological cause of what it investigates: it has nothing to say regarding being as such, or how it is that anything exists at all, or what makes the universe to *be*. But this is not to say that it has somehow disproved the reality of these other kinds of causality. It is even arguable that it has never been able entirely to dispense with formality or finality, at least as heuristic devices for defining what the researcher is seeking to discover (as, for instance, Dennett's *cui bono?* rule shows). Still, though, these causes lie for the most part outside the purview of modern science, and one believes in them, if one does, for reasons of an entirely different order.

This rather elementary truth proves surprisingly elusive for some persons. A particularly vivid and poignant example would be Richard Dawkins, who — unencumbered as he is by any philosophical training or aptitude — has an obliging habit of placing his largest logical errors either in the opening paragraphs or on the covers of his books. The subtitle of his already solecistically entitled *The Blind Watchmaker* informs us that "the evidence of evolution reveals a universe without design": a claim that seems superficially in keeping with his frequently reiterated assertion that what we find when we look at the evidence of biological evolution is precisely what we should expect to find if we assume that the entire process is governed by nothing but random chance. But, in fact, while the latter claim is true, the former is only a false inference drawn from it. It is, after all, one's prior expectations that are always at issue. For what one sees when one looks at the evidence of evolution is also what one might expect to find if one assumes that the entire process is the consequence of a transcendent intelligence drawing all things from nothingness and endowing them with form according to an internally coherent sequence of causes and a collection of magnificently intricate mathematical laws. All judgments regarding final causality — chance, design, necessity, and so on — are, by virtue of their quite irreducible ultimacy, metaphysical in nature. They reflect the primordial convictions of the observer, not his impartial conclusions; they may appear to be valid deductions in the eyes of the philosophically naïve, but in fact they concern that which lies outside the system of immanent causation that the material sciences can investigate. Neither intuitions of general indeterminacy nor discoveries of special complexity authorize us to pronounce any final verdict on the whole of being. This is as true in the case of Dawkins's clodhopping metaphysical materialism as in that of the disastrously misguided Intelligent Design movement (that odd occult discipline devoted to the ingenious demiurge who invented syphilis for us). The question of which judgments of finality are most plausible can be answered only metaphysically, for ultimately it is the question of whose primordial convictions are most rational and defensible (a standard according to which, happily, the strict materialist must always lose).

Of course, one is always free to regard formal and final causality as fictions (though they tend to reassert themselves, even if only subtly, in the oddest places); and one may dismiss the question of being as meaningless or imponderable (though it is neither). But one should also then relinquish ambitions for empirical method that it is impotent to realize. This applies to every discourse that aspires to the status of a science. If one wants to pursue a science of religion, one should know from the first that one will never produce a theory that could possibly be relevant to whether one should or should not believe that, for example, the transcendent God has revealed himself in history or within one's own life. Certainly, at any rate, the Christian should be undismayed by the notion that religion is natural "all the way down." Indeed, it should not matter to him whether or not religion really is the result of evolutionary imperatives, or of an inclination towards belief inscribed in our genes and in the structure of our brains, or even (more fantastically) of memes that have impressed themselves upon our minds and cultures and languages. All things are natural. But nature itself is created towards an end — its consummation in God — and is *informed* by a more eminent causality — the creative will of God — and is sustained in existence by its participation in the being that flows from God, who is the infinite wellspring of all actuality. And religion, as a part of nature, possesses an innate entelechy, and is oriented like everything else towards the union of God and his creatures. Nor, most emphatically, should the Christian expect to find any lacunae in the fabric of nature, needing to be repaired by the periodic interventions of a cosmic maintenance technician. God's transcendence is absolute: he is cause of all things by giving existence to the whole, but nowhere need he act as a rival to any of the contingent, finite, "secondary" causes by which the universe lives, moves, and has its being in him. Certain varieties of fundamentalist — evangelical Christian, atheist, or what have you — may think otherwise; but they are in error.

In the end, however, nothing of any significance is decided by talking about religion in the abstract; it is a somewhat inane topic, really. It is relevant neither to belief nor to disbelief. It touches upon neither the rationales nor the experiences that determine anyone's ultimate convictions. Neither certainly is anything important to be learned from Daniel Dennett's rancorous exchanges with nonexistent persons regarding the prospects for an impossible science devoted to an intrinsically indeterminate object. If Dennett really wishes to undertake a "scientific" investigation of faith, he should promptly abandon his efforts to describe religion in the abstract, and attempt instead to enter into the actual world of belief in order to weigh its claims from within. As a first step, he should certainly — purely in the interest of sound scientific method and empirical rigor — begin praying, and then continue doing so with some perseverance. This is a drastic and implausible prescription, no doubt; but it is the only means by which he could possibly begin to acquire any knowledge of what belief is or what it is not. Rather than court absurdity, though, I should probably refrain from pursuing the issue any further.

PETER HEATH observed some decades ago, in his wonderful *The Philosopher's Alice,* that Lewis Carroll was not a writer of nonsense, but was rather an absurdist; and a Carrollian character is absurd precisely because he does not blithely depart from the rules, but rather "persists in adhering to them long after it has ceased to be sensible to do so, and regardless of the extravagances which hereby result." When Carroll's characters assume the authoritative tone, the opinions they express are invariably ridiculous, but those opinions "are held on principle and backed by formal argument. . . . The humor lies not in any arbitrary defiance of principle, but in seeing a reasonable position pushed or twisted by uncritical acceptance into a wholly unreasonable shape."

I would hesitate to say that *Breaking the Spell* is, in this sense, entirely absurd, as I doubt that it is tightly reasoned enough to merit the description. What does seem clear to me, however, is that, in its general form, the book's argument is one that strives (not always successfully) to preserve the outward shapes of reason, logic, and method, even while evacuating them of all rational, logical, or empirical content. To put the matter very bluntly, I cannot believe that anyone could mistake it for a genuinely substantial argument who was not firmly intent upon doing so before ever reading the book. For, viewed impartially, Dennett's project manifestly leads nowhere, and its diffuse and flimsy methods are clearly altogether unequal to the task of capturing the complex, bewildering, endlessly diverse thing they are designed to subdue. Dennett sets out with perhaps a pardonable excess of ambition — in the words of the Butcher,

> In one moment I've seen what has hitherto been
> Enveloped in absolute mystery,

> And without extra charge I will give you at large
> A lesson in Natural History.

But it soon becomes obvious that Dennett has no lesson to impart. He is, when all is said and done, merely hunting a Snark, and in a sense he can hardly avoid sharing the Baker's fate. One need only read *Breaking the Spell,* and then attempt to apply it in some meaningful or illuminative way to the terrible and splendid realities of religious belief, to confirm this; because, once one has done that, one will immediately discover that the book's entire argument has "softly and suddenly vanished away." And this, to the reflective reader, should come as no surprise, given the nature both of Dennett's quest and of the quarry he has chosen to pursue — "For the Snark *was* a Boojum, you see."

Acknowledgments

1. "Christ and Nothing (No Other God)" originally appeared in *First Things*, October, 2003.
2. "Notes on John Paul II's Pontificate, 2001" originally appeared in *First Things*, March, 2001.
3. "A Most Partial Historian: On Maurice Cowling's *Religion and Public Doctrine in Modern England*" originally appeared in *First Things*, December, 2003.
4. "Sheer Extravagant Violence: Gogol's *Taras Bulba*" originally appeared in *First Things*, January, 2004.
5. "Religion in America: Ancient and Modern" originally appeared in *The New Criterion*, March, 2004.
6. "When the Going Was Bad: On Evelyn Waugh's Travel Writings" originally appeared in *First Things*, May, 2004.
7. "Freedom and Decency" originally appeared in *First Things*, June/July, 2004.
8. "The Pornography Culture" originally appeared in *The New Atlantis*, June/Summer, 2004.
9. "The Laughter of Philosophers" originally appeared in *First Things*, January, 2004.
10. "Tremors of Doubt" originally appeared in *The Wall Street Journal*, December 31, 2004.
11. "Tsunami and Theodicy" originally appeared in *First Things*, March, 2005.

12. Copyright 2006 Christian Century. Reprinted by permission from the January 10, 2006, issue of *The Christian Century*. Subscriptions: $49/yr. from P.O. Box 378, Mt. Morris, IL 61054. 1-800-208-4097.

13. "Roland Redivivus" originally appeared in *First Things*, February, 2005.

14. "The Soul of a Controversy" originally appeared in *The Wall Street Journal*, April 1, 2005.

15. "Beyond Disbelief: On Alister McGrath's *The Twilight of Atheism*" originally appeared in *The New Criterion*, June, 2005.

16. "The Anti-Theology of the Body" originally appeared in *The New Atlantis*, Summer, 2005.

17. "Ecumenical War Councils" originally appeared in *Touchstone: A Journal of Mere Christianity*, November, 2004.

18. "The Angel at the Ford of Jabbok: On The Theology of Robert Jenson" originally appeared in *First Things*, October, 2005.

19. "Infinite Lit" originally appeared in *Touchstone: A Journal of Mere Christianity*, November, 2005.

20. "Theology as Knowledge" originally appeared in *First Things*, May, 2006.

21. "On the Trail of the Snark with Daniel Dennett" originally appeared in *First Things*, January, 2007.